Difficult Women, Artful Lives

Parallax Re-visions of Culture and Society

Stephen G. Nichols, Gerald Prince, and Wendy Steiner, Series Editors

Difficult Women, Artful Lives

Olive Schreiner and Isak Dinesen, In and Out of Africa

Susan R. Horton

The Johns Hopkins University Press
Baltimore and London

Published 1995
Printed in the United States of
America on acid-free paper
04 03 02 01 00 99 98 97 96 95
5 4 3 2 1

The Johns Hopkins University Press
2715 North Charles Street
Baltimore, Maryland 21218-4319
The Johns Hopkins Press Ltd.,
London

ISBN 0-8018-5037-1
ISBN 0-8018-5038-X (pbk.)

Library of Congress Cataloging in
Publication Data will be found at
the end of this book.
A catalog record for this book is
available from the British Library.

Certainly, the whole of the story is not written here, but it is suggested. And the attribute of all true art, the highest and the lowest, is this—that it says more than it says, and takes you away from itself. It is a little door that opens into an infinite hall where you may find what you please.

Olive Schreiner, *The Story of an African Farm*

Contents

Illustrations ix

Preface xi

1

Disclaiming, Claim Staking, and Vacillatin' Rhythms 3

2

Alone by Design: Precarious Enclosures 41

3

The Subversion of "Woman" and the Triumph of Women 75

4

Mythic Times, Gothic Images, and the Role of the Dice 107

5

Sketching Landscapes, Stretching Genres 139

6

African Landscapes, Fauve Painters 169

7

African Gossip and the Two-Way Street 193

8

Conclusion: "Remembering" and the Chain of Tradition 237

A Note on Texts 249

Notes 251

Works Cited 279

Index 305

Illustrations

1 L'il Miss Singing Mermaid; Mami Wata 9
2 Denys Finch Hatton 20
3 Olive Schreiner and Samuel Cronwright-Schreiner 21
4 Modernism as a graph or table 27
5 Isak Dinesen 49
6 The author 56
7 Henri Matisse, *Le bonheur de vivre* 172
8 Albert Marquet, *Le Pont-Neuf* 176
9 The Mami Wata 229

Preface

In what is probably the best-known passage from all her writings on Africa, Isak Dinesen expresses her greatest fear: "[If] we nations of Europe . . . who do not fear to floodlight our own inmost mechanisms, . . . [turn] the blazing lights of our civilization into dark eyes . . . essentially different to ours," we will "dazzle and blind" them and "bring upon them a longing for darkness, which will drive them into the gorges of their own . . . unknown minds."[1] This rhetoric of a European Enlightenment shining light into the recesses of consciousness, forcing self-reflection and self-awareness, is of course familiar. J. W. T. Mitchell associates it with the rise of interest in optics in the nineteenth century that produced a spate of metaphors of "rational transparency" in writers from Burke to Marx.[2] Anthropologists Jean and John Comaroff trace the ways this rhetoric was tailored to particular purposes by Christian missionaries, whose first gifts to Africans frequently were mirrors. This gift of the mirror was coupled with exhortations to let "brightness illumine their hearts," transforming cultural imperialism into moral duty.[3] These are by now parts of a familiar story, well and frequently told by writers in social theory, anthropology, African history, art history, and literary and cultural studies. But what has struck me is how wrong Dinesen was, and how wrong we still are, in assuming that it is "we," those of us of European extraction, who do not fear the floodlight. In so much analysis of colonial or postcolonial Africa and the contact zone between Africa and its others, it is the First World critic who too frequently remains in darkness, and I have thought with more than a little bemusement that Ezekiel Mphahlele would surely still feel some of the "anthropological creepy-crawlies" he confessed to experiencing while reading white writings about Africa in 1962.[4]

In First World writings, "Europeans" too frequently seem to be abstractions every bit as much as are the "Africans" to whom Africanists have taught us to refer only in citation, and I intend my project as a gesture of rectification. It is a modest one. Rather than rehearse again the story of "European" encounters with "Africans," I have tried to speculate only on what two particular white women, Olive Schreiner in South Africa and Isak Dinesen in Kenya, *got out of* their particular encounters; to consider the part Africans played in each woman's psychic economy; and to regard their "Africa" as one piece of the very artful bricolage that was their work of self-construction. In the process I have tried hard to keep that Enlightenment floodlight firmly trained on them, and on my own imbrication in constructing this particular story of them. But this does not mean the pages that follow here contribute in any way to what Peter Brooks sees as a regrettable recent trend toward the personalizing of criticism that seduces the critical personality into flaunting its idiosyncrasies. Instead I have tried to submit to what he refers to as the "test of that otherness which is culture," undergoing "the discipline of listening to the voices of cultural traditions before, and at the same time as, one speaks in one's own voice."[5] Since the cultural traditions to which I have tried to listen include those presented in both African and European history and art history as well as those newer ones created in and by postcolonial and feminist writings, this study is far more an experiment in critical method than an exercise in biography or autobiography, though it does necessarily contain elements of both.

Even the most disciplined glance into the mirror of self-awareness inevitably encounters resistance; strong impulses to flinch or look away. To resist them as much as possible, I have chosen as my subjects two difficult and complex white women, each of whom was in her own way as restless, as resistant to race, gender, and ethnic categorization as I have always experienced myself to be, two women whose strategies of self-presentation in the face of those difficulties are similar to my own. Olive Schreiner was what some might think of as a rather mannish woman, more than a bit like that other famous Olive, Henry James's Olive Chancellor. A political activist, a realistic and at times rather flat-footed writer, she believed among other things that her novels, speeches, and political tracts might help to bring about substantive political and social changes for women and for native South Africans. The flip side of the stolid, sensible, diligent political activist was, perhaps inevitably, the frustrated head banger she quite literally was. Isak Dinesen was the hyperfeminine woman, a bemused *bricoleuse,* a romantic teller of dreamy tales—a sucker for the aristocratic and the beautiful, for transcendently true and everlasting love. The flip side of that romantic, sentimental lover of love and the beautiful is, perhaps just as inevitably, the self-ironizing, laughing fatalist *she* so surely was. Despite our putative postmodernity, most of us remain cryptomodernists whose identities depend on the same kind of shuttling between oppositions, and I suspect not a few of us ride the daily shuttle between exactly these same extremes. This is part of what makes them a perfect occasion for this small piece of a genuine Enlightenment project, one that has as its object shining light not only on the writings and histories of these two white women, but on the First World critic and on the Africa of her imagination.

From its earliest beginnings this project has had about it an aura of personal urgency of the sort that must have been experienced by all white explorers journeying to "Africa" to discover their own interiors. In my own journey I have had bountiful help. The numerous Africanists, feminists, and art historians solicited by the Press who remain unknown to me provided insightful, lavish, and generous reports. For all of their commentary, both supportive and critical, I am exceedingly grateful. I hope I have responded with the respect it deserves. The graciousness and openness of Professor Bogumil Jewsiewicki in sharing with me so generous a selection from his private research collection of slides of the Mami Wata have been an inspiration. So also was the help that Professor Valentin Mudimbe, perhaps unwittingly, provided at crucial moments in the form of a few supportive comments he offered to me during various conferences over the past several years. It has been a special pleasure and honor to work once again with Eric F. Halpern, editor in chief of the Johns Hopkins University Press. I am extremely grateful for his patience and support. To two of my former graduate students from the University of Massachusetts at Boston, Ali Erritouni, who provided research assistance, and Pamela Nova Wolf, whose enthusiastic responses to an early draft provided my first real experience of an audience beyond myself, I owe many thanks. To my brother, Michael L. Seibenick, are due love and gratitude for his epistolary offerings posted from Defiance and for companionship and guidance along the Path.

In "The Storyteller" Walter Benjamin tells us that *Mut,* or courage, is the greatest gift. In fairy tales it is divided dialectically into cunning (*Untermut*) and high spirits (*Übermut*). The mature, liberated man is happy, says Benjamin, for as long as he is able to meet the forces of the mythical world with those same qualities. This book is dedicated with admiration and much love to my son, John Joseph Horton, who has always exhibited both in abundance.

Difficult Women, Artful Lives

1

Disclaiming, Claim Staking, and Vacillatin' Rhythms

If there is a lesson in the broad shape of [the] circulation of cultures, it is surely that we are all already contaminated by each other, that there is no longer a fully autochthonous *echt*-African culture awaiting salvage by our artists (just as there is, of course, no American culture without African roots). And there is a clear sense in some post-colonial writing that the postulation of a unitary Africa over against a monolithic West—the binarism of Self and Other—is the last of the shibboleths of the modernizers that we must learn to live without.

Kwame Anthony Appiah,
In My Father's House

An earlier title for this book was *Cross Talk,* intended to signal that it was, as an earlier draft had announced, "cross-cultural in at least three senses, crossing boundaries between male and female, black and white, Africa and Europe as its argument requires." But since the book was begun a great deal of very powerful work aimed at challenging essentialist notions of bounded categories of race and gender has appeared, all making it much easier to talk about what had captured my attention about Dinesen and Schreiner from the start: the stupendously original ways in which they were themselves consummate crossers and double-crossers of race and gender categories in the production of their own identities. The restless boundary crossing that characterizes the lives and works of these two women makes them subjects who require a critical method characterized by disciplinary border crossings as well. The original title was also meant to suggest the irritability that can often be detected in their writings; a crossness I attribute to their frequent feeling of restless confinement in the category "woman."

Isak Dinesen produced two very popular romantic chronicles of her years in Kenya, and essays and radio broadcasts advocating, among other things, extremely traditional—one might even say feudal—roles for males and females. The prolific writer of gothic tales often either set in Renaissance Italy or played out "on a full moon night . . . [on] a dhow . . . on its way from Lamu to Zanzibar,"[1] she may actually be best known as the architect of her own flamboyant persona. She was born in Denmark in 1885, lived in Kenya for seventeen years beginning in 1913, and survived until 1962. Olive Schreiner is more the sturdy woman in sensible shoes: the author of political tracts on the injustices inflicted on both black and Boer during the Anglo-Boer War, speculations on the future of South Africa and the rights of women, collections of what she called allegories and dreams, and three novels set mostly in South Africa: *Undine, The Story of an African Farm,* and *From Man to Man,* which she still regarded as unfinished at the time of her death in 1920. Her relentless earnestness prompted Rider Haggard, an early admirer of her novels, to express to her his strong wish that she would try writing "something more cheerful."[2] She was born on the dusty Karoo of Cape Colony in 1855. Her father was a British Lutheran minister; her mother, the daughter of Nonconformist missionaries.

Schreiner's novels have caught the attention of feminist readers in recent years; her political writings have engaged the attention of others. Feminist readers have found in some of Dinesen's tales elaborately coded explorations of woman and language or of woman and the body. A parallel track of Dinesen criticism produced increasingly by Africanists continues to mine her two memoirs of her years in Kenya. The only actual point of contact I can find between these two women is a tenuous one.[3] Though their paths never crossed and their temperaments were radically different, philosophically and psychically they were kindred spirits, and I believe the two sets of narratives that critics have produced in recent years about these separate women can usefully be read as parts of the same story of self-production, one relying heavily on the unwitting collaboration of "Africans" to bring it about. Both in and out of Africa, Schreiner and Dinesen were inevitably entangled in both the colonial and the sexual politics of their times and places. But if we get more particular about those times, places, and women, the story becomes ever more intricate and interesting. "Out here," Dinesen says of Africa, "it comes naturally to me to be myself."[4] Exactly how and why she came to find "being herself" more possible in Africa than in her native Denmark is a large part of my subject.

But if my study insists on the importance of both Africa and Europe to Schreiner's and Dinesen's work of self-construction, it also insists on recognizing how much imaginative energy each invested in constructing an identity that made it possible to see herself as something other than woman. To put it bluntly, both Schreiner and Dinesen saw "Woman" as a continent "out there" far more than Africa ever was. This may seem an outrageous claim to make either about Schreiner, a self-avowed new woman, or about Dinesen, a champion of "the eternal feminine." But in my reading of their lives and works, both women worked hard to make woman their cross-cultural other, a move made possible partly because as white women in Africa each was able to operate to some extent as an honorary male.

I believe Olive Schreiner's recent acceptance into the feminist canon has been purchased at the cost of a serious disambiguation of her own feelings about being "woman," and though feminist readings of some of Dinesen's tales have enriched us all,[5] most of them that seem to advocate extremely traditional roles for male and female have been almost completely sidestepped. Because of this, the resistance to femininity that can be read in Dinesen's exaggerated, metaleptic troping of it both in her self-presentation and in those tales has gone largely unremarked.[6]

One of the earliest images to haunt my imagination, for instance, is of Isak Dinesen standing in the kitchen of her farmhouse in Ngong late in 1928. Her former husband Bror Blixen is sending "bearishly affectionate" letters from Sweden announcing his impending remarriage, but Dinesen seems largely unaffected, because the home she has constructed for herself in Kenya crackles with an erotic energy she both sparks and fuels.[7] Her lover Denys Finch Hatton is in and out of her house and life at his whim, if not always at hers. In letters to her family back in Denmark she describes her efforts at orchestrating the marriage of the Kikuyu Kamante Gatura to a young woman Dinesen insists on referring to as "the lovely Wamboi" by helping him amass the requisite bride-price. Insinuating herself not just into the working lives of the Kikuyu, like any "good" colonial, but into their personal lives as well, her identification here—as so often—is not with the African woman, but with the desiring African man.

Standing in that kitchen in Ngong, Dinesen also feels at home because she has absolute confidence in Kamante's ability to prepare expertly the specifically European dishes—turbot, truffles, partridges—she's ordered for her latest dinner party. The necessary ingredients will appear on schedule, because she's ordered "her" Maasai to bring them. She knows Kamante will cook them to her specifications, because she's taught him herself. Her dinner guest will be the Prince of Wales. Even sweeter, he's coming not just because she's *asked* him; he's pretty much invited himself. Dinesen had piqued his interest with her confident assurances that African chiefs in the area, among them Kioi and the great Kinanjui, will stage an *ngoma* for her—if she asks them to. She's sent "her" Somali Farah to drive out and extend that request. Her lover Denys has committed himself to pay for the drinks and cigars. "It is not so easy to make a good ngoma at this time of year," Dinesen writes to her mother, "because the actual dancing season is over."[8]

Dinesen's is not just a simple statement of difficulty: it is a boast. Out of season, inappropriately staged as a spectacle for European visitors, this *ngoma* is out of context and out of time. But the natives will dance at and for her pleasure. The *ngoma* is the dance of liberation, the dance of ecstasy, Fanon tells us. Dancing it would of course be unseemly for a European woman, so Dinesen doesn't dance. But through the power of her own will and the power that being a European woman in Africa makes available to her, she does become the triumphant architect of the "home" of her desires, orchestrating the movements of males on two continents to erect it. Hardly a figure for woman's harmony with the landscape or a representation of the eternal feminine for which she advocated, here she can be seen instead as the figure for a very "masculine" manipulation of people and landscape to the end of her own self-production.

When *Jungle Fever* was released, Houston Baker predicted that Spike Lee's movie would spark a renewed interest in jungles. We'll soon be seeing reruns of old Tarzan movies, he said, watching Tarzan make love to Jane all over again.[9] Mine here is an invitation to watch Jane make love to Tarzan. "If I know a song of Africa," Dinesen asks in *Out of Africa,* "does Africa know a song of me?"[10] I intend to read Dinesen's and Schreiner's lives and works here as a series of efforts to devise elaborate mechanisms for constructing both themselves *and* Tarzan—everyone knows you can't have one without the other—producing in the process an aesthetically and erotically charged place of the imagination that became the only place either woman could comfortably call home.

This is of course a stupendous accomplishment, if we think about the extent to which space and the struggle for space are at the heart of all cultural politics.[11] Schreiner's and Dinesen's space clearing and home building should be read differently because their erections are female rather than male, and because those "homes" required the more or less willing collaboration of males on two continents, and often either overrode or ignored their active resistance.

No one just plants a flag and declares that here is my home, of course. Spectacular acts of self-construction and home building require rather large audiences of erstwhile participants. Gayatri Spivak suggests that anytime women theorize themselves as women they must adopt a dual focus: "Not merely who am I? but who is the other woman? How does she name me?"[12] How did Schreiner and Dinesen name other white women? How did they name white men? How did they name black women? How did they name black men? And how did their naming of others produce themselves? Clearly, more is at stake here than an expanded appreciation of Schreiner's and Dinesen's works and lives. If we've spent the past decade talking about the way social forces have produced various versions of the gendered, ethnic, and racial self, *this* decade requires that we start talking much more particularly. What we *do* to and with our selves and one another is as various as our individual histories; sometimes feeling our selves to *be* that other; sometimes, in my own experience, quite consciously constructing our selves as the other's other. David Roediger's *The Wages of Whiteness,* for instance, points to the exact moment and reasons the working class in the United States first constituted itself as "white," and Ruth Frankenberg's *White Women, Race Matters* has at its heart a variant of that same project. When we become the other's other, at least some of the time I suspect we do so out of grace and generosity, recognizing that every human being needs the resistance someone else's othering provides in order to carve out a space to own as "me" simply and precisely because and insofar as it is *not* "you." Sometimes we declare ourselves other out of self-defense, sometimes—who knows—out of simple human perversity, boredom, curiosity.

Some of us quite systematically play at being the other. Probably this is partly a matter of wanting to be inside the other to see what it feels like in there. Partly we imagine ourselves there to see what *we* look like from that other place. Such moves are often a consequence of our not feeling at home inside the constructions the social order produces and expects us to inhabit: the modernist exile lurks within. But if I am in exile, the corollary is that someone else must be inhabiting my real home. And if I could get inside that other's place—skin, gender, race, ethnicity, ancestral

Figure 1. L'il Miss Singing Mermaid. © 1991 Mattel, Inc.

Mamba mantu, a Zaïrian Mami Wata image. (See fig. 9.)

religion, national ethos, class—who knows but that I might feel more at home there than in here.

I understand all this to be part of the profoundly serious play of identity going on in the space between the little mermaid doll shown in figure 1, which Mattel promises will change color when you put her in water, and contemporary black African artists' paintings of the Mami Wata, which often represent her either as a white woman (vain, rich, capricious, but generous if the whim strikes her) or, in the Papi Wata, as a man rather than the woman legend and myth have told us she is. Either of these two mermaids—Hans Christian Andersen's filtered through Hollywood and Mattel, or those such as Zairean urban artist Cheri Samba's, produced in part for the white tourist trade—represents the quintessential figure for a creature both at home and *not* at home in his or her element. Mermaids always do that. But if we juxtapose them and let the eye oscillate between the two, what can be seen in the afterimage is an instance of artistic production both inspiring and requiring one eye on the other. This is precisely what both Schreiner and Dinesen did in their works and lives. Schreiner named her earliest novel and its heroine *Undine,* a common name for the mermaid in Germanic mythologies. Dinesen's tale "The Diver" can, I believe, be seen as a complex interweaving of Hans Christian Andersen's little mermaid and the Mami Wata. The mermaid happens also to be the perfect figure for Schreiner and Dinesen themselves: creatures caught in the act of various metamorphoses, living on the line between resistance and accommodation to various categories of race, gender, and nationality. This is of course the place where the individual subject is born.

Gender, race, and ethnic boundaries will be treated here as mythologies in the sense Roland Barthes describes. In "Mama's Baby, Papa's Maybe," Hortense Spillers considers the efficiency with which ethnic and gender categories allow us to lock one another into the same kind of mythic timelessness created by Western inventions of the notion of African "tribes." [13] In that process particular human bodies function largely as raw material for metaphor. To the extent that "white" and "black" get locked into "a constant opposition of binary meanings" [14] as the signifier begins to reproduce "the physique of the *alibi* (which is, as one realizes, a spatial term): in the alibi . . . there is a place which is full and one which is empty, linked by a relation of negative identity ('I am not where you think I am; I am where you think I am not')." [15]

Schreiner and Dinesen worked mightily all their lives to defeat mythic binaries of race, gender, and nationality in three ways. First and paradoxically, by embracing them in an effort to explode them from within in the ways Walter Benjamin advocates. Second, by affirming on one stratum of representation what they confound or overturn on another; and third, by doing exactly what

Barthes describes here, working in both obvious and subtle ways to put themselves in some other place: to live in the alibi. Announcing that "I am not where you think I am" and its corollary, "I am where you think I am *not,*" is probably far more common than we admit, and as we return more and more often to specific histories and biographies to retrieve the ways particular subjectivities get formed, we may find identifications across gendered, racial, ethnic, or sexual boundaries beginning to emerge. (The word *emerge* is chosen deliberately here to beg the question of how much of this will be discovery and how much production.) Some different senses of otherness will also begin to be articulated. It may be, for instance, that a white girl growing up in Defiance, Ohio, whose progenitors were factory workers who learned to control their destinies largely, if at all, through strategies of improvisation, a self-demeaning humor, mimicry of the powerful, and a Roman Catholicism characterized more by stoic resignation to the dictates of a whimsical fate than by a conviction about the presence of God's loving hand, might find in herself a great many affinities with the colonizers' construction of colonized Muslim black Africans. Her affinities with those Africans might be as strong as those experienced by, say, an African Africanist whose progenitors were respected elders, leaders, colonial administrators, judges, bishops, and professors. For instance, my experience of otherness as I read the moving concluding chapter of Kwame Anthony Appiah's *In My Father's House,* which recounts his father's funeral in Ghana, arose not so much because he is a black African male and I a white European American female as from my enviousness that he could refer to "the king of Ashanti, my uncle,"[16] whereas I have never been able to find a relative who knew for certain who my ancestors were, what they did for a living, where they came from, or why.

My own positioning and self-construction here have nothing to do with a race to the margins, or with an attempt to win some game of economic, social, class, racial, or ethnic one-downmanship. They instead constitute an attempt to explore with as much honesty as I can muster the question of whose other I'm playing today, who I'm identifying with today, who I'm casting as my other today, and what I gain in each instance.

My focus for answering these questions will be on what I call the aesthetic and survival strategies (the two turn out to be more or less synonymous) devised by Olive Schreiner and Isak Dinesen in the face of what they regarded as too rigid categories of race and gender, coupled with the various intractabilities of world and will they experienced as they faced those categorical imperatives. Dinesen passionately loved the works of Nietzsche, whom she encountered through the writings of her countryman Georg Brandes. Schreiner's formative years were spent as a governess in leaky Afrikaner farmhouses where the identifications germinating in her were not with other women serving as governesses, but with male writers like Schopenhauer, whose ideas had provided the ladder Nietzsche used to reach his own. Both women were to that extent extremely male identified. They were also women of idealistic temperament who out of principle and stubbornness resisted believing that they or the world could be less than ideal—if everyone just tried hard enough. Their strategies of resistance in the face of these and other intractabalities provide the structure for this book and its chapters.

Its title *Difficult Women, Artful Lives* is intended to be read chiasmatically. Combine an unyielding belief in the ideal with an unrelenting need to advocate for that ideal, house both in bodies and psyches with the usual human fallibilities, and you have a complex mix, one that seems to have made both Dinesen and Schreiner exceptionally difficult women for those around them. Biographers and critics still find them difficult. Yvonne Kapp's biography of Eleanor Marx, daughter of Karl Marx and close friend of Schreiner's, in the space of less than a page describes Schreiner as guilty of "rampant egotism," "possessive and domineering in her friendships, venomous in her dislikes . . . and putting little curb upon her expression of these violent loves and hates," having a "tendency to delusion about her health and also a slight touch of persecution mania, accompanied by its opposite: the conviction that everyone admired and revered her if they were not positively in love with her." She didn't so much "captivate" friends as "capture" them.[17] After her death Schreiner's own husband is reputed to have called her a liar.[18] Seen as people whose idealism, absolutism, and passion outran their capacity to do and be what they enthusiastically espoused, both Schreiner and Dinesen unequivocally were stupendously untruthful.

I do not mean to suggest that sympathetic portraits of either woman are hard to find. But such portraits seem by and large to have been achieved only by building firewalls between the critic or biographer and the more incendiary and problematic aspects of each woman's personality and pronouncements. In trying to paint portraits simultaneously sympathetic and honest, I will refer collectively to Olive Schreiner's and Isak Dinesen's literary works, lives, letters, essays, memoirs, and self-presentations as their *lifeworks*. In collapsing distinctions between art and life in this way and assuming the artful life functions as a major survival mechanism, I admit to adopting a position much like that of early ethnophilosophers of Africa, such as Janheinz Jahn, who represented as typically African the notion that art is not so much what gets written or painted as it is an "ongoing activity or attitude" of life itself.[19] My citing Jahn here should not be taken to imply uncritical acceptance of ethnophilosophic or anthropological constructions of "Africans." Instead, it reflects my belief that art functions in this way for anyone in any culture. In suggesting as well that Dinesen's and Schreiner's aesthetic and survival strategies are syncretic ones, I do not intend to reinscribe syncretism as a distinctive feature of African cultural formations; I mean that *all* art, no matter what its cultural origin, is to a greater or lesser extent inevitably syncretic. The most evocative art coming from the United States, that of Cindy Sherman, for instance, is radically so.

To survey Schreiner's or Dinesen's lifework is to recognize both women as distinctly modernist spirits. Whatever else, this spirit is characterized by two things: attempts to replace the real with the ideal and the personal with the impersonal, and attempts to produce artful, visually and emotionally satisfying configurations of space, material, movement, and gesture. Despite the apparent differences in the genres in which each worked, the voices adopted in every one are for the most part distinctly impersonal. Schreiner's novels and Dinesen's tales and memoirs all reveal the tones and stances of allegory, folktale, legend; their literary prose is most often austere, ceremonial, or mythic. Recordings of two of Dinesen's recitations from memory, "Barua a Soldani" or "The King's Letter," originally written for Danish radio and included in *Shadows on the Grass,* and "The Wine of the Tetrarch," one of the many tales within a tale in "The Deluge at Norderney" from *Seven Gothic Tales,* strongly suggest a quite conscious decision on her part to emulate the disembodied voice that would be characteristic of Benjamin's storyteller, one auditors at her recitations regularly described as having a "wraithlike transparency."[20] My own listening to tapes confirms this description. That same transparency is evident in her photographic portraits. The voices of the heroines or narrators of Schreiner's three novels nearly always seem to be straining toward some universalized, mythic voice of woman, and though some might argue that her letters are full of impassioned and very personal confessions, the *content* of those confessions places her firmly in the camp of the modernist impersonalists. Habitually, in times of trial she repeats some version of what she says in a letter to her friend Edward Carpenter: "It isn't really the intellect and nature that are at war, it's the PERSONAL and the IMPERSONAL."[21] In the months before her novelist friend Amy Levy committed suicide, Schreiner had desperately tried to offer her support. She sent Levy a copy of "Do Not Hurry, Have Faith" from Carpenter's *Toward Democracy,* for instance. But in writing to thank Schreiner Levy confided, "Philosophy can't help me. I am too much shut in with the personal."[22] She killed herself the next day. When Schreiner returned to South Africa after one of her extended stays in Europe, her first letter to Havelock Ellis back in England detailed what she missed most: the loss of "talk about anything that [is] in any way impersonal."[23]

If Dinesen and Schreiner shared modernism's preference for the impersonal over the personal, like it they also preferred those artful configurations that deny or defy the "natural" in favor of configurations presumed to be more ideal, pleasing, or satisfying. I am not the first to suggest that such a definition has several prior implications embedded within it. Denial of the natural, the real, and the past (which would include, obviously, one's race, gender, and "own" history and origins) implies unhappiness with exactly those things. It implies the *need* for rejection of them, implying in turn that the past, the real, and the natural all possess a fascination and a power that precipitate the need for rejection or denial in the first place. Above all else, it reflects the belief in and need for the deliberate assertion of *will* or imagination over the natural or the real.

Schreiner and Dinesen fulfill every piece of this prescription. One finds few real Africans in their writings, for instance. Schreiner's sleepy Boers, slow to anger but flaring like tinder if provoked, are Schreiner herself. Dinesen's Africans have been read by Robert Langbaum as mythical reenactments of Europe's lost Edenic past, and more recently by Abdul JanMohamed partly as evidence of her unwitting contribution to the production of a colonialist discourse having as its major aim the commodification of Africans into exchange value. But while it's true there may not be any real Africans in Schreiner's or Dinesen's writings, there are no real husbands there either. Dinesen uses exactly the same strategy of affectionate diminishment to describe Africans and men in general. In the process she manages to reserve for herself a self-protective distance from both: "In my dealings with Farah and his tribe [the Somali], I felt that whatever else I might risk from their hand, I did not run the risk of being pitied—no more than I would do in my dealings with a young boy at home. Personally I have always had a predilection for boys, and have at times reflected that the strong sex reaches its highest point of lovableness at the age of twelve to seventeen—to get it back, in a second flowering, at the age of seventy to ninety. So were the Somali from the first day irresistible to me."[24]

Anyone looking for a fair rendering of Dinesen's husband Bror Blixen probably ought to read not Dinesen's letters, her memoirs of Africa, or even her short book *On Modern Marriage,* but Beryl Markham's *West with the Night.* More can be learned about Bror Blixen in a few lines there than in all of Dinesen's writings: "Blix—Blickie—Baron von Blixen. . . . He is six feet of amiable Swede and to my knowledge, the toughest most durable White Hunter ever to snicker at the fanfare of safari or to shoot a charging buffalo between the eyes while debating whether his sundown drink will be gin or whiskey."[25] Markham's is also a more revealing portrait of the lover Dinesen and Markham seem to have shared. The Africans' name for Denys Finch Hatton was Makanyaga, which means "to tread on you." "He could tread upon inferior men with his tongue," says Markham. "He can punish with a word—and that is a wonderful skill."[26] This observation has about it far more of the messily real and human than any of Dinesen's far more romantic constructions, where Finch Hatton tends to figure mostly as sultan to her Sheherazade. This is not to suggest that Markham's is an entirely clear-eyed vision either, especially not a clear-eyed apprehension of Africans' understanding of Europeans. Underestimating the extent of their ability for ironizing, and for laughing at the European colonizer, Markham here either does not know or neglects to mention that Africans also referred to Bror as Wahoga. Blixen thought it meant "wild duck"; it actually means "waddler."[27]

In Schreiner's universe as in Dinesen's, men vacillate. Sometimes they are childlike creatures toward whom she can safely feel affectionate. She writes to Edward Carpenter describing "a dear old Swede [who] has just been to say goodbye to me. Such a beautiful *childlike* nature. . . . He wanted me to marry him."[28] The father whose death devastated her when she was twenty-one is resurrected in her portrait of Otto the old German in *Story of an African Farm,* and there the epithets used to describe him at his death replicate the move Schreiner makes around males in general whenever she admires them: he had been, she says, "a loving, simple, childlike old man."[29] At other times Schreiner's dances of deference in letters to male correspondents seem to suggest that these portraits of men as childlike are designed to counteract the unimaginable powers she bestows on them elsewhere, especially when she considers them as sexual partners or objects of desire. In her two-volume biography of Eleanor Marx, Yvonne Kapp recounts what she takes to be Schreiner's heartless response to news of her friend's death. She writes from Kimberley, South Africa, "I am so glad Eleanor is dead. It is such a mercy she has escaped from [her husband]."[30] Although it is true that Marx's husband was the almost universally despised Edward Aveling, that Olive Schreiner, new woman and freethinker, could imagine no escape for her friend but death is more than a bit disconcerting.

Schreiner exhibited all her life an alternating idealism and cynicism about specific males and about mankind writ large. Her idealism about marriage was absolute and nonnegotiable: "The one and only ideal is the perfect mental and physical lifelong union of one man and one woman."[31] Her letters to friends are full of protestations of how wonderful her marriage to "Cron" was. He was the mate to her soul, the financial and moral equal her ideal of marriage required, the life companion her social writings espoused. It is quite a shock to discover at the end of Ruth First and Ann Scott's biography the bitter diary entry written by her husband three years after her death, describing their marriage as "so many weary years."[32]

First and Scott suggest that Schreiner was "ideological about personal life."[33] So was Dinesen, who insisted in *On Modern Marriage* that the *ideal* of marriage should always supersede the demands of the real. "If a sufficiently attractive illusion can be created the reality automatically follows."[34] This sentiment could be taken as just one more piece of the characteristic Dinesen perversity designed to shock, a bit of homage to the Nietzsche or Kierkegaard whose works she loved so much. But it is also at least two other things. It replicates a conception of love she and Schreiner held in common with other modernist women. Lou Andreas-Salomé, intellectual companion to Nietzsche and others, articulated a similar belief in ideal love as a "shared love for and dedication to a third instance, something that exceeds them both."[35] This privileging of ideal over real is also a sign of Dinesen's belief in Lamarckian evolution. The giraffe constantly stretching to reach the tenderest leaves eventually grew a long neck. All that is needed is sufficient exertion of will over enough time. For Schreiner, who even as a teenager read Schopenhauer, this need for exertion of *will* over nature, desire, and feeling was absolute.

Though Schopenhauer's writings reached their height of popularity among Europeans in the 1850s,[36] Schreiner discovered him only shortly after 1870, during the years she spent as a governess in mud-floored Afrikaner homes. His influence on her was profound. But the conception of will she found in his writings that so intrigued her is not uncomplicated, and it certainly provided no license for a young girl to set her teeth and go after what she wanted. "The highest ideal of human nature," she insisted in *Woman and Labour*, is one "in which intellectual power and strength of will are combined with an infinite tenderness and wide human sympathy."[37] At the very least, this Schopenhauerian view of the function of will carries with it no necessity for individual choice or self-assertion, as Walter Benjamin recognized in his *Origin of German Tragic Drama,* where he associates the Schopenhauerian will not so much with conscious self-assertion as with "the slumbering will to life" to be found in "Nirvana" once man recognizes that we are "merely images and artistic projections for the true author." We achieve our highest dignity, that is, only in our significance as works of art.[38] Both Schreiner and Dinesen consistently struggled to enact, or in the most literal sense to *embody,* this philosophical stance, even as their behavior frequently contradicted those principles. Terry Eagleton's blunt assessment of will's function for Schopenhauer and Nietzsche helps to account, perhaps, for Schreiner's and Dinesen's consistent contradictoriness. Finally, says Eagleton, for Schopenhauer "the will is quite futile and purposeless." But it nonetheless serves one very important purpose: it "shields us from a knowledge of its own utter pointlessness by breeding in us a delusion of intellect."[39]

To no small extent this emphasis on the will and on the ideal the will might bring into being helped generate the unhappiness both women experienced. In *Story of an African Farm,* imagining herself inside the head of Napoleon Bonaparte, Lyndall muses, "When he said a thing to himself he never forgot it. He waited, and waited, and waited, and it came at last." And when Em concludes that "he must have been very happy," Lyndall's response is, "I do not know . . . but he had what he said he would have, and that is better than being happy."[40] The priority Dinesen and Schreiner gave to straining toward the ideal rather than living in the real, among other things, provided both with a rationale for running from more ordinary kinds of intimacy. In real, everyday relations each woman apparently feared she could not control either her own emotions or those of the one with whom she might be intimate. Dinesen was quite clear about the power of the erotic. "There is actually not a little to be said for the sensible views of the old folk," she muses in a letter to her brother Thomas, "who tried to protect themselves in every way they could and equip themselves with both safety valves and fireproof walls; this perilous power was necessary to life, but no one should be permitted to set it free, play with it without being under control or run around with it by themselves."[41] Every human being is ultimately a secret to every other, and no analysis, no matter how complex, can uncover what lay deepest in either woman's heart. But I do suspect that both women's fear of erotic attachment stemmed partly from their recognition of their own tendency to give away too much of themselves once they were in one. Schreiner's letters are full of disconcerting confessions of a desire to open her veins and pour out her own lifeblood to nourish someone else. Dinesen's desire is more deeply coded, but it can be read nonetheless in such places as her story "Babette's Feast" and can be seen even during the Danish occupation, when she adamantly refused to do anything that might resemble hoarding, leaving her home at Rungstedlund with an empty pantry.

This belief in the destructive power of erotic attachment is, I believe, partly responsible for the self-containment and the private, unreachable core each woman so clearly cultivated. That unreachable core, in turn, seems to have frightened men to whom they might be attached, and partly as a consequence each ultimately lived her emotional life alone.[42]

If their psychic makeup, fierce passion, and idealism combined with strong will caused others to see them as difficult and to stay a safe distance away, their lives must have felt every bit as difficult from the inside. Since each *thought* she wanted real emotional attachment, each made endless deferential or conciliatory gestures to get and retain men's affections. But each had an uncanny knack for choosing husbands, lovers, or male friends either constitutionally incapable of commitment or less than their equal in intellectual or spiritual energy or will. Bror Blixen was a playboy and great white hunter but was no intellect. Denys Finch Hatton, the man Dinesen by all accounts really loved, was classically educated and classically beautiful, as figure 2 makes clear. He was also a man with a pathological fear of emotional commitment of any kind, and she may have chosen him as a lover not only because of his dashing good looks but also because his emotional distance replicated her own intuitive fear of being trapped.[43]

Like many of the new women of the 1880s, Schreiner spent

Figure 2. Denys Finch Hatton. Photographer and date unknown. Photograph courtesy of the Royal Library, det Kongelige Bibliotek, Copenhagen, Denmark.

most of her adult life insisting that marriage was unnecessary. Samuel Cronwright was a South African farmer eight years her junior. A lawyer and eventually a powerful political force working for the rights of native Africans in South Africa, he did some writing himself, including a paper on ostriches and a book called *The Angora Goat*. When Schreiner at the age of forty announced to feminist friends that she intended to marry him, they all wondered why. Her response was graphic and to the point. She stood up, strutted around the room, and said, "because I like his forearms."[44] The portrait of Olive and the man she called "Cron" standing in the doorway of their South African farmhouse in Cradock shortly after their marriage, Cron with his shirtsleeves rolled up above his elbows, suggests that he had good forearms and she had good taste (see fig. 3).

One source of both women's difficulties lurks in these anecdotes. Impossibly idealistic, each feared disappointment and protected herself from it in advance. Schreiner admired the poetry of Robert Browning, but when she had an opportunity to meet

Figure 3. Olive Schreiner and Samuel Cronwright-Schreiner in their farmhouse near Cradock, South Africa, soon after their marriage in 1894. The Carpenter Collection, the Sheffield Archives. Photograph Courtesy of Keith Crawshaw, director of Sheffield Libraries and Information Services, Sheffield Central Library, Sheffield, England.

him in London she declined, fearing disillusionment with the real man.[45] Both were obviously committed to following their physical desires, whatever that might cost in the way of spiritual or enduring companionship. But a good bit of their difficulties began at this site of desire. The passion of Schreiner's Undine is aroused not by the gentleness or potential for intellectual camaraderie embodied in the one man who expresses a desire for her, but by his cruel and more handsome brother, whose magnetic attraction consists—exactly as does Grandcourt's for Gwendolen Harleth in George Eliot's *Daniel Deronda*—in his mastery of the art of mastery. Schreiner's biographers have speculated that sadomasochism played a part in her erotic life. "You love me," Lyndall says to her stranger, "because you cannot bear to be resisted, and want to master me. You liked me at first because I treated you and all men with indifference. You resolved to have me because I seemed unattainable." Her stranger's response is a question: "And you loved me—?" To which Lyndall replies without hesitation, "Because you are strong. You are the first man I ever was afraid of."[46] Both Dinesen and Schreiner are drawn to an erotics of power, and the pain each experienced in her relations with European men might best be seen as a consequence of this attraction toward "masters" rather than as an attraction toward pain or toward being mastered. "Africa" in their psychic economy obviously became another site for this same exchange, in which identification with Africa and Africans was alternately an identification with mastery over Africans and the masculinity implied by that mastery and an identification with those who had been mastered. Schreiner's identification with "England" was alternately an identification with its mastery and with what she called in *An English South-African's View of the Situation* the "shell of hard reserve" characteristic of the English she constructed. "There are probably few of us," she confesses, "who have not some consciousness of this defect in our own persons."[47]

Alternately master and mastered, each woman all her life found men simultaneously absolutely essential and completely irrelevant. Each was capable of great self-reliance, running a farm or a career or both, helping to lead a feminist movement, living a life largely self-supported in all senses of that word. Schreiner was the sixth of twelve children. She was put out to work as a governess by age fifteen and was virtually homeless for the next ten years. It should come as no surprise that one of her early heroes was Ralph Waldo Emerson or that her first published novel, *The Story of an African Farm,* which she carried in manuscript from Africa to England on her first trip in 1881, was published under the pseudonym

Ralph Iron and contained characters named Waldo and Em.[48] But despite their self-reliance, each woman still saw herself by turns as waiflike and lost when she was not the center of some male gaze. Each consequently lived in varying degrees of misery or profound restlessness.[49]

In Africa, Schreiner thought she would feel healthier in England. In England, she longed for Africa. She loved South Africa but hated British imperialism there. Since 80 percent of the white population in the Cape Colony were Afrikaners with no love of the Brits or "Rooineks," and since most of the British were virulently nationalistic, as she was not, Schreiner was an outsider even in her "own" country. Her resistance to the Boer War in 1899–1902 got her labeled anti-British by other white women interested as she was in universal suffrage, so even membership in the international community of feminists was problematic. She was allowed into the International Women's Suffrage Alliance only after much resistance. Her opposition to the British during the Boer War did not necessarily endear her to native Africans. For instance, it put her in opposition to King Cetshwayo. This great Zulu tactician and leader welcomed British annexation of the Transvaal because British control might serve as a defense against Boer encroachment into Zulu lands.[50] In England Schreiner found intellectual companionship, but she was mercilessly harassed during World War I for her German surname and pacifist views. And as a woman raised in Africa, oblivious both by temperament and by cultural upbringing to the niceties of ladies' manners, she encountered smirks and hostility wherever she went in Europe because of her inattention to proprieties of dress and demeanor. In *Thoughts on South Africa* she describes her position as an Englishwoman born in South Africa and returning to it after many years' absence. In a telling metaphor she describes herself as "in a somewhat twofold position . . . half . . . outsider; half . . . lover."[51] But hers was a profound psychic restlessness transcending—if that is the right word—any external causes. On November 16, 1884, she would write to Havelock Ellis, "My real life is here, and if I leave England, . . . I am dead."[52] Only three weeks later and still in England, she is full of nostalgia for South Africa: "I want," she says, "to go back to the old life."[53]

Both Schreiner and Dinesen were clearly creatures of their

times. Their belief in the necessity for willful, imaginative reconfiguration of the real makes them part of the modern spirit. Both enacted much else of what is true of the modern, most especially its tendency toward oscillation: between fascination with and rejection of the past, nature, the real. Their desires oscillated between embracing the unconventional and the orthodox. They oscillated as well between believing in the necessity for the exertion of will and in the need to surrender to fate (in Dinesen's case) or to the dictates of nature (in Schreiner's), each woman devoting huge amounts of literary and extraliterary writing to speculating on just what the nature of woman might be.[54] Obviously there is more than a bit of contradiction in the notion that one must will oneself into being what "by nature" one presumably already is. Psychosexually, both oscillated between wanting to be desiring subjects and desired objects.

Despite their best intentions, both also participated to some extent in the construction of "Africa" and "Africans" as concepts in Western epistemology. Participating in late nineteenth-century discourses of eugenics and sexology and sharing friendships with central figures in those explorations like Havelock Ellis and Karl Pearson, for instance, Schreiner actively contributed to the debates not just about the "nature of man" and the "nature of woman," but about the "nature of Africans" as well. In this regard she can be grouped with other liberal British settlers living in the Cape Colony during this period who, while trying to resist what by 1905 would become apartheid, unwittingly helped to legitimate it. Sympathetic liberal British residents of South Africa like Schreiner tended to assume that the nature of Africans suited them to an agricultural self-sufficiency that could only be crippled if they were not shielded from the "harsh world of industrialization" and the laissez-faire capitalism whose consequences in England during this time were painfully obvious.[55] The eugenicists who formed a major part of Schreiner's intellectual circle were also worrying about protecting the "racial purity" of every group. Schreiner's constructions of Africans are never uncomplicated. The same Olive Schreiner who wrote powerfully about the sufferings inflicted on native Africans as Boer and British struggled for possession of South Africa regularly referred to "dirty little Bushmen" in her novels.[56] The same Isak Dinesen who wrote eloquently of her great admiration for the natural nobility and endurance of Somali and wrote matter-of-factly about her day-to-day working relations with Kikuyu and Somali men regularly romanticized and infantilized both.

As women whose roots were European, they were necessarily participants in what Achille Mbembe calls the intimate tyranny at work in everyday life in the colony and postcolony.[57] But they also gave every evidence of identifying with colonized Africans. I suggest no equation between their sufferings and those of black Africans—only that Dinesen's and Schreiner's *own* perceptions of insufficient liberty are evident in their assumption of survival strategies that are sometimes analogous to those of black Africans, in Dinesen's case, and of South African Boers or Afrikaners in Schreiner's.[58] "A human being only becomes human at all by imitating other human beings," says Adorno, and though one might regret Dinesen's and Schreiner's appropriation of what they thought of as African survival strategies, for Adorno acts of imitation like theirs constitute the primal form of love, in which can be traced the "scent of the utopia which could shake the structure of domination."[59]

Dinesen's and Schreiner's borrowings from Africans are many. Their visual representations of African landscapes, for instance, sometimes replicate European desires to render the changes their presence had wrought and sometimes approximate strategies more akin to Africans' efforts to take back their own territory by depicting it as it was before those intrusions. They oscillate between a desire to be seen as they are and an equally strong desire to hide, dissemble, mask: to confound the gaze of those who would try to understand them, as did those Africans Dinesen portrayed as longing for darkness. Addressing himself to African artists in *The African Image,* Ezekiel Mphahlele tells them that "the needle that registers your response as an artist swings between protest and romantic writing, and then, when you are spiritually emancipated, the needle quivers around the central point—the meeting point between rejection and acceptance. Then you know both how excruciating and exciting it is to be the meeting point of two streams of consciousness and the paradoxes they pose." He adds that "if there is any *negritude* in the black man's art in South Africa, it is because we are African." "Simply because we respond intensely to situations is no reason why we should think non-Africans are incapable of doing so, or that we are the only section of the human race who are full of passionate intensity."[60] Schreiner and Dinesen, full of their own passionate intensity, oscillate between these same two poles.

To trace the major forms of oscillation I see as constituting these two white women's survival and self-presentation strategies, I have carved out a path that is itself an oscillation between biography and criticism, or more accurately an easement across both as well as across theories of modernism, subaltern studies, feminist and colonialist discourse, and theories of African philosophy and history, particularly recent work critical of what Paulin J. Hountondji and others refer to as "ethnophilosophy." In doing so I hope to make some small contribution to the dialogic project V. Y. Mudimbe suggests might constitute one heuristic available to members of one culture attempting to understand itself and its relation to an other.[61]

This is not infrequently a negative hermeneutic, and mine draws together strands of discourse from art history and postcolonial theory that at first glance seem quite disparate. Homi Bhabha, for instance, is one of those postcolonial critics who, following Frantz Fanon, uses a psychoanalytic paradigm to understand the mechanisms of the postcolonial condition. "Racist man," he suggests, "turns on the idea of man as his alienated image, not self and other, but the 'otherness' of the self . . . inscribed in his behavior and his writings," producing in the process the "bizarre figure of desire [that] splits along the axis on which it turns."[62]

In the diagrammatic schema she constructs in *The Optical Unconscious,* Rosalind Krauss produces and emphasizes a different axis as she represents the closed field she sees the modern to be. Krauss suggests we have tended to think of modernism as a history, one that moves from impressionism, through neoimpressionism, to fauvism, from there to cubism, to abstraction, and so on. But she believes more can be learned about the political implications of modernism by representing it diagrammatically. For her the "universe" of modernism is best represented by a version of the

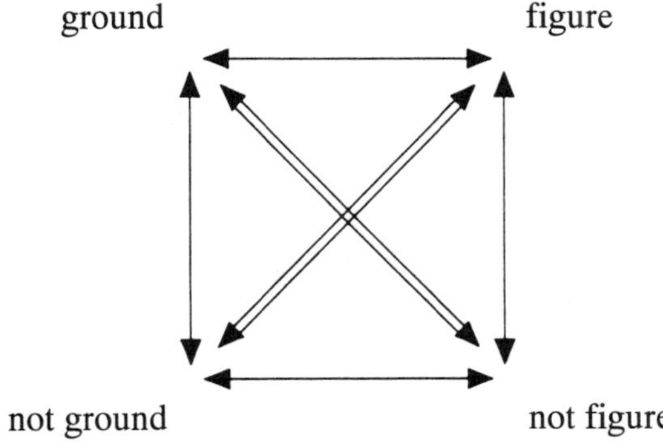

Figure 4. Modernism as a graph or table rather than as a history. From Rosalind Krauss, *The Optical Unconscious,* p. 14.

structuralist's Klein group reproduced here from Krauss's book (fig. 4), representing modernism "not just [as] a binary opposition or axis" but as "a fourfold field."

The beauties of Krauss's diagram are many. It can be read all around the square, so that the usual oppositions of the visual field, "field" and "ground," can be reread: "All around the square we find the same thing stated over and over—field *versus* ground—except not stated the same way."[63] The universe of visual perception mapped by a distinction between figure and ground instead becomes one in which there is more than just the axis of field and ground, and more than just its inversion. What becomes available for consideration is work going on along what she calls the *neutral* axis or, following the structuralists, the deixical axis of not-figure and not-ground, or even the axis of not *not*-figure and not *not*-ground, a "neutral axis for the maybes."[64] In *Vision and Painting* Norman Bryson notes that *deixis* suggests "utterance in carnal form." It not only points back to the body of the painter (or speaker, I suggest) but points to a here, there, then, and now, all of which deixical references he says Western painting is predicated on disavowing.[65] In place of Bhabha's psychoanalytic image of racist man "splitting along the axis" of his own figure of desire, then, Krauss's rewriting of the modern can be substituted. Not only does her figuration incorporate the psychoanalytic dimension present in Bhabha's model, but it opens up at the same time a "space for the maybes."[66] "There is," says Krauss, "for every absolute—marriage yes; incest, no—its more flexible, shadow correlate: the kind of maybe, maybe of the not-not axis."[67] Here, on the slash of that deictical axis, is the place where Dinesen and Schreiner carefully construct themselves. It is the place they come to call home—to return to Mphahlele's metaphor of the African artist, the psychic place where their "needle quivers" midway between acceptance and rejection. They were not travelers to Africa, and generically speaking they did not produce travel literature. But what they produced is not quite *not* travel literature either. In their production of works that are not travel literature and not not-travel literature; not memoir but not not-memoir, they managed to produce lifeworks that could be at the same time more self-revelatory and more powerfully political than could have been produced in generically more determinate works. Self-defined as both not European and not African, they take pains to construct themselves as not *not*-European and not *not*-African either, representing themselves also as not male/not female but also not *not*-male and not *not*-female; they are not white/not black; not colonial/not *not*-colonial. If we consider their lifeworks in toto, it becomes abundantly clear that living on the slash became their line of flight from construction of gender, race, and nationality they found too confining.

My reading of their positionality as not male/not female is among other things an attempt to read feminist theory through the lifeworks of Olive Schreiner and Isak Dinesen rather than reading Schreiner and Dinesen through the lens of any feminist theory. I settled on this method for several reasons. First, because in general theories tend to be valued as much for what they allow us to *avoid* seeing as for what they bring into view. No matter which critical paradigm one applies to a reading of Dinesen's and Schreiner's lifeworks, what is most molten and highly charged in their works seems always stubbornly to evade its explanatory power. Each woman's strategies of resistance seem to reveal themselves always and only in the quotidian, and in the "residue" theory leaves behind: in all those messy particulars of behavior and style; in offhand and especially in parenthetical remarks in letters; in each woman's carefully constructed, mutually self-canceling gestures and postures. Though post-Enlightenment theory has strongly advocated attention to such concrete particulars, the largest proportions of it still seem to exist in the form of generalized recommendations that the critic be specific. In considering the role of academic feminists in theorizing difference for women, Nancy Hartsock asks whether it is either possible or desirable to develop a general theory and considers that the search would better be abandoned in favor of making a space in which a number of heterogeneous voices might be heard. "What kind of common claims can be made about those of white women and women and men of color? About the situations of Western peoples and those who have been colonized? . . . Is it ever legitimate to say 'women' without qualification?"[68] V. Y. Mudimbe asks virtually the same questions in "Which Idea of Africa?" concluding that in African literature as in all matters African "each text is . . . particularized according to the ideological and the literary inclination of its author."[69]

Close study of the particulars of the lifeworks of Schreiner and Dinesen yields more and more instances of oscillation between contraries: between their private production of gender and their public pronouncements about and performances of that gender; between public embracing and private rejecting of belief in something like the eternal woman. Judith Butler's *Gender Trouble,* which I read in part as suggesting that it's possible to talk about the somewhat "woman"-alienated woman as something other than necessarily self-alienated, woman hating, or male identified, has helped this project immensely. So also have Eve Sedgwick's musings at the 1991 English Institute. If a female can't "come out" as *not* woman (because she is not queer), and she feels confined and constrained by all available constructions of woman, what public or private places might she construct where she can negotiate how and who to be? Perhaps, Sedgwick suggests, the binary poles of sexuality are neither female/male nor heterosexual/homosexual, but closeted/out, and gender is a product of the constant negotiations made as we shuttle between private and public performances in the public and private spheres.

Readers will undoubtedly ask what I intend to make of Schreiner's and Dinesen's complicated mutually self-canceling performances of their gender—of what both Foucault and Habermas would regard as split subjects. But the question of whether Schreiner's and Dinesen's elaborate and artful survival strategies of oscillation ought to be seen as pathological will be bracketed here. We have Foucault to thank for reminding us that by and large frameworks produce pathologies rather than pathologies' producing frameworks. At several junctures in the pages that follow I will also make claims for the function of particular elements of Schreiner's or Dinesen's practice that rely on no particular theory of feminist or colonial discourse, even claims that might be regarded as somehow retrograde. But there is always a gap between consistency with the hypotheses of theory, which is always *textual,* and lives, which are always *actual:* stubbornly untheorizable, messily and mercifully particular. In instances where Schreiner's and Dinesen's lifeworks seem to be functioning in ways no theory accounts for, my only defense is to say that I recognize the particular aesthetic/survival strategy being employed because I see in it a form of one of my own, or that in my fifty years on earth there have been friends, lovers, or family who either have acknowledged or seem to have demonstrated similar strategies of survival and self-presentation. Were someone to push me to the wall when I make such assertions I would respond exactly as H. L. Mencken did when asked if he believed in infant baptism: "Believe it," he answered, "Hell, I've *seen* it!"

Insofar as I do have a guiding spirit, that spirit is Walter Benjamin. As my practice in these pages has probably already made clear, my stance is very much that of a flaneur of theory. But Benjamin's usefulness extends far beyond this. His privileging of story over novel points the best way toward a fuller appreciation of Dinesen's and Schreiner's lifeworks. He also provides inspiration for a discussion of Dinesen and Schreiner because each woman's most common subversive survival strategy turns out in my reading to be a kind of master oscillation between an apparent embracing and an actual subversion of mythic categories, either of some mythic Africa or of some mythic idea of woman. Exactly this was the example of Benjamin's own lifework, which often focused intensely on such imaginative refigurations, most often by burrowing inside mythic categories in order to explode them from within. Finally, as a Jew in Europe during the 1930s Benjamin was of course engaged in his own valiant struggle to find or create a home or haven.[70] Whereas Benjamin in part survived by becoming the bemused, detached flaneur, Dinesen and Schreiner seem to have insisted on being fully engaged, both feet within both poles of the oppositions and oscillations out of which they produced themselves. But though there may be no *flâneuse,* even here Benjamin provides a kind of proleptic commentary on Dinesen and Schreiner, noting in his study of the romantics and of Novalis in particular that the movement between apparently preexisting extremes seems not only to precede those extremes but to produce them, creating in the process the raw materials of self and art.

These raw materials are as various and complex as the refigurations they undergo in Schreiner's and Dinesen's hands. What appears to be embraced on one level or in one sphere—"womanly" self-effacement, for instance—is often overturned on another. Each woman's lifework is a kind of montage. Schreiner's is made up of the earnest rhetoric of the new woman coupled with far from sympathetic portraits of what she often refers to as the solid, "sheep-souled" Boers. The latter are seen ambivalently, sometimes with distaste at their lack of imagination, their literal-mindedness, their complacent focus on their own creature comforts. But sometimes they are portrayed more sympathetically, especially when Schreiner sees them through her Schopenhauerian belief in the will. Yet there are times when either of these constructions is confounded by Schreiner's own self-presentation, which, as her biographers and biographers of her friends are quick to point out, is often as "demanding" and "egotistical" as that of the heroines she produces. The earnest philosophical questioning characteristic of her heroines and of her own prose alternates with a lyricism that from time to time overtakes her and her prose, especially in her short allegories. Her earnest fictional explorations of the new woman are laced with themes characteristic of modernist novelists, especially with musings about the nature of man and the nature of woman echoing explorations like those in Virginia Woolf's 1915 novel *The Voyage Out.*[71] Her novels' explorations of the new woman are set in African landscapes that are sometimes rendered in emotional terms after the fashion of avant-garde painters of the modern era. Those same landscapes sometimes offer instead a rare, straight-ahead look at the degradation brought about by the colonial order in South Africa.

Dinesen's montage includes the fairy tales of Hans Christian Andersen fused with folktales she heard in Africa, borrowings and behaviors inspired by the paradoxical, puckish philosophy of Kierkegaard and Nietzsche strained through what she saw as the similarly puckish and paradoxical philosophy of the Kikuyu[72] or the serene acceptance of the Muslim Somali she claimed taught her so much about how to survive and endure under less than ideal conditions. Of Kamante, her majordomo during her years in Kenya, for instance, she remarks that "sometimes I had the feeling he was really impersonating himself for me—playing the outcast, the *destiné,* the jester, the muse, the servant of a great master."[73]

One of the most interesting things about Dinesen's use of Africans to construct her own identity is the extent to which she professed to identify with the Kikuyu—the more "sensible," "get ahead" people who worked closely with her at Karen Coffee—rather than with the Maasai, who were so much more like her: aristocratic, proud, fatalistic. Temperamentally far too much like her to be safely othered, the Maasai she mostly observed respectfully, if romantically, from a distance. If descriptions of natives by Westerners represent a kind of naming of alterity, then Dinesen's elaborately detailed descriptions of them from the outside, coupled with her silence about her affinities with them, are explicable as evidence of her recognition of their uncanny "sameness." In *Out of Africa* Dinesen tells us the Maasai *moran* (warrior) has "that particular form of intelligence which we call *chic;* —daring, and wildly fantastical as they seem, they are still unswervingly true to their own nature, and to an immanent ideal. Their style is not an assumed manner, nor an imitation of a foreign perfection; it has grown from the inside, and is an expression of the race and its history."[74] Dinesen's extremely admiring and minutely detailed description of the Maasai goes on for many pages. But that minuteness is by no means complete, and the lacunae are interesting. Dinesen explicitly neglects to tell her readers whether those morans walking so majestically past Karen Coffee are Keekonyokie, Purko, or Ildamat. Dinesen needed those Maasai to be members of *her* "tribe," since she was convinced she had learned a great deal about—to cite Gayatri Spivak citing Derrida citing Nietzsche—woman playing woman "playing woman,"[75] and she learned it largely from the Maasai, whom she saw as enacting a corollary self-ironizing self-presentation, and doing it with intelligence, wit, and grace.

Sara Suleri suggests that the female colonial in India experienced a similar sense of alternating identity and alterity from Indian women, which resulted in the creation of an attraction/repulsion so strong the Anglo-Indian women writing about Indian women seemed incapable of focusing on faces or describing physiognomy, even as they described minutely the Indian women's clothing. One consequence was an aesthetic produced by the European woman writer in India that Suleri suggests moved "veil" from the female subject to discourse itself.[76] But the relation between Dinesen and Schreiner and their discourse of Africa is more complex, or at least different from that of the Anglo-Indian women Suleri describes, in part because Schreiner and Dinesen believed themselves to be in Africa as *independent* women rather than as wives, at least in their own self-constructions. They also enacted the oscillation Ann Bermingham aptly delineates in *Landscape and Ideology* as one between "spectacle and specimen." Victorians had a taste for nature as spectacle, but they were at the same time developing a serious interest in the naturalist's study of nature. "One appears to celebrate the seeing subject, the other to investigate the objects seen." One effect of viewing nature in this way, Bermingham suggests, "is to naturalize the spectator's role. . . . The sheer obviousness of the spectator's presence thus facilitates the viewers' 'objective' attention to what is seen."[77] But Dinesen's and Schreiner's obvious identifications with Africans result in a discourse revealing them to be uncomfortable with the positionality of distanced spectator at the spectacle of Africans. Dinesen, for instance, regularly alternates between minute descriptions of individual Maasai and a discourse that seems designed to allow them the kind of privacy and freedom from the gaze that she herself desires. Dinesen hated to be what she called "brass-serpented"—seen as an image—by Africans or by Europeans. Of one member of the Maasai, Kabero, she says that "he had acquired the Maasai carriage of the head, with the chin stretched forward, as if he were presenting you his sullen arrogant face upon a tray. He had," she says, "the general rigid, passive, and insolent bearing of the Moran [warrior], that makes of him an object for contemplation, such as a statue is, a figure which is to be seen, but which itself does not see."[78] Dinesen replicates not just the spirit but even the particulars of this posture, pose, and attitude in her own photographic portrait taken many years later by Reimert Kehlet in Denmark (see chap. 2). Only by considering her production of her own visuality in her photographic portrait and her portrait of Africans in her memoirs as part of the same lifework does it become possible to recognize both her strong identification with the Maasai she describes here and her reluctance in her two memoirs of Africa to subject them to the same kind of surveillance she found repugnant when it was trained on her.

Cheryl Bentsen's *Maasai Days,* a record of her stay in Kenya beginning in 1980, has all the advantages of a personal memoir with no pretensions to ethnographic analysis. Her account of her friendship with members of two extended Maasai families offers some glimpses into the day-to-day life of Dickson, a young Maasai who has reluctantly given up the life of a moran to attend college. Dickson and his roommate, also Maasai, tack a sign on the door of their dorm room: Strangers in a Strange Land, it announces. Bentsen remarks, "He liked spy thrillers in which the CIA, the KGB or the Mossad were featured. He asked if I had any Marvin Gaye or Kenny Rogers tapes. He liked them both, and his roommate had a cassette player. His desk was spread with charts and books, geometry exercises, drawing tools. Other students asked to 'rent' his notes. Above his desk, he had put up a snapshot of himself as a moran, under which he had written: 'The Desert Wanderer: Further Studies in the Bush.' "[79] Dinesen produced for herself a similar perspective on woman, investing a great deal in living with style what she referred to, in one of my favorite double citations, as "what is generally known as 'one's life.' "[80]

Dinesen also produces tales exhibiting her own very modernist reaction to the overcooked sensualism of Danish romantic novels such as Jens Peter Jacobsen's *Niels Lyhne,* which she loved. All these gestural, generic, formal, behavioral, attitudinal borrowings both European and African are not sources and influences. They serve instead as raw materials refigured and played off against one another. Juxtaposing these separate borrowings and tropings lays bare some of the mechanisms whereby Dinesen, for instance, turned her writings' calls for the submission of women into a triumph for her own self-determination as a woman, and by which Olive Schreiner managed to parlay her writings' calls for woman's selflessness not into self-erasure but into her own self-assertion. Each woman seems to have been able to convert the admonishments in her writings to do one thing into a life performance in which she herself did the opposite. This is a familiar strategy. In *Daniel Deronda* George Eliot turns her own "selfishness" in upsetting social convention by living with George Henry Lewes into a fictionalized plea for self-abnegation in the face of the social and moral obligations assumed to come with gender (in Gwendolen Harleth's case) or race (in Deronda's).

Borrowing from both European and African forms and the spirit behind each, through complex sets of reversals both women invented for themselves a liberatory performative logic in discursive space and simultaneously a discursive logic in performative space, with everything in their lives and writings functioning homeostatically. In this respect they seem to have devised a survival strategy in the face of difficulties that resembles those that Belgian missionary Placide Tempels attributed to Africans in his *Bantu Philosophy*, published in 1959. Tempels proposed that African behavior and belief rest on "a single principle" representing "a single value: vital force," growing out of a desire to achieve "a balance of forces." African cultural formations, then, were all to be understood as "mechanisms for maintaining that balance."[81] I am by no means uncritically accepting such simplistic conceptions of African "philosophy" as these that Hountondji, Mudimbe, and others have brought under critique; I am positing instead what Dinesen and Schreiner constructed as African behavior and belief and then turned to their own use. What I am calling the *homeostatic* is one of those borrowings, and the truth of course is that *all* artists, whatever their nationality, gender, or "race," forage among the materials of their ambient culture(s) to produce lifeworks that are homeostatic for both artist and audience. "The great genius," as Schreiner suggests, is the person who "gives voice to the great wants of his age."[82] Kikuyu oral narratives function in the same way: they are the collective efforts of people "persistently rummaging through their physical and mental environments in a concerted bid to overcome impediments to a desired moral equilibrium."[83]

In saying that Schreiner's and Dinesen's lifeworks functioned homeostatically, I mean far more than that they wrote to ameliorate the pains and disappointments of their lives, though that is surely true. Dinesen began telling stories to take her mind off her problems during a particularly bad drought in Africa and, like Scheherazade, to hold the attention of Denys Finch Hatton as well, beginning "in the evening to write stories, fairy tales and romances that would take my mind a long way off, to other countries and times."[84] Back in Denmark after her years in Africa, she continued to tell stories to take her mind off the claustrophobic life to which she had returned. Schreiner wrote for some of the same reasons. "Just now I do not exist, my book [probably *From Man to Man*] exists; that is all, as far as my daily life goes. . . . That is why writing makes me happy, because then my own little miserable life is *not,*" she confesses in her diary.[85] When Dinesen compares the poet's tale to pearls, because "both are disease turned into loveliness,"[86] she implies this homeostatic function as well. She wrote *On Modern Marriage* at precisely the moment when she was separated from her husband and her lover was refusing to make any commitment to her. It is a book written from a perspective of some olympian detachment, behind various masks and carnivals of literary quotations and with an air of authority about her subject she distinctly must not have felt at the time. The more disenchanted Dinesen became with marriage, the more her writings advanced its sanctity. The more distant she became from Africa, the greater the immediacy with which she described it. The more hampered she felt by her status as woman, the more she wrote tales in which traditional roles for women are at the center. The further she moved financially from the position or comfort of the aristocrat, the more she wrote of the aristocracy. The more fate dealt her knockout punches, the more she worshiped fate as a force.

Schreiner's passionate pleas for the strength and self-reliance of women, her need in *Woman and Labour* and in her novels to rail against the dangers of women's "parasitic" attachment to men, fly in the face of the inclinations of half the heroines in her fiction, and of her own life. Her valiant attempts to articulate her ideas and to be understood are countered by her portrayal of her most sympathetic heroines, such as Undine, who falls silent or misrepresents herself whenever anyone tries to understand her and then suffers from having been profoundly misunderstood.

A few final disclaimers are necessary. First, what is offered here has not been designed to yield a generalized assessment of colonial relations, except insofar as specific expositions of how "Africa" and "Africans" functioned in Schreiner's and Dinesen's construction of their own psychic economy can be construed as one small part of such a project. Second, as will already be apparent, no particular distinction will be made here between literary productions, biography, letters, and even landscape. All will be treated as one continuous text that can as well be painted as written, as well lived as turned into fiction. Biography will be enlisted, but not to explain literary texts, memoirs, or political writings. Instead it will be assumed that *all* "texts," including the body, can be most fully read if, as far as possible, all the contexts impinging on those texts—political circumstances, historical record, personal biography, aesthetic strategies—are consulted in the construction of that reading. I also mix the verbal and the visual, assuming that the visual carries messages that can be extracted and that the verbal is visual or visualizable, making this a very postmodern study with a tendency to sweep over surfaces rather than plumb the depths. But a full exploration of just one of the things I mention here—such as Dinesen's or Schreiner's debt to visual strategies of the avant-garde, or their use of exterior landscape to render their inner landscapes—would have cost me the chance to trace that nexus, for instance, where the modernist "impersonal," Benjamin's rehistoricized "mythic," Dinesen's Lamarckian or Schreiner's Schopenhauerian "ideal," and the abstraction Westerners have historically regarded as a hallmark of African art all combined to open up a space that offered each woman a kind of custom-made home that served as a refuge from a day-to-day life that was less than ideal. Asked to draw a picture of a lion, the

Khoisan of South Africa are said to draw only the eyes and feet. They show what's important: tracks by day, eyes by night. I too have tried to draw what's important, moving in rapid oscillation between Africa and Europe, between Schreiner and Dinesen, and between these two women and my own "stuff."

If these oscillations are experienced as some version of intellectual whiplash, I argue only that this rapid oscillation—between Boer and Schopenhauer, between Kierkegaard and Kikuyu—is worth the danger because what can be seen in the afterimage those oscillations produce is not only a more complete picture of Schreiner and Dinesen but, I think, something of us all.

My own shuttlings and oscillations here have sometimes felt both as personally urgent and as opportunistic as nomadic border crossings always must. I am bemused, to say the least, to have discovered how often in these pages I have resorted to descriptions of my project as mapping or surveying the terrain. Such language choices signal my recognition of my own imbrication in the continuation of the process of mapping of other peoples' territories in order to appropriate them for one's own needs that reached its full force in the nineteenth century and continues in more subtle forms into the present. Self-aware travelers have always recognized the extent to which their mappings were easing the way not just for their own but for later travelers' appropriation of the terrain. Appropriations of course are rarely only geographic or economic, and I acknowledge my ambivalence at being not so much even an armchair appropriator of African aesthetic and survival strategies as an appropriator of other Europeans' appropriations of African materials to the end of increasing my own self-knowledge—a participant in what seems to be the most recent form of mining the African continent.

But the most kindly disposed understanding of this book is probably one that sees it as my own valiant attempt to produce a refiguration of a past—Schreiner's, Dinesen's, Africa's, and my own—to produce a more salutary future. Benjamin, I think, would absolutely approve of this attempt to build a contingent, provisional home on the precarious edge produced at the convergence of all these ethnic, racial, gendered, continental, critical, methodological borders. In *Ideology,* Terry Eagleton provides the most efficient summary of this model that Benjamin's work offers. For Benjamin, "the only image of the past which counts is that which appears unexpectedly . . . at a moment of danger." This is perhaps, says Eagleton, "what 'theory' means to Benjamin; that which under extreme pressure can be hastily thrown together and kept ready at hand. His project is to blast open the lethal continuum of history with the few poor weapons available to him: shock, allegory, estrangement, heterogeneous 'chips' of Messianic time, mechanical reproduction, Kabbalistic interpretive violence, surrealist montage, revolutionary nostalgia, reactivated memory traces, readings which brush left-handedly against the grain."[87] Benjamin would be entertained by my seeing similarities between these women and the Africans whom they lived among, and between these women and myself, believing as he did that the gift for seeing similarity represented always "nothing but a weak rudiment of the formerly powerful compulsion to become similar; to behave mimetically."[88]

All of this could mean that the pages that follow are of interest only to me. But if in talking about Olive Schreiner and Isak Dinesen I have managed to produce something that resembles even a bit the kind of universalist biography Michel de Certeau has recommended,[89] I will have succeeded. As Femi Ojo-Ade says, only a mad person beats the drum and dances to the music alone.[90]

2

Alone by Design: Precarious Enclosures

Both in speech and writing, she had so strongly proclaimed her opinion of the iniquity of the [Boer] War that certain minor officials were inclined to persecute Aunt Olive. When one of these wired: "Have got Olive Schreiner here," the only reply he got was: "Leave the woman alone"—an incident which absolutely delighted my aunt, who ever had . . . a chuckle for so sensible a man.

Lyndall Gregg, *Memories of Olive Schreiner*

In *Techniques of the Observer* Jonathan Crary draws a sharp demarcation between the modern world and that of the eighteenth-century traveler-observer. The latter had achieved conceptual mastery over the world through a combination of what was presumed to be a kind of transparent reporting and recording that purported to make available to readers the simple visibility of a world apprehended through straightforward acts of seeing. But during and since the nineteenth century, as a consequence of studies on the physiology of the eye and the nature of vision, clearer understanding of the ease with which both can be tricked, and a blossoming of visual technology, we have come to live in a world of visuality rather than visibility. Whereas visibility represents objects and people as a duplication of what the eye can see, visuality challenges exactly that possibility. What Crary calls the techniques of visuality—the manipulation of what is seen and how it is seen—produce both very different observers and very different subjects, who know themselves to be the subject of observation and conduct themselves accordingly. While writers like Schopenhauer were trying to shape the observer by advocating sharpening one's powers of observation, heightened awareness of the techniques by which one might do so also came to provide clues that would allow the observed to take some control over how they might be seen. Both senses of the term *visuality* will come into play here.

Visuality is of course fundamentally an issue of the relation between the body and the operation of social power.[1] Verbal, gestural, or visual strategies enlisted to manipulate or control this relation are part of what Jean and John Comaroff talk about as the "deeper dialogue of forms" operating in the colonial context, in which even to say that events "*take* place" implies the struggle people encounter in trying to be seen in a space that is their own.[2] The concern Dinesen and Schreiner had for preserving their autonomy—a concern that seems at the very least to have fallen at the outside edge of the normal range—could only have been born out of a recognition of how much at risk they felt themselves if they allowed anyone to step into their space, to get close enough to see them clearly or deeply. It's no surprise, then, to discover the prodigious quantities of Nietzschean or Schopenhauerian will and the great amounts of imaginative energy each devoted to carefully designing and positioning her own body for viewing both in and out of the African landscape, and then to careful reporting or representing of those positionings. Their fictional heroines often occupy themselves in the same way. True modernists, they also engage in various space-clearing gestures, their prose often designed either to frame their bodies in space and thereby call attention to them or, alternatively, almost to merge them into the landscape itself. Since their space clearing, posturing, and apparent self-erasure by wrapping themselves in "Africa's darkness" take place both in an actual physical world where their bodies can be seen and in a more strictly verbal/textual one, a term might be borrowed from Gaile McGregor's study of cross-culturality, language, and landscape in Canada, a terrain he refers to as a *langscape*.[3]

Over and over Isak Dinesen assures us that Africa *is* Isak Dinesen, and vice versa. "The grass was me, and the air, the distant invisible mountains were me, the tired oxen were me."[4] This circuit of identification is particularly clear in Meryl Streep's portrayal of her in Sydney Pollack's film version of *Out of Africa,* which begins with "Isak Dinesen's" almost incantatory "I had a farm in Africa" and ends, "Does Africa know a song of me?" In choosing this frame Pollack taps what might be the single most powerful appeal of Dinesen's book, a rhapsodic rhetoric that successfully conflates the identity of its author with that of the African continent:

> If I know a song of Africa,—I thought,—of the Giraffe, and the African new moon lying on her back, of the ploughs in the fields, and the sweaty faces of the coffee-pickers, does Africa know a song of me? Would the air over the plain quiver with a colour that I had had on, or the children invent a game in which my name was, or the full moon throw a shadow over the gravel of the drive that was like me, or would the eagles of Ngong look out for me?[5]

If Africa was the dark continent, and if, as Freud suggested, female sexuality was the same, such a conscious identification enabled the kind of metaleptic troping Gates and others have described. But more is going on. If in the modern world visuality and power go hand in hand, it is interesting to read closely enough here to discover that Dinesen declines to produce a picture of herself that can be seen at all. What she does instead is construct a report of how she is *looked at*. Its emphasis is emphatically on the optic rather than the haptic—one doesn't ordinarily touch moons or eagles—suggesting distance from the African landscape rather than a merging into it. Large, powerful, and aloof, her very presence produces effects on landscape, flora, fauna, and children, even as she herself remains entirely unreachable, untouchable, and unseen. From one point of view this is all the more impressive when we recall that she is producing this vision of Africans' vision of her for consumption by European and American readers while she sits in her mother's house in Denmark, where she has retreated after Karen Coffee in Kenya has failed. Far from being a defeated ex-farmer, this woman controls her visuality to such an extent that she soars with eagles instead—hardly a bad deal for the Danish daughter of the Westenholzes on the verge of financial ruin. She manufactured a kind of massive power for herself through her identification with the African continent—with its largeness, its distance, as well as with the prodigious sexuality associated with the continent in European imaginations. Her lush rhetoric sexualizes everything; the juxtaposition of "the new moon lying on her back" with a "plough in the fields" hardly needs explication. The very air quivers. "A colonialist gaze," as Hal Foster suggests, "seems to double a sexual gaze in a vision of masculinist mastery," a mastery that in fact "may not be so secure." Here, just as in Paul Gauguin's paintings of Polynesian women—supine, exposed, yielding—what is represented, Foster suggests, is not only a figure of and for masculinist desire, but also one of identification with the very visible supine *object* of desire; a figure of control, but also of surrender.[6] Displacing her own sexuality onto the continent itself, Dinesen remains quite literally above it all; vulnerable and exposed and aloof and invincible at the same time.

In part Olive Schreiner's paeans to Africa are designed to invoke in women readers recollections of what was by her time a long-standing tradition that allowed European women access to a kind of freedom by lighting out for South Africa.[7] But Schreiner's paeans to Africa are also functionally the equivalent of Dinesen's African identifications. "There is nothing measured, small nor petty in South Africa," she says. "South Africa is like a great fascinating woman; . . . those who come close to her fall under [her power] and never leave her for anything smaller, because she liberates them."[8] But even as she and Dinesen insist *l'Afrique, c'est moi,* they also do two other things. They work to construct themselves as modernist works of art, which necessarily means they work to clear away all reference to themselves as part of "nature," African or otherwise, and they employ every available means to manufacture plenty of protective space separating them from African landscape and from other people. The explosion in the second half of the nineteenth century of discourses presuming to offer scientific studies of race and sex both women found constricting in the extreme. When Olive Schreiner went to England in the 1880s hungry for intellectual companionship, she walked right into the thick of them. Her closest friends, Edward Carpenter and Havelock Ellis, were prolific writers on such things as what they called "the confusion of the sexes": minute study of every sexual impulse, fantasy, behavior, or possibility like Carpenter's works, all of which have titles like *Intermediate Types among Primitive Folk*. Among Ellis's numerous books on sexuality at least one, subtitled *A Study of Secondary and Tertiary Sexual Characters,* was severely out of balance, and its title, *Man and Woman,* was a misnomer. Casting its probing gaze largely at *female* sexuality, its chapters gave nothing like equivalent attention to males. The chapter titles give the game away: "The Periodicity of Women"; "The Pelvis"; "The Affectability of Women."

This intense interest in the study of sexuality and free love became the excuse for the notorious lives and careers of people like James Hinton and Edward Aveling, who took advantage of the principles of free love to take advantage of freethinking new women. By 1884 disillusionment, especially with Hinton's attitude toward women, would strike Schreiner hard, and by 1885 she referred to herself as a "strong anti-Hintonian." But the same letter shows her confessing shame at having revealed her own sexual proclivities in a previous letter. I was, she says, "somewhat ashamed the other day after what I had said about sexual feelings."[9] Clearly, a freethinking new woman like Schreiner had every day to walk a careful line: espousing sexual freedom and spontaneous sexual activity as a natural condition of woman's nature, yet being cautious lest they be "used" by men whose creeds countenanced free love; revealing unabashedly their innermost sexual feelings or "perversions" in a demonstration of their lack of shame around matters sexual while managing not to feel violated—too visible—as a consequence of those confessions. One necessary reading of Dinesen's and Schreiner's lifeworks would see them as a set of attempts to find a comfortable place to *be* somewhere between these two sets of oppositional projects: alternately espousing and quite visibly enacting "womanly" behavior and at the same time confounding or trying to clear away or wall themselves off from both the womanly and the prying eyes of those who would study them to determine exactly what the womanly might be.

One *formal* manifestation of their very modernist desire to erase the hold of nature on woman and to escape the prying eyes of those social Darwinists, eugenicists, and sexologists who would try to penetrate to woman's "essence" is a writing style that works to clear out the claustrophobic overelaboration of the romantic writings to which in part it was a response. Jens Peter Jacobsen's *Niels Lyhne* was a favorite novel of Dinesen's. Its plot bears remarkable similarities to many of Dinesen's tales. A dreamy, romantic mother, Bartholine, has a practical-minded husband, and she compensates by pouring into the ready ears of her son Niels all her dreams of romantic adventure. In consequence he grows up a daydreamer with impossibly high ideals and an excruciating contempt for the ordinary. He becomes, that is, a version of Isak Dinesen, and formally and stylistically her tales can be read as clearing out the underbrush of elaborated sensation so characteristic of *Niels Lyhne*. One small example, mercifully, will suffice:

> [Temma] had given herself entirely to his embrace, and with her gaze lost in his, her lips murmured strangely sweet words of love, half muted by her breath, words repeated after him, as if she were whispering them to her own heart.
>
> The cessation of the voices in the street made her stir restlessly. Then they came back to the firm, rhythmic accompaniment of a cane striking against the cobblestones, crossed over to the other side, lingered long in the distance, sank to a murmur, —died away. And the silence again welled up around them, flamed up around them, throbbing with heartbeats, heavy with breath, yielding. Speech had been seared away between them and lingering kisses fell from their lips fraught with unspoken questions, but giving no solace nor any

present bliss. They held each other's gaze and dared not take their eyes away, but neither did they dare to put meaning into their looks; they veiled it rather; withdrew behind it, silently hiding, brooding over secret dreams.[10]

Among other things the spaciousness of the two women's "Africa" represents a geographical release from the claustrophobia born of this endless mining of the personal, the probing and limning of sensation and nuance. De Aar was a railway junction on the Northern Karoo where Schreiner lived with Cron beginning in 1905. It was a spot she loved, both despite and because of its dusty, desolate character. She also loved it because it enabled a quick getaway. Her niece Lyndall Gregg reports, "Aunt Olive said there was one great thing about living at De Aar, and that was the knowledge that you could always get away, that you could take a train any day."[11]

But neither Dinesen's nor Schreiner's strategies for clearing space or achieving a quick getaway always took the form that might be expected. A clearing of the interior or mental landscape is surely characteristic of the prose of Dinesen's tales, even if the same cannot be said for Schreiner's novels. But the detailed descriptions of African landscape and African people that both women produce frequently capture a moment transforming from one thing to another. "Out on the Safaris I had seen a herd of Buffalo," says Dinesen, "one hundred and twenty-nine of them, come out of the morning mist under a copper sky, one by one, as if the dark and massive, iron-like animals with the mighty horizontally swung horns were not approaching, but were being created before my eyes and sent out as they were finished."[12] Giraffes appear "not [as] a herd of animals but a family of rare, long-stemmed, speckled gigantic flowers slowly advancing,"[13] looking suspiciously like one of the paintings in Van Gogh's sunflower series. Schreiner describes "Bushmen" as "a race caught in the very act of evolving into human form."[14]

An analysis with different aims than mine would consider Schreiner's rhetoric here in the context of that of eugenicists of her time. But this same rhetoric served personal functions as well. In his discussion of modernism, Frederick Karl sees the "contingency of effects, in which analysis and description serve not to limn an object, but to keep before us an object in the process of becoming itself"[15] as constituting part of the power of Mallarmé's poetry. Homi Bhabha suggests that the subaltern voice finds itself able to speak "betwixt and between lines and phrases" of any narrative of "meanwhile."[16] If Dinesen could produce an Africa caught in the process of "becoming itself" and Schreiner a "race" of Africans doing the same, and if they positioned themselves as witnesses and reporters in the midst of that becoming, then perhaps each had managed to clear a space there for her own becoming. If Schreiner participated in a racist discourse that saw Africans in the process of "becoming human," her purpose was in one crucial way that of inscribing herself within that same discourse.

If such impulses to clear a space or shake up an existing order of being in order to create a world and an identity de novo are some of the manifestations of modernism's desire to erase the hold of nature on woman, then conscious production of one's image and awareness of the materials out of which one creates one's self-presentation are modernist as well, and both women were decidedly modernist in this sense. In his biography of Schreiner Johannes Meintjes suggests that few people have been so unfortunate as she was in the violation of their privacy.[17] But a closer look at her friendship with Havelock Ellis complicates that assessment. It was in one crucial way a mutually rewarding affair that married Schreiner's need to confess—to be *exposed*—with Ellis's need to gather material for his studies of sexology. Equally valenced drives for evasion and invasion go a long way toward explaining both Schreiner's and Dinesen's verbal and visual self-presentations. Dinesen's dramatic eyes darkened with kohl, her turbans, and her carefully cultivated emaciated body, as well as Schreiner's insistence on wearing her familiar faded blue serge and her matter-of-fact stride, suggest that both women were intending to comment on their own "materials." But this commentary needed to be seen to be heard.

To look at photographs taken of Karen Blixen at any time in her life, for instance, is to see an avant-garde painting. My favorite is the 1934 photograph by Reimert Kehlet reproduced as figure 5. Dinesen chose it specifically as her way of representing herself to

Figure 5. Isak Dinesen, 1934. Photographer, Reimert Kehlet. Photograph courtesy of the Royal Library, Det Kongelige Bibliotek, Copenhagen, Denmark.

her American public "after the identity behind the pseudonym of Isak Dinesen had been revealed."[18] It hardly reveals who Karen Blixen was, but it does suggest how "Isak Dinesen" wanted to be seen.

In her reedlike slenderness, the forty-nine-year-old Karen Blixen of this photograph creates a vision of herself as almost prepubescent. All edges and angles, she comes close to making her body a representation of a cubist painting. Virginal in white and photographed from the side, she shows less surface to the viewer than had she presented her body frontally. Rosalind Krauss suggests that modernism by and large and despite its intentions accepted the traditional oppositions between field and ground, inverting rather than subverting those categories. By contrast the avant-garde—surrealism, dada, cubism—succeeded in challenging these structural relations, thereby challenging the nature of visuality itself. Isak Dinesen's photograph here achieves the status of the avant-garde by continually shifting the relation between figure and ground. Appearing to be all figure at one glance, at the next it becomes all ground. In so doing it resides on what Krauss calls the deictical or deixical axis. Neither not figure nor not *not*-figure, not ground but at the same time not *not*-ground, the photograph presents her body as part of the flat plane and so figures—literally embodies—the alternating egotistical arrogance and abject insecurity characterizing Dinesen's and Schreiner's psychic makeup.

Since the fictional characters Dinesen and Schreiner produce in tales and novels rarely exhibit the sophisticated development we expect in the characters of realistic fiction, they too can be seen as "flat" rather than "round" in the sense E. M. Forster first developed in *Aspects of the Novel,* which was based on his 1927 series of Cambridge lectures. If we transvalue Forster's categories in such a way as to privilege the production of flat characters over round, precisely because the former preserve the protective isolation of fictional characters by withholding the character's interior from the prying gaze of viewer or reader, and because *formally* they speak to the poststructuralist dream of subverting the relation between figure and ground, those characters might be far more subversive than has ordinarily been recognized. In a kind of double reverse conflating visual and verbal, Dinesen's making her body part of the ground rather than the field of her photograph can be read as a visual play on the verbal categories of visuality—field and ground—themselves. Even a cursory reading of their letters suggests that both women for the most part felt not "grounded" insofar as they had no emotionally present males in their lives. Biographers insist that great affection remained all their lives between these women and their legal mates—in Dinesen's case even after her divorce from Bror in 1923—but at best both marriages provided something less than the solid spiritual and intellectual grounding each might have wanted. Bror was known to be a rake and a philanderer, and Dinesen confessed that she would have been willing to "let [him] have his 'freedom' while remaining nominally married to him so long as he avoided any scandal."[19] The unreliability of Denys Finch Hatton as a grounding in her life is well documented. In addition to his pathological fear of commitment, there is the matter of his response to her pregnancy. The two had always referred to any child that might be conceived during their liaison by the code name Daniel. When she thought she might be pregnant, Dinesen sent off a note to which Finch Hatton immediately fired back a telegram: "Strongly urge you to cancel Daniel's visit."

Schreiner was forty when she married Samuel Cronwright-Schreiner, who took her surname when they married. Though they stayed married until her death, they spent relatively few years actually living together. Asthma and other ailments separated the two, since she often left South Africa to live in England, where she hoped she would feel better—on one occasion for a nine-year stretch. During those trips Cron stayed in Africa. Even at the end of her life the two seemed perpetually to miss one another: she was in England while he was in Africa; he was in England when she returned to Africa. He learned of her death by reading about it in the morning papers. In some ways the Cronwright-Schreiner marriage enacted the ideal of marriage espoused by the new women of the time, one that advocated a kind of nominal marriage involving living under the same roof only occasionally. In *Testament of Youth* Vera Brittain articulates her own doubts about marriage, in distinctly modernist terms. "In spite of the female traditions and the relentless social pressure which had placed an artificial emphasis on marriage for all women born, like myself, in the 1890s, I had always held and still believed it to be irrelevant to the main purpose of life," she writes. "For a woman as for a man, marriage might be enormously helpful or devastatingly hinder the growth of her power to contribute something impersonally valuable to the community in which she lived."[20]

Dinesen was also older than the man she married. Judith Thurman surmises she married Bror partly as the young girls in her tale "The Dreaming Child" are said to marry: *par dépit,* "to save their self-respect, deny[ing] their first love and mak[ing] the excellency of their husbands their one point of honor."[21] Thurman refers here to Dinesen's decision to marry Bror Blixen when she was unable to marry her first choice, his older brother Hans. But though Dinesen may like her Copenhagen girls have married *par dépit,* "out of spite," the phrase has its roots in *dépetrer*—to extricate, free oneself, to get out—and Bror Blixen and the Africa to which he promised to take her were one escape from the confinements of marriage.

What was confining to both women was not just marriage, but feeling itself. Even after his enthusiastic advocacy of and participation in free love cooled her personal admiration for James Hinton, Schreiner continued to admire his novels. "One thing that draws me to him very much," she says, "is his *fear of feeling.*" "Some people," she confides in a letter to Havelock Ellis, "*dare* not feel fully—all life must be a long self-repression."[22] Ever the lover of Kierkegaardian paradox, Dinesen believed suppression of feeling was necessary to make play possible. "Much is demanded of those who are to be really proficient at play," she says in *On Modern Marriage.* "Courage and imagination, humor and intelligence, but in particular that blend of unselfishness, generosity, self-control and courtesy that is called *gentilezza.*"[23] The words *play* and *self-control* have equal valence here, and the state of "groundlessness" Dinesen embodies in her photograph and that Schreiner replicates in letters and in her dispositions of her female heroines in her novels all are explicable as homeostatic responses to a desire for passionate connection, coupled with an equally passionate fear of feeling.

The lack of grounding staged in Dinesen's photograph is a deliberate choice. Because her body takes up so little space while being surrounded by so much of it, it seems to hover in something like the universal space characteristic of modernist architecture's open plan. Krauss suggests that these "Mies van der Rohe 'universal spaces' articulate no function whatever. They are space frames within which anything might be accommodated."[24] Dinesen inhabits just such a floating, luminous space in which anything could happen—*if* the viewer could ever be so bold as to violate that space. On the one hand, hers is a body so ethereal that her actual corporeal presence casts barely half a shadow. The reality of even that half shadow is called into question by the strange cloudlike curving shaded area trailing upward from just above her extended elbow, like some shadow of a shadow. The image she presents here is like her persona in all of her lifework. Simultaneously unapproachable and coyly inviting, and framed in a luminous space, the subject of this photograph becomes not Dinesen's body at all, but the inhibiting expanse of space the viewer would have to traverse to get to the object/subject standing serene and unapproachable inside it. Standing so close to the backdrop, Dinesen seems to hug that space and to back as far away from the viewer as possible. The side view, the angle of the camera, the line of the body virtually uninterrupted by pattern, object, or even bodily protuberance of any kind all combine to give the photograph the elongation characteristic of a Giacometti sculpture, an elongation that further enhances the sense of "seeing at a distance. The object carrie[s] as its meaning," as Krauss says, "the mark of the viewer's separation from it."[25] In his famous essay on Baudelaire Benjamin sees such unapproachability as a primary quality of "the ceremonial image."[26] Dinesen in fact frequently confessed that she had "a real horror of being 'an object,'"[27] professing to hate what she called the "brass-serpenting" of her to which Africans were prone. But she found her defense not so much in resisting becoming a ceremonial image as in trying mightily to control the ways she would be "brass-serpented": in controlling her image and its framing.

Jameson tells us traces of imperialism are always to be found not so much in the content or representation in modernist texts as in their disposition of space itself,[28] and if objects in a painting or photograph form a system or a world as Krauss suggests,[29] the world of this photograph has to be seen as one in which its subject—Karen Blixen's body—rules supremely alone, reproducing the imperialism of modernist spatiality by reserving for herself the luxury of *lots* of her own space. This is partially explicable simply as a *formal* decision: a consequence of the concern she shared with Scandinavian modernist painters to create space around the figure. A preoccupation of several of Matisse's Norwegian pupils, it is especially evident in works such as Rudolph Thygesen's 1914 painting *Mimi,* looking for all the world as if Dinesen might have been its inspiration. But the isolated figure Dinesen makes of herself in her photographic portrait is truly modernist in that it hardly represents form apart from function. It functions precisely as do many descriptions of the prelapsarian landscape produced by colonized peoples: it becomes a kind of retrospective decolonization [30] of the continent of her body.

A Lacanian framework brought to bear on this photograph would no doubt suggest that Dinesen's self-presentation makes her the object of a male, gazing subject and interpret its femininity as necessarily constructed "in reference to the masculine sign [of the phallus], insuring its nonidentity, impelling a corresponding effort to cover or *disguise* that fundamental lack." Citing Lacan, Kate Linker suggests that "woman's desire to be the phallus, the signifier of the other's desire, leads her to 'take refuge in this mask.' Hence," says Linker, "the flaunting or foregrounding of femininity involved in dressing up or 'disguising' oneself as object of the masculine gaze evoke[s], through covering, the constitutive absence of woman in the patriarchal order." [31] One could in fact say this analysis handily explains what Dinesen is up to in her photograph. But Dinesen's entire elongated body *itself* becomes a kind of phallus here, precisely as Norman Bryson suggests Géricault's elongated paintings of French soldiers do, or for that matter as do those old photographs of Arnold Schwarzenegger, fully pumped, when he was known more as a bodybuilder than as a Terminator. Bryson suggests that the minuscule trunks in photos of the fully pumped bodybuilder cover very little indicating a penis, that position having been shifted in the viewer's gaze to the entire *body,* whose bulging veins make it resemble entire a tumescent penis.[32]

The eyes of Reimert Kehlet's sublimely solitary subject are cast downward and aslant, but they reveal not the dreamy, far-off gaze characteristic of either the female subjects of the Pre-Raphaelite painters or of so many of Tennyson's poems—"Maud," "The Lady of Shallott," or "Mariana," who in the John Everett Millais painting inspired by Tennyson's poem declines to look at the viewer, turning viewer into voyeur. Dinesen looks down and away, but with a half smile as if to make perfectly clear that it is *she* who presents—even flaunts—this figure to the observer's gaze, a figure whose sharp edges and outlines oscillate between representing the quintessentially fragile feminine and the defiantly asexual. The position of the camera, combined with Blixen's downward gaze, constructs a viewer who must look *up* at this subject, as she of course looks *down* on the viewer. Richard Avedon's portrait of Dinesen is not a full-body one, but it too captures the same relation of observer and observed. Both portraits reveal the mix of reticence and arrogance, seductiveness and aloofness that Dinesen attributes to Somali women. Attaching the modifier "coy" to every invocation of them, Dinesen's descriptions are invariably full of admiration. "The great sweetness of" their demeanor for her "lay in the play of opposite forces within it. Behind the eternal principle of refutation, there was much generosity, behind the pedantry what risibility, and contempt of death. These daughters of a fighting race went through their ceremonial of primness," she says, "as through a great graceful war-dance; butter would not melt in their mouth, neither would they rest till they had drunk the heart's blood of their adversary, they figured like . . . ferocious young she-wolves in seemly sheep's clothing. . . . Heavy weights of life, strenuous pressure, high waves, and long ages, must have gone to turn [them] into such hard, shining amber." If the "play of opposite forces" she projects onto Somali women is the same as that in herself, one that comes from the "heavy weights of life [and] strenuous pressure," she at least projects onto them admiration due herself for the same skillful management of those forces. This "Somali system," she says, "was at once a natural necessity and a fine art, it was both religion, strategy, and ballet, and was practised in all respects with due devotion, discipline and dexterity."[33] Here indubitably are the Africans of her imagination; the Africans who embody the ideal self-presentation she imitates in her own portrait here.

There is surely nothing natural about Dinesen's pose. No body at rest holds an elbow at quite the angle she adopts here. The arm

Figure 6. The author, 1964. Photograph by Paul March. Photograph courtesy of Rod Brown Photography, Defiance, Ohio.

can only have been pulled back explicitly so the viewer can see the ribcage with no padding, the absence of waist. The side pose and the ultimate *purpose* of such a photograph I recognize only too well, because thirty years ago I chose precisely the same elongation, the same angles and pose for my wedding photograph (fig. 6). Though my own self-starvation was obviously far less successful than Dinesen's, I did struggle toward a similar thinness, striving for the same sharp angularity and "edginess" evident in her photograph. I also chose to drape that body not in a wedding dress with frills and petticoats, but in a sheath designed to accentuate what I hoped were all those sharp angles. Caught in the camera's eye for presentation to a public in the newspapers, I also insisted on presentation from the side, to show off the angularity I thought I'd achieved. If the culture required that brides be presented as virginal though fecund female, in what even then felt to me like the distinctly confining role of the new wife, at least I could determine the shape of that body and dictate the form of visuality in which I would be seen. Unlike Dinesen's, my own portrait frames its subject/body not in a luminous empty space, but in a space embarrassingly cluttered by objects that announce, however unconvincingly, the social/economic space that body inhabits. Had I been as old, wise, and brave as Dinesen when it was taken, my portrait would surely have been like hers: of the figure aloof, mysterious, unapproachable, with a look registering the same come to me/go from me look.

From February to August 1993, the Museum of African Art in New York hosted an exhibition titled "Secrecy." Exploring secrecy "cross-culturally within Africa as an aesthetic and political strategy, as a social and spiritual boundary marker, and as a form of property and power," the exhibition presented objects that had been selected to demonstrate how African artists have recourse to particular aesthetic strategies or devices that permit the artist simultaneously "to suggest the presence of the secret and to camouflage it." The exhibition pamphlet listed four such strategies explicitly: coding, obscurity, accumulation, and containment. Obviously written by someone steeped in Lacan and Foucault, this pamphlet insisted that the emphasis of the exhibition, like that of the artists included in it, was "not on the content of secrets, but on the ways artistic works from Africa all have visible, public dimensions, and invisible or secret ones as well." Works "conceal and reveal knowledge by attracting attention to secret realms, distracting viewers away from secret places, or containing and enclosing secret things." Discussing Bamana initiation masks, for instance, the pamphlet quotes a Bamana man explaining them: "The Komo mask is made to look like an animal. But it is not an animal, it is a secret."[34] The abstract shape Dinesen makes of her body and the come to me/go from me look of her eyes replicating that of Dinesen's Somali women produce a photograph that depicts not a woman, but a secret. It is in this form that Dinesen chose to represent herself when it came time for the "real" woman behind her literary pseudonym to reveal herself to her American public. Behind the secret, another secret.

Admittedly, the effects attributed to this Kehlet portrait are partly the product of artistic choices made by the photographer rather than by his subject. But it is well known that Dinesen from her earliest years thought of herself as a piece of art. When she was complimented on her looks once by an acquaintance, her immediate reply was, "Well, I did attend art school in Paris, you know."[35] No photographer has control over the shape of the body he photographs, and for the most part the choice of costume remains in the subject's hands as well. Surely the selection of a particular portrait from a portfolio of possibilities would have been left to the subject of those photographs. The Giacometti-like abstract shape that is Dinesen's body reveals her lifelong habit of starving her body to achieve all those sharp angles and then wearing dresses and hats that accentuate the angularity. The syphilis Bror Blixen gave Karen—the wedding gift that kept on giving, making pain her lifelong companion and making eating ever more difficult as her life went on—plays its part in the construction of the emaciated form we see in her photographs too. But the sharp angles predate the syphilis. Other photographs taken after marriage and therefore after the onset of the syphilis show her at times distinctly heavier, and the necessary conclusion is that she cultivated the emaciated image by which most of us know her.

Judith Thurman attributes Dinesen's lifelong tendency toward anorexia to a resistance to the stolid family dinners of her childhood, which Dinesen at least once referred to as horrid eight-course meals with two bottles of wine apiece. In 1900, at age fifteen and on her way to an art class, Dinesen would throw her lunch out the window of the train in what Thurman calls "the first of many fasts, undertaken in an effort 'to achieve greatness' through human suffering."[36] In a letter to her sister Elle in 1928 Dinesen reports, "As the years go by one learns to . . . sort out the minor phenomena of life, that are necessary to enable one to be oneself. . . . I know that I must not get fat; it is preferable for me to suffer the pangs of hunger, because being overweight '*cramps my style*.' "[37] Even in old age, dying of emaciation and never weighing more than eighty-five pounds, Dinesen maintained her anorexia. The Africa Dinesen produces projects this anorexia onto the continent in order to cement her identification with it. *Out of Africa* opens with Dinesen's particular praise that "there was no fat on it . . . anywhere."[38]

One can celebrate this remarkable portrait while regretting the anorexia that made it possible; can admire the particularly imaginative use of one of the few gestures of defiance she apparently felt were available to her. I am inclined to agree with Terry Eagleton, who suggests we ought not be too harsh on either women or colonized peoples who find themselves enmeshed in efforts at resistance or transformation that seem vexed, retrograde, or muddy. To achieve any transformative politics, a resolute, self-confident agent is necessary. But if such an agent existed, resistance and transformation would be unnecessary.[39] In her portrait, Dinesen does what she can. She imitates the Somali of her imagination, tropes the figure of the slender virgin, identifies herself with the continent, and even constructs at least a moderately successful version of the powerful act of defiance in contemporary Bengali writer Mahasweta Devi's short story "Draupadi." The final gesture of Draupadi confronting Senanayak, the army officer who captures and whips her, is to reject his insistence that she "in the name of modesty" cover the visible effects of her degradation. " 'I will not let you put my cloth on me,' she says. 'What more can you do? Come on, *counter* me—*counter* me—?' . . . and for the first time Senanayak is afraid to stand before an unarmed *target,* terribly afraid."[40] In Dinesen's story "The Caryatids" Childerique grieves "because she had not been born a boy." When it becomes no longer possible for her to conceal her gender, she makes a decision. "As the truth could no longer be concealed, the world might as well have it point blank."[41] Goethe observes in *Elective Affinities* that people seem to have a natural aversion to looking at portraits, because "they always seem to be uttering a silent reproach,"[42] and Lacan suggests that the object or victim of the gaze often resists by saying, "You want to see? Well, take a look at this!"[43] All these resistances can be detected in Dinesen's portrait by the viewer willing to read its codes. It catches her coming as close as she ever comes anywhere in her life to revealing herself "point blank," and it finds her thrusting in viewers' faces the horrible consequences of the "femininity" for which she advocates in her tales.

Since Olive Schreiner was born so much earlier than Dinesen, one would think hers could not possibly be strategies of the avant-garde, not at any rate of the avant-garde construed as the ever-forward-moving cutting edge of modernism interested in control of visuality. But for many of the same reasons and just as imaginatively, she was often doing just that—producing her life as an artful fiction and her body as an exercise in a visuality she wanted to be "read." Much to her friends' chagrin, she wore virtually nothing but her "immortal green suit" for ten years; she refused to go corseted, walked the streets of London sans hat and gloves, took pains to get married in her old blue serge, and remained oblivious to clothes to the extent that the sneers and stares of ladies she encountered in the dining rooms at Swiss spas sent her in tears to eat alone in her room. But an apparent disregard for fashion that deliberately emphasized her "short sturdy vigorous body in loose shapeless clothes"[44] is itself of course a deliberate fashion statement.

But the physical distance Schreiner constructs around herself is evident not so much in her physical persona or photographs as at two other sites: in her self-presentation in her letters, and in the distance she creates around her fictional women, who all pour remarkable amounts of time and energy into erecting figurative or actual enclosures around themselves. Although Schreiner's protestations that she was utterly different from people around her grew in frequency and intensity as her life progressed, both early and late letters are riddled with protestations that she feels herself to be utterly separate from all others. This sense reaches its crescendo toward the end of her life, when she muses to her own husband, "It is funny why I have always to be out of everything. The day will never come when I can be in the stream. Something in my nature prevents it I suppose. Sometimes I don't seem to be alive at all, but only creeping about in a ghastly dream. No one wants me. I'm in no relation with the life or thought in England or Africa or anywhere else."[45] The immediate occasion for her declaration of separateness here is her lack of sympathy for England's participation in World War I,[46] but characteristically she attributes her feeling far more broadly, to "something in my nature."

Returning to South Africa after a nine-year stay in England, she describes herself as being in an "utter separation" from people there too. People are "so good, so kind, so nice—and yet, not a common bond between us." She feels, she says, "like a live white elephant."[47] Even when people surround her they function to enhance her isolation. At the end of her life she must have received a letter from a woman friend, Frances Smith, expressing concern that being around other people might "tire her." But her response is telling. People don't tire her, she says. "It's good to have human beings around you. It stops you from thinking and feeling too much." Far from being companions with whom one might intertwine one's own ideas or feelings, she calls human beings instead "a narcotic" in this letter, because she finds it "so restful to sit and watch them and sort of live through them."[48] Virginia Woolf's *The Voyage Out* is similarly modernist in its focus on the isolation of the individual consciousness from others and from its own deepest awareness: "Cows . . . draw together in a field; ships in a calm," Hewet says, and "We're just the same when we've nothing else to do. But why do we do it?—is it to prevent ourselves from seeing to the bottom of things?"[49] Schreiner's earliest heroine, Undine, is convinced that "the path through life in which each soul must tread is single; no two walk abreast. Heaven on earth is only found in perfect solitude."[50]

Shifts in genre produce no shift in attitude. Her description of the feminist movement in *Woman and Labour* turns even a mass social movement into an experience of isolation: the women's movement may "resemble strongly . . . the gigantic religious and intellectual movements which for centuries convulsed the life of Europe. . . . [and] looked back upon . . . presents the appearance of one vast, steady, persistent movement." But, she says, "to the mass of individuals taking part . . . it was fought out, now here, now there, by isolated individuals and small groups, and often for what appeared small and almost personal ends" (p. 138). Looking for earlier heroes to whom she can compare the heroes of this revolution, she settles on a catalog of earlier isolates: "Spinoza cut off from his tribe; an exiled Rousseau or Voltaire" (p. 139).

The "primal battleground where . . . reform and human advance must ultimately be fought" is "the depths of the individual consciousness" (p. 142). The leaders of the battle can expect to "find themselves at last in solitudes where the silence is deadly" (p. 285).

The Story of an African Farm and *From Man to Man* are riddled with the same concern for isolation. The opening scenes of each find a young heroine creating for herself a circle of private space. The opening chapter of the former consists of an ever-narrowing series of concentric circles enclosing the two girl children in their beds. "The full African moon poured down its light from the blue sky into the wide, lonely plain. . . . The low hills that skirted the house, the milk-bushes with their long, finger-like leaves, all were touched by a weird and an almost oppressive beauty as they lay in the white light." In the circle of moonlight is the kopje surrounded by a heap of stones; within that circle is the homestead, then a low brick wall enclosing a bare patch of sand and two straggling sunflowers, the series of concentric circles exacerbating the essential isolation of the girl child. In the opening pages of *From Man to Man* the birthing mother and her small daughter are each encircled in a separate, private space:

> The little mother lay in the agony of childbirth. Outside all was still but the buzzing of the bees, some of which now and then found their way in to the half-darkened room. The scent of the orange trees and of the flowers from the garden beyond, came in through the partly opened window, with the rich, dry odor of a warm, African, summer morning. The little mother groaned in her anguish. (p. 3)

Outside this solitary circle Rebekah constructs one of her own:

> Step[ping] onto the stone slowly. . . . She was building a house here. It stood in the center of the stone floor; it was a foot and a half high and about a foot across, and was built of little flat stones placed very carefully on one another, and it was round like a tower. . . . She took a few polished flat stones out of her pocket and began to place them carefully round the top to form a turret. (pp. 4–5)

In the absence of character development, complexity accrues to the female characters in Schreiner's fables, allegories, and fictions, and to those in Dinesen's dreamy tales, only if and so far as we recognize that the *physical,* material conditions in which they find themselves—isolated by sex or cultural conventions or both, living as isolates or nomads (as Europeans in Africa or as Europeans convinced Africa is "home," even as they are "stuck" in Europe), or living as isolates because men have disappointed them—are translated into the architectural moves female characters are shown to be making, into the descriptions of the settings in which those female characters find themselves or the milieus into which they have actively maneuvered themselves.

My analysis here hovers between proposing that the isolation of Dinesen and Schreiner and their fictional characters is imposed from without and suggesting it was self-produced. That fluid and even molten teleological question was part of what propelled this book in the first place, and I'm no more certain now than when I began in which proportions their isolation was cause, and in which, consequence. Either way, it's clear the strength of Schreiner's female characters rests solidly on their ability to design and inhabit their own private spaces as surely as their weakness and downfall as grown women comes about when they forget the importance of fortress building. The pubescent heroines of Dinesen's tales carry the same wisdom:

> She came into possession of a world of her own, inaccessible to the others. . . . The others would never understand her, were she to tell them that it was both infinite and secluded, playful and very grave, safe and dangerous. She could not explain, either, how she herself was one with it, so that through the loveliness and power of her dreamworld she was now—in her old frock and botched shoes, very likely the loveliest, mightiest, and most dangerous person on earth.[51]

These are the same convictions expressed by Virginia Woolf's modernist young heroine Rachel Vinrace, whose first act on setting foot on South American soil in *The Voyage Out* is to scrutinize "this inch of the soil of South America so minutely. . . She noticed every grain of earth and made it into a world where she was endowed with the supreme power."[52] The title of Woolf's novel has come to be synonymous with the European imperialist venture,[53] but if the male European colonizer's impulse was to encircle and claim entire countries and continents, the European woman's seems to have been to draw a minute circle within that circle that produced the room of her own that Schreiner's Rebekah creates and that Woolf, inspired by Schreiner, came to advocate.

Despite her professed belief in a "unity underlying all nature," Schreiner's relationship with Havelock Ellis—a relationship in which the two were interested in one another insofar as they were so alike that they *were* each other and repelled insofar as they were individuals—is full of what First and Scott refer to as Schreiner's "language . . . express[ing] a terror of invasion." Perhaps needing physical distance from Ellis "to gain the detachment of a writer," Schreiner's fear of invasion was even more profound. She "would never find health while dependent on any human creature," and her impulse "was to withdraw from any relationship less than ideal, for it meant her disinterestedness had failed her."[54] She defined happiness all her life as a state of being "in a condition to master my own feelings and keep them from rending me." To Havelock Ellis she confesses that "——loves me very much [Ellis and Cronwright-Schreiner have censored the name here], but now I keep all men who love me at a great distance," calling him "boy" throughout the letter—as she frequently calls him "baby," just for good measure.[55]

Anthropologists Jean and John Comaroff note the extent to which nineteenth-century discourses of sexology claimed "woman's" constitution "was passionate and intuitive, susceptible to nervous disorders and responsive to control by males—particularly by men of science."[56] Schreiner's intellectual companions were all "men of science" like those to whom the Comaroffs refer, and she preserved herself from them by constructing in the rhetoric of her letters and in the landscapes of her fictional heroines strategies allowing her and them to stay alone by design, exactly as Dinesen manipulated her distance from others in order to control the manufacture and distribution of her image, turning herself into an abstract object of art in the process. In so doing, like Rachel Vinrace both produce enclosures that are "a fortress as well as a sanctuary."[57] "Art," says Schreiner in a letter, "is the little crack in the iron wall of life which shuts one in awful isolation through which the spirit can force itself out and show itself to one's like-minded fellow spirits outside; or rather can creep in through the cracks in their terrible walls that shut in the individual life and say, 'you are not alone.'"[58] The curiously garbled syntax and confused sense of exactly what is entering what in her assessment of the place of art in life here only makes clearer the ambivalence and charge that surround Schreiner's vacillation between what she and Dinesen obviously thought of as the two inevitable poles between which they had to choose: either evasion or invasion.

One thing these self-representations accomplish can best be explained by reference to Wilhelm Worringer's *Abstraction and Empathy,* the small but influential book of 1908 that has come to the attention of most of us through T. E. Hulme's references to it in his *Speculations.* Worringer identifies two polar aesthetic urges: one toward empathy, another toward abstraction. Until recently, Westerners have tended to assume that the abstraction of form characteristic of "primitive" art denotes a childlike inability to produce representational versions of nature. But Worringer hypothesizes that abstract art comes about as a deliberate artistic choice. Cultures favoring abstract art over representational, the Egyptian, for instance, show in their production of everyday objects every evidence of their ability to produce representational art with ease. It follows, then, that the production of abstract forms must be seen as the deliberate artistic choice of cultures that fear and distrust nature or believe it to be "Maya," or illusion: a conscious choice, in other words, of people who distinctly do not feel at home in the natural, external world. "Whereas the precondition for the urge to empathy is a happy pantheistic relationship of confidence between man and the phenomena of the external world, the urge to abstraction is the outcome of a great inner unrest inspired in man by the phenomena of the outside world; . . . We might describe this state as an immense spiritual dread of space." While the "rationalistic development" of some cultures "pressed back this instinctive fear conditioned by man's feeling of being lost in the universe," the more "civilised peoples of the East, whose more profound world-instinct opposed development in a rationalistic direction," retained their unblinking awareness of that knowledge, and thus "they alone remained conscious of the unfathomable entanglement of all the phenomena of life, and all the intellectual mastery of the world-picture could not deceive them of this."

> Tormented by the entangled inter-relationship and flux of the phenomena of the outer world, such peoples were dominated by an immense need for tranquility. The happiness they sought from art did not consist in the possibility of projecting themselves into the things of the outer world . . . but in the possibility of taking the individual thing of the external world out of its arbitrariness and seeming fortuitousness, of externalising it by approximation to abstract forms, and in this manner, of finding a point of tranquility and a refuge from appearances. Their most powerful urge was, so to speak, to wrest the object of the external world out of its natural context, out of the unending flux of being, to purify it of all its dependence upon life, i.e., of everything about it that was arbitrary, to render it necessary and irrefragable, to approximate it to its *absolute* value.[59]

This urge toward abstraction, the urge to wrest the object out of its context, render it isolated, and "suppress representational space," is dictated "through the mere fact that it is precisely space which links things to one another, which imparts to them their relativity in the world-picture, and because space is the one thing it is impossible to individualize. Insofar, therefore, as a sensuous object is still dependent upon space, it is unable to appear to us in its closed material individuality. All endeavor was therefore directed toward the single form set free from space."

> The artist was forced to approximate the representation to a plane because three-dimensionality, more than anything else, contradicted the apprehension of the object as a closed material individuality, since perception of three-dimensionality calls for a succession of perceptual elements that have to be combined: in this succession of elements the individuality of the object melts away. On the other hand, dimensions of depth are disclosed only through foreshortening and shadow, so that a vigorous participation of the combinative understanding and of habituation is required for their apprehension. In

both cases, therefore, the outcome is a subjective clouding of the objective fact, which the cultural peoples were at pains to avoid.[60]

Stephen Clingman points to distinct differences between the fictions of Africa produced by Olive Schreiner and those of Sol Plaatje—each in a way a founder of modern South African fiction—and he is one critic who recognizes that while Schreiner's *Story of an African Farm* "purports to be firmly 'settled' in its African setting," it actually bespeaks its "*alienation* from its environment, though—perhaps unsurprisingly," he suggests, "it naturalizes that colonial condition by seeing it in 'universal' terms." This observation is shrewd. But Schreiner's female characters are neither wholly alienated from their African environments nor yet quite at home there. Clingman recognizes where their alienation comes from: It "ha[s] to do with the gender of both [*The Story of an African Farm*'s] author and of its chief character Lyndall, [where] it becomes apparent how in the colonial setting, it is white femaleness which marks out the boundaries of the licit and illicit; and how, for those who venture beyond those boundaries, the threat of mental destabilization appears." This is, he rightly notes, "something which affects Lyndall in the novel, and affected Schreiner in her own life."[61]

But there is a bit more to be said. Sol Plaatje grew up in one of the Barolong communities of the Northern Cape. His novel *Mhudi* was written about 1917 and published in 1930, but its setting is the 1830s, the period of the Difaqane or "great scattering" of South African peoples after the Shakan wars. Rather than depicting the separation of character from the landscape as one might expect, Plaatje's novel instead makes a different kind of claim, "that of *belonging*." But although Clingman and I agree on the function writing serves—his own analysis is close to describing what I have called the "homeostatic" function of Schreiner's writing—clearly the homeostatic functions the South African novel serves for the white South African woman writer and for the black South African male writer are very different. In Plaatje's novel, in contrast to Schreiner's, Clingman sees a very different image of the place of women:

> Not only does every person appear to have his or her proper position in society, and to be valued in that capacity, but Plaatje actively venerates women in his novel—something Schreiner certainly would have envied. The presentation is no doubt idyllic and idealized, but if one thinks of fiction as "writing out" certain problems this in itself should be suggestive for the historical mind.[62]

Whenever she was in any kind of psychic distress Schreiner invariably did speak of needing to "write herself right" again, and in a way my entire project is an attempt to delineate the ways she and Dinesen "wrote out" certain problems. Yet the idyllic and idealized position women hold in Plaatje's fictions would hold no comfort for either of them but would instead figure among precisely those confining categories they would have felt it necessary to write themselves *out of*. Some years ago Elaine Showalter suggested that in part Schreiner's fictional works were trying to render what she referred to as the claustrophobic inner landscape of the new woman.[63] Part of the psychic charge Schreiner's novels still generate today originates in their attempts to break out of those claustrophobic inner landscapes against the expansiveness of the African Karoo through which she moves. But one looks at these African landscapes as they are produced in and by Schreiner's fictions a bit differently if they are read against the same landscapes as they are produced in her letters to European friends.

In a particularly eloquent letter to Havelock Ellis, for instance, Schreiner described the landscape of her South African environs at the time she was writing. She and Cron were living near Kimberley Hole, the site of the largest man-made pit on the African continent. This hole was the product of mining activities begun in earnest just at this time,[64] and in a letter dated July 1884—and signed "Your little Child Olive"—Schreiner makes a characteristic conflation of landscape and personality: "It is so beautiful here to me, Henry. On the hill opposite are some great stone quarries. It is as though something tore the hill open and said 'Here you shall see not only the smooth but the hard strong stuff that is inside too.' Somehow I like quarries," she says, immediately adding, "some people think them ugly."[65]

In *From Man to Man* Rebekah valiantly tries to make that "hard strong stuff" inside her self visible to her stubbornly oblivious husband Frank who, busy running from one affair to another, ignores her attempts to be "seen"—to be *visible* to him. After the final affair he walks out the door of her study, itself a precarious enclosure, and Rebekah stares at the door he has just shut.

> Then she sat down in her armchair and leaned her head back against it. She folded her hands over her head and looked up at the dark little ceiling. She drew a long breath; but it was not the ceiling of the little room she saw as she sat there staring upwards. It was as though a vast dome were reared over her, as though a dark pall, which for years had been stretched out just above her, were folded up and removed and she looked up into almost infinite space. So wide, so still, so peaceful; and she was alone there![66]

Having failed to make the "hard strong stuff" of her nature visible, Rebekah produces compensatorily this expanse of space around the isolated woman. All through her novel Schreiner tries to make visible to her readers this same hard strong stuff. The magnitude of this effort in her own mind goes a long way toward explaining why Schreiner spent over thirty years trying to complete this novel, why she never could finish it to her own satisfaction, and in part why so many readers don't like it.[67] The same earnest philosophical, psycho-spiritual-sexual meditation, the same urgency and intensity of that speculation that Frank runs from very nearly defeats any pleasure readers might take in the novel. At its center, long chapters like "Raindrops in the Avenue" are made up of excerpts from Rebekah's personal diary, detailed records of the crimes and deceptions committed against her by her philandering husband, meditations recording Rebekah's struggle to understand the nature of truth that seem to record Schreiner's own attempts to explore philosophical questions in the guise of fiction. This same fictional diary also stands as eloquent evidence of Rebekah's—and Schreiner's—self-sabotage of those same efforts. Philosophical speculation on the interconnectedness of all things alternates with passages where speculation trails off into phrases like "then she scribbled on about . . . ," which effectively shut out any possibility of comprehension.[68]

The same thing happens in Schreiner's letter to Ellis. In it Kimberley Hole becomes not, as might be expected, a figure for the raping of the African continent by European mining interests, but instead a figure for Schreiner's own project of making the "hard strong stuff" of *her* inner layers visible to Ellis. But though she trains attention on the quarry as a representation of her own inner world in a move presumably designed to lead to closer intimacy because of the self-revelation it implies, she concludes by subverting her own efforts. After flashing a glimmer of the inner, private Kimberley Hole—and I mean to suggest the "flash" to have the erotic charge Roland Barthes suggests when he notes that the most erotic part of the body is "where the garment gaps"—Schreiner instantly retreats. "You *perfectly* understand my old self," she tells Ellis, immediately adding, "but not in the same way my new self. It is this last four years . . . that makes the difference. I don't understand myself now, and how should you?"[69] Here is the verbal equivalent of Dinesen's photographic portrait, the figure set apart from its ground or "groundings" and from all hope of being understood, all the while insisting on the inevitability of that separateness and foreclosing in advance all understanding.

Dinesen's version of Kimberley Hole, an ideal in which the inner is bravely exposed and made visible, is probably most evident in her fascination with the stretched-out bodies of lions lying skinned on the African plain after a hunting expedition. Among the things she appreciates is the perfect conjunction she sees there between their outer mien/mane and inner being. "The dead lions . . . looked magnificient in their nakedness, there was not a particle of superfluous fat on them [the anorexic ideal again], each muscle was a bold controlled curve, they needed no cloak, they were, all through, what they ought to be."[70]

Both Dinesen's and Schreiner's rhetorical gestures here might best be seen not as one more instance of the modernist grappling toward significance that Jameson frequently decries, but as a struggle toward style in the most productive sense: as attempts to achieve something like the highly eroticized and stylized freedom Foucault describes in his *History of Sexuality,* most particularly in what he calls the great themes of sexual austerity, in all kinds of interdictions, dietary prohibitions, admonitions to self-denial or self-mastery that are no strangers to Dinesen's or Schreiner's psychic makeup and that he sees as means to enhance sexuality.[71] Or more recently, as style in the productive sense suggested by bell hooks, who uses the term to signify a kind of performance in which "to style" is "a sign of value, uniqueness, and seriousness."[72] Schreiner flashing a glimmer of the inner woman and then instantly suppressing it is Schreiner "styling."

Cultivating their position as "exotics," surrounded by admirers in Dinesen's case and by new women and intellectual companions in Schreiner's, but ultimately alone on purpose and by design, in at least one sense both women inhabited the same bit of ground as Marilyn Monroe and Greta Garbo. "I believe—perhaps illogically—," mused Garbo, "that if I bring people closer to myself, they may discover my real character and through their maneuverings and gossiping I might lose my legend . . . [which] is everything to me now. I would not sell it for life, happiness, or anyone. . . . As a matter of fact, I would even sacrifice my own life so as not to jeopardize it."[73]

Unfortunately, this fear that if people "really knew" the "real Olive" she would lose power, lose her "legend," is evident in a great many of Schreiner's letters, especially to male correspondents. It's dismaying to say the least to read seriatim the great bulk of her halting, deferential letters to Karl Pearson, Ellis, and Edward Carpenter as she struggles to share her views on what she's read. It's dismaying also to recognize how consistently she hedges, backs off, qualifies, ending so many of her forays into philosophical or social speculations with "Don't you think?" or beginning them with "I may be wrong but. . . ." It's even more distressing to recognize how much Schreiner shows this deference toward male correspondents who, though they may not have been less intelligent than she, were surely less socially egalitarian or morally expansive. Karl Pearson, for instance, was commonly regarded as one of the theorists of capitalism who firmly believed in the inherent superiority of the white race and the necessity for Europeans to expand into virgin areas of the world as a kind of holy mission—convictions Schreiner distinctly did not share.

Schreiner's husband collaborated with Havelock Ellis in producing an edition of her letters after her death, and Ellis made sure the letters she had written to her other close intellectual confidant Karl Pearson were left out. He also shared with Schreiner's husband his assessment of her as an intellectual: she had "never really *developed* in all the forty years I knew her, and I had no influence on her."[74] If we take the latter half of Ellis's sentence as his attempt to prove the accuracy of its first half, then the entire sentence seems not so much to demonstrate Schreiner's lack of development as an intellectual as to validate her fear of invasion and the wisdom of her need for those protective enclosures and evasions that so characterize her life.

Isak Dinesen's cloches and large hats, her carefully constructed photographic representations, her ethereal storyteller's voice all separated her from a crowd even in its midst. Schreiner's exasperated insistence that no one could possibly understand her, even as she tried desperately inside and outside her fiction to explain herself, speaks to a profound ambivalence, strongest around European men, about being visible and being known. But identity does require an audience, and if that audience needed to be European, Schreiner and Dinesen not infrequently constructed "Africans" as a kind of mediating screen through which they would become visible. In their extraliterary writings—in Dinesen's memoirs and Schreiner's social and political tracts, that is—both the production and the dissemination of their identity were controlled by a process of alternately setting themselves off against and setting themselves comfortably among Africans whom they variously constructed: Dinesen constructing them as workers/helpmates, as children in need of protection and defense, Schreiner sometimes constructing them as children in this same way and sometimes, as she does in *Closer Union,* as less evolved creatures deserving sympathy and protection, if not respect. Africans also serve each woman at times as a kind of audience in attendance at their identity formation, and sometimes as a defense or shield against Europeans who would come too close.

The persona each produces might be described as the surrealists described their images: as precarious enclosures[75] carved out of a *langscape* of Africa. Their self-constructions at that site prove the truth of Adorno's observation that "man is the site or arena of his philosophy rather than a being for himself."[76] Their identity formation is played out at other sites besides the ones at which they present or represent their physical bodies, the same struggle going on in their tropings and amalgamations of both African and European materials. These other sites or arenas will be the subjects of later chapters.

3

The Subversion of "Woman" and the Triumph of Women

Oh it is awful to be a woman. These women are killing me. . . . Give my love to Louie, but I don't want to see her or any other woman. I want to live *alone, alone, alone*. . . . I wonder if I shall ever come back to England among these women again. . . . Oh please see that they bury me in a place where there are no women. I have not been a woman really, though I've seemed like one.

Olive Schreiner, *Letters,*
ed. Cronwright-Schreiner

It is often said that trousers are not suitable for women, and I agree. But I must add they are not suitable for *men* either. . . . The great dramatic scenes of antiquity—Socrates' death, the murder of Caesar at the Capital—are incompatible with any image of trousers. Moses in trousers could never have brought forth water from a rock.

Isak Dinesen,
Daguerreotypes

Writing to the sister of Havelock Ellis she called Louie, Olive Schreiner confides, "I want to wear boy's clothes and *will* as soon as I can get other women to join me."[1] Dinesen's favorite literary character was Shakespeare's Viola, another pants wearer. Behind all this interest in trousers were issues going well beyond the sartorial. Whether they were positioning themselves in relation to femaleness, to maternity, or to their own mothers, Schreiner and Dinesen worked hard to distance themselves from the category "woman," often by the most ingenious means. As early as age twenty Schreiner was quite matter-of-factly referring to "my woman hatred" as if it were already an old friend.[2] The two epigraphs here do suggest some differences between the two, and though those differences seem largely a matter of style, style turns out to matter a great deal. The intense earnestness that suffuses all of Schreiner's writings about women, including periodic protestations that "the work of [her] life [was] to try and teach women to love one another" and to "put [her] arms round all the tired lonely women in the world and help them"[3] makes her occasional distancing of herself from them register particularly harshly, and it's difficult not to hear Nietzsche's voice lurking behind her own: "Women themselves always still have in the background of all personal vanity an impersonal contempt for 'woman.'"[4] Whereas Dinesen's apparently more benign distancing tends to be expressed with a lighter touch, often in the kind of ironic, bemused humor evident in her discourse on trousers, Schreiner's fear of confinement in the category "woman" virtually screams at readers—even when what she has written ostensibly has nothing whatever to do with women.

In *Closer Union* Schreiner advocated a federation rather than unification for South Africa, and in doing so she anticipated precisely a dialogue going on in 1994 at the moment of elections in South Africa. "The Eastern Province taal has a saying: 'Trouw is nie paere koop!' ('Marriage is not buying horses')—neither is Closer Union. He that is in cannot get out! It is best to clear the ground before you pitch your tent!"[5] "Getting out," or trying to, turns out to be a major activity of *Story of an African Farm,* as its heroine first tries to burn her way out of a locked room, later rescues Waldo from entrapment in a shed, later still runs away for four years to live incognito, and at great cost chooses to live out her belief that marriage is a form of entrapment. After succinctly listing all these moves in his 1991 study of Schreiner, Gerald Monsman concludes that what "salvages the figure of Lyndall" in the end is her relationship with Waldo.[6] But some will regard Lyndall's frantic attempts to keep herself from being ensnared as exactly the things that make her, and Schreiner's book, most intriguing. With a strong need all her life to see where the windows were and to be assured they could be opened, when she and Cron traveled by rail in Europe Schreiner is reported to have instigated "occasional scenes with other passengers in the matter of fresh air, which sometimes ended with Cronwright holding open the window by force; on one occasion, at least, with a threat on his part of physical violence."[7] Her lifelong asthma partly accounts for this obsession with window opening, and I do not count myself among those critics who want to read Schreiner's asthmatic symptoms as largely psychomatic. But speaking as another who can live only where there are plenty of windows and plenty of opportunities to see the way out, I can readily understand her impulses. Considered in tandem with other gestures she makes throughout her lifework, this attention to the exits seems to require explanations going beyond the purely physiological.

A reasonable balance of sympathy and judgment needs to be

cultivated as one looks at these women's ambivalence about being female and at the strategies it inspired. Since this ambivalence was necessarily both exacerbated and exorcised by the aesthetic and self-presentational strategies each adopted in her lifework, to identify those strategies is often to point to a possible pathology and to name its palliation at the same time. In all cases I believe what G. K. Chesterton said of Dickens could fairly be said of Dinesen and Schreiner: their peculiar genius was one that avoided itself as a sleepwalker avoids an open window. Schreiner at least, despite her endless philosophic explorations, confessed as much. "I don't know how it is," she says, "but I've never analysed, I never analyse nowadays. I just live on and act as my first impulse directs. Even to analyse and look at myself as much as this letter requires is acutely painful to me."[8] The complicated positionalities, shifting identifications, distancings, and otherings she and Dinesen enacted require careful mapping, since the ambivalence they expressed toward women and toward being women characteristically is simultaneously expressed on one stratum of representation and exorcised on another.

Neither woman's resistance to womanhood was primarily a resistance to female biology. Of all critics who have broached this subject concerning either of these women, Patricia Meyer Spacks comes closest to understanding Dinesen's position relative to gender questions when she suggests they were largely "irrelevant" to her actual life as she lived it. It would be impossible to make the case for any resistance to female biology on Schreiner's part, given the amount of space she devotes in her letters to praising maternity and expressing joy at her many pregnancies, all but one ending in miscarriage.[9] Insisting more than once that her "true destiny" was to have been the mother of many children, she devoted substantial portions of *Woman and Labour* to developing the argument that maternity has always been an important piece of woman's labor the worth of which has been seriously undervalued. But she praises this important work of bearing children in quite unorthodox terms. Unlike Schopenhauer, or Havelock Ellis and Karl Pearson, Schreiner does not argue that bearing children is woman's work and supporting them man's, either because that's how it's always been done or because it is part of man's and woman's "natures" to enact that particular division of labor. Instead she writes a different history. Women have always performed the hard physical labor of planting, sowing, and hauling "in order to obtain the right to bear men."

In his advice to Western scholars struggling to understand Africa, Mudimbe suggests that we reject anthropology or ethnography in favor of history, even though history is by and large an invention of the present,[10] and those of us struggling to understand the history of woman might consider the extremely interesting history of maternity Schreiner invents in this same spirit. Though historically childbearing was the *prize* awarded to woman as a reward for her other hard physical labor, now Schreiner fears "the world wants to turn the prize into an obligation"; to bar women from certain forms of work and spheres by presuming a division of labor that never existed.[11] Here is a glimpse of an Olive Schreiner about as Kierkegaardianly perverse as Isak Dinesen, and in the gap between the ideal or *fiction* of maternity espoused in her social writings and the actuality of maternity played out in her fictions, Olive Schreiner is either the liar her husband is said to have called her or the impossibilitarian her idealism made of her. Either way, the amount of modernist space she clears for herself is so vast that neither one—possibility or ideal—need touch her at any point.

The paeans to maternity and maternal power in her feminist writings are entirely inconsistent with the portraits of absent, uncaring, distracted, even brutal mothers in her novels, and despite the remarkable fact that it is a scene of childbirth that opens *From Man to Man,* her novels obsessively repeat the same set of relations between every mother and every child: if "Africa" is their "true home," every child's "true mother" is someone other than her mother. Raised by various relatives, Undine ends up mothering the Snappercaps' children while their own mother knocks them about quite unmaternally. Lyndall and Em in *Story of an African Farm* are raised by the grotesquely unmaternal—though very sexual—Tant' Sannie. Biological mothers capriciously give away their daughters, as happens to Griet in *From Man to Man,* "the little Bushman girl" whose drunken mother has sold her to Bertie "for a pair of old shoes and a bottle of wine" (p. 75). Schreiner's paeans to maternity in letters are also inconsistent with her view of her own mother. She protects herself from the latter using a strategy exactly analogous to the one she adopts to protect herself from the power she bestows on adult males. As adult desiring males are referred to by diminutives, as "dear, child-like creatures," in letters her mother frequently becomes either "poor little mother," or "my own little Mothie." In *Undine* Schreiner produces a complicated portrait of someone uncannily similar to Schreiner herself. Protecting herself against maternal power and all other kinds by becoming arrogant and self-abasing in roughly equal proportions, Undine muses to herself with little self-awareness "how easily the word 'poor' falls naturally before some names" (p. 122).

Such references to "little" women or to her own "poor little mother" have been the topic of a few feminist analyses at least since Kathleen Blake's article on the subject appeared in 1980,[12] and there's no escaping the fact that in part Schreiner aggrandizes her own position as woman by diminishing that of every other female. But she also regularly signed letters to her mother "Your little daughter Olive," and associating herself and her mother with the word "little" may have been one way of allying women with a uniquely "African" source of power. In "Bushman" mythology the great whimsical antihero of many tales is the littlest animal, the praying mantis, who regularly outwits far larger adversaries.[13] Still, referring to herself in letters to her mother as "your little daughter" was at the same time a peculiarly poignant and valiant kind of wish fulfillment, since Schreiner felt keenly all her life a lack of attention and support from a mother whose self-absorption in time became so complete that she cut herself off from her children, living out her later years in a Catholic convent.

Rebecca Lyndall Schreiner's history makes it easy to guess the origin of the distraction and emotional absence her daughter experienced. Schreiner saw her mother not only as not her nurturer, but as one who instead needed to be protected: from Olive's radical political views, and from her disenchantment with Cecil Rhodes, whom her mother adored. A governess by age fifteen, Schreiner found her closest companions during those formative years to be not women, and surely not her mother, but the writers she read so voraciously. They were all male. Her fictional heroines are often taken to be instances of self-portraiture, and what both she and these heroines read most were writers who espoused various kinds of willed self-reliance: Emerson, Schopenhauer, Herbert Spencer. Schreiner saw herself, then, as necessarily being her mother's mother, confiding to Cron more than once, "My mother has never been a mother to me. I have had no mother. She is a brilliant wonderful little woman, all intellect and genius." But, she notes, "the relation between us is a very curious one; it is *I* who have always had to think for, guide and nurse her since I was a tiny child. *She* seems . . . like a very favorite brilliant child of mine!"[14]

Her mother's ardent nature had led her to choose as a husband a young German missionary with "immense physical strength and . . . [a] dreamy silent nature," and in the end Schreiner's most sympathetic constructions of her mother portray her as a woman trapped, who might better have kept her eyes on the open windows. She was like "a grand piano kept permanently locked up and used as a common dining-table."[15] In recognizing that erotic attraction to the hypermasculine male had resulted in her mother's becoming "locked up," Schreiner saw a discomfiting representation of femaleness with which she could very easily identify. But insofar as such an identification was repugnant, it needed to be projected outward onto all women. Yet the projected and the repressed always return. Part of the attraction drawing Olive Schreiner to Samuel Cronwright and him to her was in my view the constant and intricate play of gender role reversals that went on between the two in this heterosexual marriage. Cron's initial attraction to Olive was based on admiration of her intellect: he had read her writings and admired their moral force and rhetorical power. But once he had seen her in the flesh, it was her robust physicality, even masculinity, that attracted him. He confessed shortly after one of their first encounters that he "would like to fight her because she was so strong." While Schreiner in turn admired *his* physical prowess, she also confessed that she admired him because "all possibilities are in your beautiful face, choked."[16] Her attraction to Cron in no small measure, then, consisted in the power with which he evoked in her psyche not her father, but her mother, and in particular her mother's own "choked possibilities." Everything Schreiner ever wrote about the condition of women indicates that she saw how their possibilities for development and self-sufficiency had been crippled, crabbed, and cut off by economic, psychological, and social restrictions. And literal-minded from childhood, demanding to know whether the bedtime stories he was being told were *really* true, Cron represented to Schreiner the same crabbed and choked imagination she saw in women in general and her mother in particular. Schreiner had assured him early in their marriage that if he would sell his farm and move to a location that was more congenial for her asthma, she could finish revising her two books and support herself completely. When later he came to call her a liar, what had happened was partly that she had underestimated his literal-mindedness, just as he had overestimated the extent to which she, or anybody, could succeed in writing on demand. Cron's face, in which all possibilities were choked, appeared beautiful because through it she could associate him with her mother and with femaleness itself.

Even as Schreiner positions her mother as her child in letters to her husband or to friends, she still needs a mother, and she fills that position with various others. Predictably it is sometimes Mother Africa. "What is true of the personal mother is yet more true of the man's native land. It has shaped all his experiences; it has lain as the background to all his consciousness; it has modified his sensations and emotions."[17] But various males are drawn into occupancy there too, including her husband, insofar as she could do it or he allow it. Writing to Dr. and Mrs. John Brown in 1894 during one of her many pregnancies, Schreiner accomplishes a kind of double reversal. At the moment when she might most be expected to construct herself or her mother as a maternal figure, she puts Cron there instead: "My husband is unspeakably tender and good to me; sometimes I feel as if I were a little baby and he was my mother."[18] But if her husband is her mother and she his child, as Old Ayah says in *From Man to Man*, "*Diss 'n snaaks se kind!*": "Tis a strange child."[19]

In *Out of Africa* Dinesen is at great pains to tell her readers how often African *watoto* (children) saw her as their mother. Africans with whom Judith Thurman spoke in 1975 who had known Isak Dinesen still spoke of her in maternal terms. Kamau, "still living in Ngong, remembered Karen Blixen as the only white person he had ever seen who picked up an African child and carried him in her arms. 'We children,' he said, 'called her our mother.' "[20] For her, enacting the maternal may have been possible or comfortable only insofar as she felt distant enough from those she mothered never to be mistaken for their actual mother—or anybody's biological mother, for that matter. Although Dinesen did not associate her own mother with self-absorption and absence as Schreiner did, she did associate her with its equally damaging obverse: with social prohibitions and interdictions and with a stifling bourgeois propriety characteristic of the Westenholz family, to which her mother belonged. Woman represented, says Thurman, "repression, self-surrender, accepting guilt, repudiating desire, living for others."[21] As Schreiner during her formative pubescent years had buried herself in the works of Emerson, Heine, and Schopenhauer, Dinesen avidly read the works of Georg Brandes. In 1883, when she was nineteen, Brandes published a critical series of essays titled *Det moderne Gjennembruds Maend* (Men of the modern breakthrough). Malcolm Bradbury and James McFarlane suggest that European modernism was born at precisely this moment in Scandinavia, with the publication of Brandes's book, which was the first to name "the modern" as such.[22] It was also Brandes who virtually single-handedly made Nietzsche, who was largely unknown before May 1888, far better known throughout Europe. This recognition was largely a result of a series of lectures on Nietzsche's works that Brandes delivered in Copenhagen. When Dinesen first encountered Brandes's works, with all the spontaneity and intellectual curiosity of a smart nineteen-year-old she sent Brandes a note inviting him to visit her at Rungstedlund. Brandes accepted. But when he arrived Dinesen's mother intercepted him and chatted with him in the parlor, forcing Dinesen to sit upstairs alone. Her mother apparently had decided it was inappropriate for a young woman to have such a meeting.[23] As an adult Dinesen, in a spirit of bitterness more characteristic of Schreiner, confessed her distress at the cavalier way her artistic and intellectual development had been ignored—the way the system had "allowed practically all my abilities to lie fallow and passed me on to charity or prostitution in some shape or other."[24]

The far more flamboyant and less constraining Wilhelm Dinesen won out hands down over her mother in Dinesen's affections and in her identifications, and his biography reads so uncannily like a prefiguring of her own that it is difficult not to suspect she was at some pains to ensure she would walk some of the same psychic terrain. The lives of both seem eloquent testimony, for instance, to the truth of Lacan's analyses of the workings of desire. After losing his childhood sweetheart to typhoid at age twenty, Wilhelm Dinesen declared that "the deepest loves [are] aroused by what could not love you in return."[25] Karen Blixen's erotic inclinations seemed destined to prove the truth of her father's judgment. Dinesen's father regularly volunteered for service in any war that came his way, beginning with the Dano-Prussian War in 1864, and Thurman suggests he cut a "nonchalant but melancholy figure" all his life. Like his daughter, Captain Dinesen escaped his melancholy by traveling. Taking the requisite romantic tour of wild America, under the pseudonym Osceola he produced travel writings about Native Americans and their virtues: "Their eyes see more than ours," he says, and they "are better than our civilized people of Europe,"[26] precisely prefiguring his daughter's assessments of Africans.

Relentlessly restless, Wilhelm Dinesen had a difficult time "making peace with peace" after his marriage. Displaying the same kind of Manichaean tendencies as his daughter, he believed that "love and peace hate, persecute, and annihilate one another." Love he regarded as being exactly "like the hunt": simultaneously "a mortal struggle" and "a form of play,"[27] a conviction that both resembles Schreiner's and goes a long way toward explaining both women's vexed relation to femaleness—given the assumption that woman would always be the weaker combatant and therefore destined to be the vanquished in any such construction of love as combat. Dinesen's identification with her father was compounded by the uncanny similarities between their lives. Wilhelm Dinesen took his own life a month before Dinesen's tenth birthday, his desperate response to the discovery that he may have contracted incurable syphilis, a fact that surely must have haunted the syphilitic Isak Dinesen.[28]

Samuel Cronwright-Schreiner suggests that Olive's portrait of the old German Otto in *Story of an African Farm* is based on her father. After he died when she was twenty-one, she never spoke of him again, the memory being too painful. Identification with father partly suggests abjection *from* mother, and Schreiner's and Dinesen's ambivalence about women can be seen in part as a form of abjection in the terms Julia Kristeva first developed in *Powers of Horror* (1982). Lacan had proposed that expulsion from the mother's breast sets in motion the infant's recognition that the world is not its own and the subsequent fall into the symbolic, the birth of the "I" being simultaneously both a recognition of the separation of that "I" from all others and a separation from the one who says "I." Kristeva posits a subject actively participating in that driving away or abjection rather than, as Freud would have it, a passive human subject unwillingly expelled. This active resister becomes for Kristeva a subject who resides comfortably in "the ambiguous, the in-between, [defying] boundaries, a composite, resistant to unity." According to her interpreter John Lechte, "the immoralist who openly flouts the existing moral order in light of a different set of principles" is not abject. But "the amoral oscillator is; he who slyly unpredictably, at one time conforms to existing moral principles, and at another secretly flouts them."[29] This is precisely the positionality Schreiner and Dinesen both cultivated, and it generated a certain predictable fallout, as it does, for instance, in Schreiner's deliberate flouting of sartorial conventions or her rejection of a mother-daughter bond and the suffering she experienced from being shunned as a consequence.

Although Dinesen's letters from Africa, like Schreiner's, frequently turn out to be confessions to other family members of all those things she could not share with her mother, in both cases that pushing away involves a pushing away from woman in general that is at least as strong. Schreiner's pushing away is partly a consequence of the disappointment she felt with white women, which in its turn is a consequence of the same idealism pervading every part of her life and thought and especially of her expectations that women ought to be more noble and more selfless than men. Writing to women, she rarely calls men to account for the social, psychic, or economic position women find themselves in, insisting instead that women must take responsibility for improving their own lot. Not infrequently she assumes that the inequalities women face are a consequence of their own deficiencies or weaknesses. "I've been so troubled and despairing about the woman question," she writes to Ellis in November 1885; adding immediately, "you know it is possible that women are absolutely and altogether the inferiors of men." "It is not against man we have to fight," she tells her friend Mary Roberts, "but *against ourselves* within ourselves." She saddles women with the responsibility not only for their own improvement, but for men's too. "A woman can call out the higher and more ideal nature that does slumber in *every* man," she tells Karl Pearson."[30] In *Thoughts on South Africa* she makes women responsible for the quality of entire civilizations: "The measure of its women is ultimately the measure of any people's strength and resistile power," she says, blaming the fall of the Roman republic on the decline in the strength of its women in its latter days (p. 20). A pacifist who had spoken out against England's entry into the Great War, she was bothered most at its close by the behavior of women: "Women gamble as they never gambled before. It seems to me they miss the excitement of the war," she says, "so they are making up for it in other ways."[31] Partly these impossibly demanding and thinly disguised woman-hating sentiments may be revealing the profound influence that an early reading of Schopenhauer, the man Henry James refers to in *The Princess Cassimassima* as "that moldy misogynist," may have had on an impressionable pubescent Schreiner. The first entry under "misogyny" in Peter Gay's *The Tender Passion* reads, "See Schopenhauer."

But the impossible demands Schreiner makes on women, presented in a rhetoric that demands that females take responsibility for uplifting the entire "race," are very much in evidence in much Anglo-American women's writing in the latter half of the nineteenth century, even if her rendition seems particularly excessive. Any failure to measure up to this rigorous standard results in her advocating forms of self-punishment much like Toni Morrison's Sula's act of "aggression" against the young boys who taunt her and her friend on their way home from school. Deliberately slicing off the end of her finger, Sula calmly tells them, if I can do that to myself, just think what I could do to *you*. "The only life I would ever punish anyone by taking," Schreiner says during the carnage of World War I, "is my own; I have always since I was a little child . . . thought the punishment one would have a right to inflict on those who had injured one too much was to go and stand before them and stab or shoot oneself and say 'my blood be upon you.' "[32]

In truth, nothing can quite describe the experience of reading seriatim Schreiner's allegories published in 1891 under the title *Dreams*. In many, a woman addresses a figure named "Life," "God," "Truth," or "Love" and, in a gesture of expiation, self-sacrifice, or supplication, offers invariably the same gift:

> Then she came to a shrine; she knelt down before it and prayed; there came no answer. Then she uncovered her breast; with a sharp two-edged stone that lay there she wounded it. The drops dripped slowly down on to the stone, and a voice cried, "What do you see?" She answered, "There is a man; I hold him nearer than anything. I would give him the best of all blessings."

The woman making this offering doesn't know what it is the man wants most, but as her prayer is answered, she learns what that is. It turns out to be as perverse as anything in a Dinesen story: "It is that he might leave you."[33]

Among the many modernist oscillations in Schreiner's temperament besides acceptance and rejection of womanhood was that between working hard to construct protective self-enclosures to protect her boundaries and a powerful desire to pour herself out in a kind of self-immolation. The most extreme instance of the latter perhaps exists in the curious sentiments she expressed to Karl Pearson, whom she regarded as the human being she felt closest to because his mind "work[ed] with its material in the same way" she believed hers did. "If I could," she gushes, "I would open a vein in my arm and let all my blood run into your body to strengthen you for your work," insisting all the while that "no element of sex . . . creep[s] into [her] thoughts or feelings" for him.[34] What therapists today would call boundary problems were clearly a part of Schreiner's psychic makeup, and despite everything—bouts of exasperation and frustration—she seemed all in all to be able to speak of those problems with relative equanimity and resignation. "Ever since I could remember," she says, "if I loved a person really, . . . then I had no self, they were everything to me."[35] Phyllis Grosskurth reports that in his private journal Havelock Ellis judged that Schreiner "has a desire—which seems a little morbid—to . . . be abnormally selfless. I think that it may be a reaction," he says, "from an opposite state of mind." To which Schreiner herself enters into his journal, "No, it is a *development*."[36]

The woman Schreiner perhaps most admired and to whom she dedicated *Woman and Labour* was Edward Bulwer-Lytton's granddaughter Lady Constance Lytton, who was sent to prison more than once as a militant suffragist who, in a remarkable act of masochism sanctioned by political purpose, is reported during her stay in prison to have tried to scratch the words "Votes for Women" on her skin with a pin.[37] Biographers have speculated based on the few bits of evidence not suppressed that Schreiner may have experienced an early love affair that had been wounding in the extreme, and it may be at least partly true that her appreciation of and attraction to Lytton's behavior here was caused by a powerful tangling and confusion not just between politics and eroticism, but between the erotic and pain, between politics and pain, and between womanhood and pain. Surely the tendentiousness in her novels and allegories makes it clear that she presumed pain was woman's lot because it had been hers, and the choices she saw as available to women were to suffer it nobly and stoically or to whine and cry. In only one place, in "The Woman Question" in *Thoughts on South Africa,* does she report direct conversation with an African woman. There she asks an African woman whether she believes in God and reports her answer. There *might* be one, says the woman, "but if there were one, He was not good. If he had been good, he would not have made women" (p. 206).

Selectively consulted and selectively reported, the African woman here can only confirm what the European male writers Schreiner read had already told her. Schopenhauer, Heine, and Herbert Spencer confirmed what her experience seemed already to show: woman was destined to sacrifice, to suffer, to be alone, and to triumph through willed acceptance of that lot. Women could improve their position in the social order by improving themselves.

They could punish others for their position by punishing themselves. They would enlarge the portion of goodness in the world by heroically being good themselves, and they would improve the world most and best by taking responsibility not only for their own moral position but for everybody else's as well. The strongest evidence suggesting that Schreiner thought of the continent of Africa as female lies in the fact that she held Africans to the same impossible standard to which she held woman. It is South Africa herself who is to blame for Europeans' rapacity: "The man at the helm who goes to sleep," she says as she pleads with the British not to initiate the Anglo-Boer War in *An English South-African's View of the Situation,* "cannot blame the rock when the ship is thrown upon it, though it be torn asunder. He should have known the rock was there and steered clear of it" (p. 58).

Still, and for all this construction of "woman," Olive Schreiner indubitably remained all her life a great defender of women. Feminists from everywhere, among them the prominent Dutch physician and feminist Aletta Jacobs, for instance, made a special point of making the pilgrimage to her home at De Aar whenever they were anywhere near South Africa, and women from around the world cite her works as inspiration. A Russian Jewish immigrant to the United States, Anzia Yezierska—an early lover of John Dewey and writer of six volumes of stories and novels about immigrant life in the 1920s—lists Schreiner's works, particularly her *Dreams* and *Story of an African Farm,* as a major influence on her own life and career.[38] Churning out tracts and letters to newspapers championing women's rights, she was unique in her day in that she fought for universal suffrage in South Africa for male and female, black and white, breaking her ties with white South African feminists when they refused to fight for the suffrage of African women. *Dreams* was reprinted twenty-two times in rapid succession, and some of her allegories were read from pulpits. Her "Three Dreams in a Desert" was read aloud to Women's Freedom League prisoners like Lady Lytton, who testified that it seemed to her "a bare literal description of the pilgrimage of women.' "[39]

She nourished friendships with women, including Mary Brown, who helped and encouraged her to write when she first visited England, with Erilda Cawood in Africa, who was probably her first real confidante there, and with Betty Molteno and Alice Greene, who were teachers at the Collegiate School for Girls in Port Elizabeth. She belonged to a number of the major socialist and feminist discussion groups popular in England during her lifetime and was a member of probably the best known of the groups formed to explore issues like the "nature" of "man," "woman," "race," and sexuality, the Men and Women's Club founded by Karl Pearson, professor of applied mathematics at University College in London. That group met regularly to discuss the nature of sexuality, the "aesthetic" aspect of sex—by which they meant pleasure separated from procreation—and the ideal form male-female relations might take, and they consistently and emphatically insisted that a woman needed financial independence, sometimes arguing that otherwise the *man* was not free.[40] Besides her *Thoughts about Women* published in 1908 by the Women's Suffrage League, in 1911 she published *Woman and Labour,* the book she refers to all her life long in her letters as "my sex book,"[41] and in 1891 *Dream Life and Real Life.* Another collection, *Stories, Dreams, and Allegories,* appeared after her death, in 1923. Her extraliterary writings are as full of appreciation for women as these allegories, articulating with passionate insistence that they deserved better treatment, a better future. And contrary to her protestations cited above that she wished she had not been born a woman, sometimes there are expressions of gratitude for having been born into that sex: "Being a woman I can reach other women, where no man could reach them. A growing tenderness is in my heart for them."[42]

I race past this portrait of Olive Schreiner as feminist not because it is unimportant, but because it is well known and well documented, most recently in Joyce Berkman's *The Healing Imagination of Olive Schreiner.* What has *not* been so well documented or analyzed is Schreiner's self-positioning in this landscape of women. A curious and interesting slippage occurs as the two sentences above unfold, for instance. At the beginning of the first, Schreiner includes herself among women. By the end of the second, women have become "them." "I sometimes think my great love for women and girls, *not* because they are myself," she writes to Mrs. Frances Smith, "but because they are *not* myself."[43] "You know it is possible women are absolutely the inferiors of men," she tells Ellis; "but still their suffering is real, and something must be done for it." And here the same positioning of women occurs: it is not "our" suffering that needs amelioration, it is "theirs." She adds immediately, "When I look into my heart, then I feel as strong and firm as a lion."[44]

Schreiner may have preferred to see herself as lion rather than woman in the same way Dinesen delighted in reminding everyone at the drop of a pith helmet that she was called lioness by her African familiars. If there had to be binaries, or when they could not manage to balance on that deictical axis of the not woman/not *not*-woman and not man/not *not*-man, both seem to have preferred a man/lion binary. In her obsessive explorations of the nature of man and the nature of woman Schreiner had had ample experience with her male friends' classificatory exercises, and she knew how confining their product was. Frequently in *Woman and Labour* she seems to be directly addressing people like James Hinton: "Scientifically speaking," she says, "it is unproven that there is any organic relation between the brain of the female and the products of art in the form of fiction, as that there is an organic relation between the hand of woman and the typewriter. . . . The tendency of women today to undertake certain forms of labor proves only," she suggests, "that in the crabbed, walled in, and bound condition surrounding women in the present day, these are the lines along which action is most possible to her."[45]

Yet if "woman" was claustrophobic, she wasn't "man." Too often European "man" represented brutishness, insensitivity. In *Thoughts on South Africa* it is the Afrikaner male who comes off best, and the Boer farmers she portrays in her political writings—if not so much those in her novels—are gentle, pacific, and unlike European males, slow to anger. In touch with the natural world, they were also childlike, a great virtue in Schreiner's gender and moral schemas. But they had no intellectual life. When sensitivity and intellectual rigor existed in a male it was linked to impotence, as in her relationship with Havelock Ellis, or with gender ambiguity like that represented in her portrait of Gregory Rose. Ellis was the first to be amused that he had come to be regarded as an authority on sex "despite how small my experience was and how temperate my estimate of the sexual act," concluding it may be "after all, the spectator who sees most of the game."[46]

The terms on which this relationship between Ellis and Schreiner rested were not unrelated to Schreiner's way of being female in the world and to her feelings about the maternal. Scattered here and there in the profusion of miscellaneous "impressions" collected in many volumes Ellis published throughout his life are frequent strong indications of his attraction toward the sexually ambiguous. He describes a person with whom he's had a chance encounter near Victoria Station and to whom he has clearly been drawn "first by a doubt as to its sex." It turns out to be a girl, with "pronounced black down on upper lip." He admires "that shy yet daring figure, flash of vision, yet sad with the incompletion of its own bisexual mystery."[47] Ellis's wife Edith carried on a long and open lesbian affair, and Ellis's attraction toward Schreiner certainly included an attraction toward her mannishness. Phyllis Grosskurth believes her attraction toward him was partly that he was a "motherer" and that the two of them were "a little like children together." "I am her own boy," Ellis croons in one letter,[48] and she in her turn not infrequently calls him "my baby" or "my sweet baby."[49] Given the precarious enclosures Schreiner set up around her own vigorous sexual nature, it's hardly a surprise to learn that at this time in her life she took to pacing the floor regularly, partly in sexual frustration, confessing to Ellis that the potassium bromide she was taking copiously, supposedly as an expectorant, was also meant to diminish her sex drive.[50] By 1885 she was disappointed in Ellis, disenchanted with "free love," which she had come to see as "a devilish thing," and "loathing" James Hinton, who as a major proponent of it was "sitting women naked on his knees to play with them."[51] Refusing urgent proposals of marriage from Freud's physician Brian Donkin and probably from Nikolai Frantsevich Danielson, a Russian writer, economist, and correspondent and translator of Marx and Engels and a friend of Eleanor Marx who was "deeply devoted to Schreiner and long cherished the hope that she would become his wife,"[52] wanting a child but not marriage, Schreiner checked herself into a convent at Harrow. She envies Ellis his caring mother. She begins to sign her letters "The Wandering Jew."

Remaining single for almost ten years more, she continued to participate with the army of European men busy theorizing on race and sex differences, sexuality, and eugenics in countless volumes in which anecdote passed for science. The catalog of those friends who allied themselves with the most aggressive aspects of colonialism is long. Karl Pearson was a student of eugenics who concluded in *National Life from the Standpoint of Science* that "we shall never have a healthy social state in South Africa until the white man replaces the dark in the fields and the mines, and the Kaffir is pushed back towards the equator. The nation organized for the struggle [of existence] must be a *homogenous* whole, not a mixture of superior and inferior races."[53] Many of Dinesen's closest male companions in Kenya also can hardly be described otherwise than as virulently racist and violent. They included the colonial administrator Lord Delamere, who just five years before Dinesen's arrival had led a demonstration against the colonial governor Sadler in Nairobi, demanding that "natives" be forced to work for European settlers[54] and supporting public whippings in front of the courthouse should they object. Schreiner's friends decided that appropriate sexual relations between male and female could be traced to "instinctual" patterns and that satisfactory sex could be achieved only by satisfying instinctual courtship patterns. Sex for males required "an exercise of power, a form of mock combat."[55] In a far more literal sense even than that Dinesen absorbed from her father Wilhelm Dinesen, Schreiner heard from her male intellectual companions that maleness was linked to aggressivity, and as such it was also inevitably linked to the violence of the colonial endeavor. "If Nature needs a truly sympathetic international animal, Nature must wipe out man and produce another species," says Ellis in *Impressions and Comments*.[56]

Given, then, their entirely explicable resistance to being either women *or* men as those categories were construed and enacted by late nineteenth- and early twentieth-century Europeans, in a very real sense both women identified with Africans. When Dinesen's mother was tormenting herself for having allowed her son Thomas to fight in World War I, Dinesen tries to lift her spirits by citing instances of stoicism and bravery that had helped *her* through difficult times. The instances she cites are "the stoicism of the Somali," her servant Farah's "unwavering submission to destiny," and the self-confidence of British aristocrats such as Lord Delamere, who "understood their own natures and acted fearlessly in accordance with them."[57]

Schreiner does try hard to identify with women. She commends Boer women as the "finest specimens" of womanhood. "Devoid of the culture of schools," they are nonetheless "keen, resolute, determined, reflective." Best of all, they escape the "frivolity, love of pleasure and uncertainty of thought" characteristic of wealthier women that render them "so markedly inferior to the male."[58] But there are two characteristic disjunctions between her theory and her practice, and between her portrayals of these women in one genre and in another. The Boer woman praised for pulling her economic weight does something Schreiner promised her husband she would do but by and large did not manage. The same Boer woman praised in Schreiner's political writings for her noble self-sufficiency existed on a steady diet of mutton and mealies and tended to reach a physical girth that offended Schreiner's aesthetic sense. Their size, their lack of imagination, and their literal-mindedness make them the target of less than sympathetic portrayals in her novels, where they exist only as the "sheep-souled," unimaginative, creature-comfort Tant' Sannies and Mrs. Snappercaps of her fiction.

Identification with British women in South Africa, whom she frequently dismisses as nothing but straw hats with paper flowers, is not possible either. Returning to South Africa in 1889 after an eight-year stay in England, Italy, and other parts of Europe and ruminating on the relative social isolation that return implied, she confesses, "It may be good for one's work, but there are times when one longs to rub one's brains up against another human's. There are plenty of women and children and niggers . . . to love here, but sometimes one wants the other side of one's nature satisfied, that *thinks*."[59] Here is radical alterity to be sure, neither Africans nor women providing occasion for identification.

Women draw close to Schreiner, but she pulls away because she sees them as incapable of "talking impersonally," and here too Nietzsche's words can be heard behind her own. "I get so weary of personalities, always that, nothing else, between women. They don't want to discuss a man's public character, even his policy, but want to discuss all the smallest little personal things about them," she confesses.[60] Since women are mired in the personal and she longs for communion with other creatures like herself who are not so mired, then identity formation here calls for some herculean act of the imagination that would produce an alternative subject position for herself. How does she do it?

One needn't look far for one answer. Even a halfway careful reading of Schreiner's letters suggests that her central life's project was not building deeper friendships with women but doing one of two other things: trying to change the nature of men—making them more womanlike—so she could be more deeply friends with *them,* or recasting herself as a man so she could converse with her correspondents "from man to man." "Heine is not understood, and I almost doubt whether anything one could do would cause him to be better understood. He belongs to his own, like Emerson. One might cause him to be more read . . . but the real man, the infinitely tender, burning, passionate heart, will be known only to a few." She ends this letter to Ellis with a postscript: "I like what you say about feeling a woman's heart throbbing in you."[61] "Oh, can't we speak the truth to one another just like two men?" asks Rebekah in *From Man to Man*. "Can't we tell each other just what we think and feel? If you can't love me, tell me so; . . . I do not ask you to love me, only to speak the truth to me, as you would if I were another man." "You must meet me, fairly and straightly," she insists, "as one man meets another, and speak to me as one speaks to one's own soul."[62]

This same cri de coeur appears in her correspondence. Havelock Ellis and Cronwright-Schreiner worked together to collect Schreiner's letters for the latter's edition, but Ellis destroyed a great many of them in the process, including most from 1886 regarding her tormented relationship with Karl Pearson. Although Richard Rive's collection of Schreiner's letters includes letters to more correspondents than did Cron's edition of his wife's correspondence, this expanded collection reveals not only that Schreiner wrote to more female correspondents than Cron's collection suggested, but that her correspondence was full of even more protestations to male correspondents that she wished she were not a woman: To

Karl Pearson, "I am always conscious that I am a woman when I am with you; but it is to wish I were a man that I might come near to you" (1:108). To Edward Carpenter, "I wish I was a man that I might be friends with all of you, but you know my sex must always divide. I only feel like a man, but to you all I seem a woman!" (1:126). To some she insisted on being regarded as a male "pal." To Karl Pearson she presented herself as the witty, self-composed "colleague researcher"[63] who frequently signed off as "your man friend, Olive Schreiner," insisting in at least one postscript, "I'm not a woman, I'm a man, and you are to regard me as such."[64] First and Scott believe these letters reveal the conflict she felt between her "intuitive, even unconscious mistrust of women . . . and a sense of sisterhood she found obligatory," and they are among those who attribute her asthma partly to that psychosomatic source.[65]

But the strenuous effort both to be perceived as a man and *not* to be perceived as a man would have been cause enough for physical symptoms. Everywhere carefully negotiating the boundary between intellectual and sexual friendship with these men, Schreiner works mightily to retain intellectual friendships while not giving off signals that could be interpreted as anything like a sexual interest in her correspondents—even when at times she clearly *does* have sexual feelings. This is true especially in the elaborately involuted letters she sends to Karl Pearson after he had begun to take a romantic interest in another woman. Insisting over and over that her interest in him has always been intellectual, she struggles unconvincingly to explain the nature of her distress because he is attracted to someone else. "I have *never* misunderstood you, *never* thought you loved me as a woman," she insists, noting that "the sex-feeling has an aberrant effect on the intellect." Her real objection, she says, is to this particular woman, who has a tendency "to put her lips" to men and "suck and suck all their life [away]."[66]

This careful negotiation of the terrain of male-female friendships must have been particularly tricky when the *subject matter* of so much of what was being shared was itself the study of sexuality and male-female relations. These epistolary exchanges also reveal an all-too-familiar dance of deference. In the earliest letters to Ellis this dance has some very familiar steps. She keeps talking about her own ideas; meditating, speculating. He keeps responding—we can surmise this from the nature of her responses to his responses—not by engaging with her ideas, but by referring her to other things she should read, including his own articles in the *Westminster Review*. She expresses some doubt about Thomas Hardy, always with a kind of deferential "don't you think, perhaps, maybe" tone: "There seems to me a certain shallowness and unrealness about his work—no, that's putting it too strongly; it seems to me as though he was only fingering his characters with his hands, not pressing them up against him till he felt their hearts beat."[67]

In subsequent months their friendship grows and deepens—always by delicate advances and retreats obvious even if we look only at Schreiner's end of the correspondence. Resorting to the familiar diminutives, she asks, "Will you please tell me a little thing about yourself, about your work and everything like that?" Deferentially trying to strike up a friendship, gesturing toward an intellectual companionship, she says, "I have read almost the whole volume of Galton, and like it very much, because it is very suggestive, but he generalizes from quite insufficient data. Didn't it strike you so? . . . If I go to Derbyshire, and you felt you cared to come into the country a bit, would that be too far for you to come?" This is perhaps an altogether understandable, even politic, deference. Schreiner's brother Fred, embarrassed by Olive's first novel, had, she said, "asked her not to contact him any more."[68]

But letters like these with all their deference can best be read exactly as Freud sees the literary: as "a mine" where we can unearth the historical tactics to which people resort in the face of what they perceive to be their necessary life circumstances. What becomes obvious in them are what Michel de Certeau refers to as the " 'deformations' they bring about in a social and/or linguistic system."[69] These letters are permeated with such deformations. If the dialogic can be recognized in any instance in which a speaker, writer, or actor's anticipation of a rejoinder from an addressee is inscribed *within* an utterance, gesture, or behavior, then the deferential indirections of Schreiner's letters do speak loud and clear. "In the ideal condition for which we look," she said in a letter to Ellis, "men and women will walk close, hand in hand, but now the fight has oftenest to be fought out alone by both. I think men suffer as much as women from the falseness of the relations." Invoking Ibsen's *A Doll's House,* she concludes, "Helmer's life lost as much as Nora's did through the fact that they never lived really together."[70] But she surely must have had the gravest doubts about any genuine rectification of that condition of separateness, since Schopenhauer had told her that "*hope* is but the confusion of the desire for a thing with its probability."[71]

In her letters Schreiner is surely very brave, always going far to test what de Certeau calls the "game strategies" we all use in social interaction with others and, defying Schopenhauer, to turn hope into reality. In letters to Ellis she tries to express not just her ideas but her deepest secrets, difficulties, ambivalence. By definition, because there is a real and not an imagined recipient on the other end of the words as there would be in fiction, she risks a great deal. It's one thing for Schreiner's heroine Rebekah to write to her husband Frank asking if they can speak to one another "from man to man." It's another and braver version of the same thing when Olive Schreiner writes to Havelock Ellis trying to make that dream concrete. How far can she go toward assuming an intellectual parity with Ellis? What are the rules? What will she win and what might she lose?

There are no small stakes here, and Schreiner knows it. In the middle of the long central chapter of *From Man to Man,* which is pretty much just a fifty-page transcription of the letter Rebekah has written Frank after discovering yet one more of his marital indiscretions, Rebekah tries one last, valiant time to say it doesn't matter how much sexual straying he does so long as he talks to her "from man to man." In the midst of that letter she writes:

> "Oh, it isn't only the body of a woman that a man touches when he takes her in his hands; it's her brain, it's her intellect, it's her whole life! He puts his hand in among the finest cords of her being and rends and tears them if he will, so that they never produce anything more but discord and disharmony, or he puts his hand on them gently, and draws out all the music and makes them strong. Oh, it isn't only her body a woman gives a man—" (This paragraph Rebekah had not finished and had scratched out).[72]

The narrator's parenthetical notation of an excision by Rebekah is interesting, especially in the light of information contained in Phyllis Grosskurth's biography of Havelock Ellis indicating that Ellis's recollections of a very similar sentiment Schreiner expressed to him were not similarly censored: "When a man puts his penis into a woman's vagina it is as if (assuming of course that she responds) he puts his finger into her brain, stirred it round and round. Her whole nature is affected."[73]

Schreiner sets herself up for that finger in the brain by confessing her innermost secrets to Ellis—even those that all evidence suggests she never shared with women friends. Although she may write to Ellis's beautiful sister Louie (Louise) about her desire to get other women to join her in wearing trousers, she shares her erotic desires for Louie only with her brother:

> You mustn't tell [Louie] or anyone things that I tell you about other people, but things that are about myself alone are in your hands; you can do what you like with them, and I shall think it right. I have such a strong feeling for Louie. When she put her arm round me on the sofa, I wanted to cuddle close up to her, but I was ashamed. I liked it. I have such an odd feeling for her.[74]

Her intense friendship with Eleanor Marx prompts Marx's biographer Yvonne Kapp to suggest Schreiner "preferred women" to men,[75] but in the absence of other evidence it seems more likely that the intensity of the friendship bespoke nothing more startling than her discovery that there were women with whom she could talk "impersonally" after all, something she seems never to have experienced outside that friendship.

In some measure Schreiner's solution to her ambivalence about confiding in women was to make herself into a kind of cubist correspondent: a woman seen always and only in fragments, from strange, nonintersecting angles. To Ellis she was the often ill and precarious invalid. To Freud's physician Brian Donkin, who proposed marriage to Schreiner, she became the sometimes stern resister of his advances, and she could say to Karl Pearson, "I feel like a mother who has lost her child. But now he can love someone else. He couldn't while he was seeing me every day." To Edward Carpenter she would be a colleague/speculator. To Pearson she would be the intellectual collaborator. Often she tried to get the "points" in this cubist correspondence to meet one another: to Pearson she writes of Donkin; to Edward Carpenter she writes of Pearson and Havelock Ellis; to Ellis, of Hinton. To Pearson: "I wish you *could* have come when Edward Carpenter was here. I think you would like him in the same way I do. I could never love him as a woman loves the man, but," she says in a very familiar formulation, "there is something childishly unworldly that you too would like."[76]

Isak Dinesen's temperamental ambivalence results in a similarly cubist correspondence. Her mother gets the cheerful face; Aunt Bess gets lectures on tolerance. Brother Thomas gets the full account of the grisly details of her life—her syphilis is acting up, Bror wants to come back to her now that he's sick, Denys has just left her, she thinks she's going to die soon—everything presented through the stiff upper lip.[77] Even though there is none of the blatantly exasperated fulminations at being female in her letters, that ambivalence is easy enough to retrieve. Her spectacularly archaic public pronouncements on women and their "place," for instance, are ostensibly intended to champion women. But her way of doing this both in her fiction and in her writings on marriage is to define them so restrictively that nothing she says about women can conceivably include her—even though here, as always, *her* self not infrequently resides quite comfortably in the projections she makes onto "Africans." In a speech explicitly written to be delivered to a group of African women, for instance, she announces, "one's real worth lies with the opposite sex."[78] "Man," she says, "is the being who acts. A man's center of gravity, the quality of his being, consists of what he accomplishes and does in life. The woman, on the other hand, has her center of gravity in what she is."[79]

This construction of women as handmaidens to males may have been directed at African women, but here and anytime Dinesen pronounces that man's role is "to do" and woman's "to be," her discourse functions like Schreiner's protestations, when she feels for women, that she has a growing tenderness in her heart "*for them.*" The same Isak Dinesen who could claim again and again that "man was for doing, woman for being," confidently wrote to her family in Denmark at the time of her coffee plantation's collapse: "I believe that I have done a good piece of work here and in many ways a unique piece of work. I am quite convinced that no one else could or would have done it, and there has been so much difficulty that anyone else would have given up; in fact I really do believe that I have deserved to be given the V.C. for my work here just as much as you did during the war."[80]

Since the years between 1929 and 1933 in Kenya saw drought, locust infestations, the effects of a worldwide economic depression that collapsed the export market for settlers' crops grown in Kenya and exported to Europe—including of course the coffee produced at Karen Coffee—driving not just Dinesen but most European farmers into bankruptcy and out of Africa,[81] the failure of Karen Coffee and with it Dinesen's exit from Kenya in 1932 definitely ought to be seen as unavoidable failures, beyond even Dinesen's very considerable powers to prevent. From her own perspective, her valiant efforts to keep the enterprise afloat as long as she did really must have felt as noble as the work of any warrior on any front. If she was one of those colonial Europeans who displaced native Africans from their arable lands, she was at the least a highly successful one. Beneath her hyperfeminine persona, turbans, and kohl-darkened eyes, beneath her feminine wiles aimed at keeping Denys attending to her, beneath her attention to her anorexic body, beneath the pronouncements about woman's place in the tales she was beginning to tell Denys beside her fireside in Africa, beneath the seductive Sheherazade, she saw herself quite as much as a *farmer*—an employer of native labor and, given her place and time, probably as a *male* one.

A woman's seeing "woman" as her other as Dinesen and Schreiner do is far from uncommon. Hearing the seductive croon of the Beach Boys' "Surfer girl, little one . . ." as a teenager, for instance, I distinctly remember finding the song lubricious not because of any sense of being the "little surfer, little one" at all. Never wanting to *be* her, I wanted instead to *have* her. This desire was never lesbian. My attraction was indubitably in part a matter of being male-identified: a desire to ally with the male who "owns" the right and power to desire rather than with the female who can never be more than the object of desire. But the attraction also bespoke a deep-seated desire to possess—not to *be* but to *own*—a kind of beauty, vulnerability, a fragile, dependent object of desire that is marked and named "girl," an object females know with absolute certainty does not exist. Not gendered at all, the surfer girl for me was instead a marker or figure standing in for an unspecified, unattainable desire, neither male nor female, heterosexual nor homosexual, but simply Desire.

There is not and probably cannot be any particular theoretical support for such an assertion, but one can come closest by considering the best work in recent feminist film criticism, particularly in such things as Constance Penley's essay "A Certain Refusal of Difference." In this essay Penley considers what she calls "the most 'impossible' task a film by a woman filmmaker can attempt, to do what women 'theoretically' . . . cannot do: create a representation of lack, the precondition of all symbolic activity, the engagement with language and culture." Psychoanalysis, says Penley, "suggests that women are not capable of representing lack because they have never possessed and then been threatened with the loss of that which allows one symbolically to depict lack—the penis." Women must then necessarily always be depicted as *being* the image; never as *having* it or *not having* it. But Penley suggests the use of off-screen female voices in Marguerite Duras's film *India Song* manages to articulate an "ambivalent and impossibly desiring relation" to exactly such an inaccessible image, which in the case of *India Song* is embodied in the figure, or more accurately in the nonappearance of a figure, of "a woman who, the film tells us, is already dead." This nonappearance "stages a representation that is fundamentally about loss and distance." This is necessarily a fantasy of desire, "a desire that cannot be satisfied, and finally a desire for an unsatisfied desire . . . [which] leaves open the question of desire, and of a feminine position in relation to it, refusing . . . to 'answer' it with an assured definition of the nature of both masculine and feminine desire, and of desire itself."[82]

Hearing the Beach Boys' "Surfer Girl" may have produced in members of my generation exactly such a gap: one between *that* "girl" and *this* "woman" that seemed to promise to open a space where woman might become the active desiring subject rather than a desired object. Dinesen's portrayals of the lovely virginal young ladies of Copenhagen in "Copenhagen Season" produces exactly such a gap for her. "Normally," she tells us in that tale, "the spiritual atmosphere of the city was masculine." But during a short period of the year when the landed country families visit the city for a round of party-going, there is "a conquest of town by country, [and] femininity, the world of woman, rose like a tide and inundated Copenhagen." What this world of femininity looks like is an exaggerated form of wide-eyed innocence, a town, if you will, populated by great numbers of surfer girls:

> Eve was to be found at her lace pillow or her household accounts or watering the flowerpots in her windows. She was the pure and demure guardian angel of the hearth; her mental color was white and her principal virtues more passive than active—innocence and patience and total ignorance of those demons of doubt and ambition which were supposed to harass the heart of her husband.[83]

With her mental color white, her nature passive, and her mind free of any demons of doubt and ambition, she is not just another version of the surfer girl, she is nothing that Dinesen *is,* but everything she might herself desire to *have*. She also serves, psychically, as a delicious bit of revenge Dinesen takes on her own mother for keeping the young Karen "locked up" upstairs when she would rather have been talking about Nietzsche with Georg Brandes. Schreiner's production of "women" in her letters, her protestations that "I have a certain sympathy for *them*"—produces the same gap in which active desire can take root.

This desire of a female to possess rather than *be* woman, or to construct herself as a woman she can never be, frequently results in a miming of "woman," replicating quite explicitly the "Negro" self-construction Frantz Fanon describes in *Black Skin, White Masks.* In Fanon's imagined dialogue between black and white, white, wanting "a break from" his whiteness, says to the Negro, "you are so real in your life." The Negro "refreshes" him; "reconciles" him to himself. Black overhears white's imagined dialogue and in response "want[s] to be typically Negro. It was no longer possible. I wanted to be white. That was a joke. And when I tried, on the level of ideas and intellectual activity, to reclaim my negritude, it was snatched away from me."[84] Later, in chapter 7,

"African Gossip," the extent to which Dinesen and Schreiner *use* Africans in exactly this way will become clear, as both women "refresh" themselves in the reflections they "see" in African eyes. But as women they also necessarily operate on the other side of that psychic exchange. If black experiences the desire not to be white but to be "black" as white imagines black to be, evidence suggests that these particular females experienced the desire not to be male but to be "woman" as male imagines female to be. Dinesen in her exaggerated femininity and Schreiner in the woman persona constructed for European male correspondents are instances of woman *miming* "woman" in the way Michael Taussig describes in *Mimesis and Alterity,* each producing "a 'nature' that culture uses to create second nature." In this respect Schreiner may outdo Dinesen in Kierkegaardian perversity. Engaging in her letters in that earnest debate with sexologists on the nature of woman, she was all the while enacting exactly that second "nature" that culture produces. Women mime woman in order to assume the power of woman, says Taussig, and in doing so they become "accomplices of the real."[85]

In his very late works like "The Subject and Power," Foucault proposes that the problem of the present time is not so much trying to discover what we are but "learning how to *refuse* what we are." What appear on first glance to be Dinesen's and Schreiner's discomfitingly retrograde or woman-hating gestures often turn out in my readings to be instances of this kind of Foucauldian refusal. In Foucault's essay the place *power* had held in his earlier *Power/ Knowledge* gets edged aside by the word *conduct.* If power is above all the "way in which certain actions modify others," then "something called Power . . . does not exist. Power exists only when it is put into action, even, of course, if it is integrated into a disparate field of possibilities brought to bear upon permanent structures." Conduct, then, supplants power as the major force for change. Unlike power, conduct is direct. It is a way of "leading" others, and at the same time "a way of behaving within a more or less open field of possibilities."[86] Dinesen's and Schreiner's exasperated fulminations at "women" and their self-constructions as not-women are all such forms of conduct: interventions aimed at expanding their own space as women. But these interventions become visible only if their lifeworks are considered entire. Only then does it become clear how what each affirmed in her fictions got erased in and by her persona; how what she recommended in her speeches or lectures got confounded in letters or behavior; how what she urged in political writings addressed to women got overturned in personal life choices. Dinesen's ambivalence about her femaleness led her to the deliciously perverse Kierkegaardian inversions and confoundings of categories like that in her discourse on trousers cited in my epigraph and led to her public persona, which I take to be often characterized by the metaleptic troping of "femininity" evident in the Kehlet photograph discussed in chapter 2. Schreiner's determinedly mannish stride and her protestations that she hated women, hated their "crabbed" nature—until she saw it embodied in her own husband's "beautiful face"—ought to be seen as imaginative if at times desperate interventions into the cultural production of the category *woman* that social eugenicists of her time were helping to shape. When Schreiner compares her own interior to Kimberley Hole, protesting to Havelock Ellis that he might *think* he understands her but really can't, because after all how could *he* understand what she herself cannot, she deliberately obfuscates and thereby protects her self, even if she does so without the nimbleness or wit that Dinesen reveals in her discourse on women and trousers.

On his first visit to Africa, Richard Wright was surprised at his own reactions to Africans. The African seemed to him "an oblique, hard-to-know man who seems to take a kind of childish pride in trying to create a state of bewilderment in the minds of strangers."[87] What he encountered was a familiar defense strategy of the colonized. It seems also to have been a strategy that comes highly recommended by Dinesen, who took Ali Baba's slave Morgana as her heroine. Discovering that the forty thieves had marked the doorway of her master's house with chalk so they could come back later to rob it, Morgana went out and chalked ninety-nine other houses with the same sign. Arabic, female, enslaved, unself-represented, Morgana impresses Dinesen powerfully. But she does so not because Dinesen identified, as did so many European women after the abolition of slavery in the colonies, with the conception of woman as enslaved. Morgana's appeal is that she became immortal not only because she had "energy and self-confidence, but [because] she knew what she was doing: her purpose was to confuse."[88]

4

Mythic Times, Gothic Images, and the Role of the Dice

In the smallest past we find an inexhaustible mine when once we begin to dig at it. . . . It is not till the "I" we tell of has ceased to exist that it takes its place among other objective realities and finds its true niche in the picture. The present and the near past is a confusion, whose meaning flashes on us as it slinks away into the distance.

Olive Schreiner, *The Story of an African Farm*

"What is man, when you come to think upon him, but a minutely set, ingenious machine for turning, with infinite artfulness, the red wine of Shiraz into urine? You may even ask which is the more intense craving and pleasure: to drink or to make water. But in the meantime, what has been done? A song has been composed, a kiss taken, a slanderer slain, a prophet begotten, a righteous judgment given, a joke made. . . . The world drank in the young story-teller Mira. He went to its head, he ran in its veins, he made it glow with warmth and color. Now I am on my way down a little; the effect has worn off. The world will soon be equally pleased to piss me out again."

Mira Jama, in Isak Dinesen, "The Dreamers," in *Seven Gothic Tales*

Dinesen and Schreiner gained a certain elbow room by erasing themselves from the category "woman." Turning themselves into the disembodied voice of the storyteller endlessly recycling the eternal stories as does Dinesen's Mira Jama was a contribution to these same ends. Psychically this netted them a sort of self-production achieved through acts of Benjaminian self-erasure, one that had among other things the distinct advantage of preserving their privacy. Readers are moved to consider the personal biography of a storyteller not in order to understand the "individual" who produced the story, but to attend instead to the ways in which material conditions in historical time were playing themselves out in that storyteller, who is always no more than a type; always and only a vessel in which are accumulated, enacted, and displayed the effects, in concentrated form, of the particular historical moment in which she lived. The object of the story is not to "convey a happening," says Benjamin, it is to "embed it in the life of the storyteller in order to pass it on as experience to those listening."[1] In becoming such storytellers, Dinesen and Schreiner each contributed to a project that is profoundly political.

Although Dinesen's memoirs and tales seem to reveal at every point a nostalgia for a lost aristocratic past and Schreiner's writings and life seem to suggest that she was in every way a new woman with eyes firmly focused on a better future, both actually shared Benjamin's more complicated conception of the relation of past and future to anything that might be called genuine progress. For Benjamin, to assume that progress is something slated to take place in some moment "up ahead" is to fall into the sloughs of the *Immergleiche* or ever-the-same, partly because our proximity to the present and the near past makes us incapable of seeing them clearly enough to learn from them and thereby avoid turning the future into nothing but perpetual repetitions of the past. For Benjamin history was what advances, not what lies behind. To see the past as Schreiner does, as "an inexhaustible mine," sets in motion neither bouts of nostalgia nor attempts to explore "the way it really was." Her word choices precisely echo those of Benjamin, who tells us in his "Theses on the Philosophy of History" that "to articulate the past historically" is to "seize hold of a memory as it flashes up at a moment of danger."[2] What meaning we are able to grasp there, says Schreiner, is what "flashes on us as it slinks away into the distance."

Considered entire, Dinesen's lifework enacts Benjamin's belief in the liberatory power that comes to those who lose themselves in the mythic in order to experience its *Sprengung*, or blasting apart.[3] The Enlightenment understood living in the mythic as a hindrance to the pursuit of the true. "Everything becomes and recurs eternally—escape is impossible!" says Nietzsche in *The Will to Power*. But he also recognized myth's potentially subversive and liberating power: "Probable consequences of its being *believed* (it makes everything *break open*)." In the face of this endless recurrence stupendous amounts of imaginative energy were required: "New means against the fact of *pain* (pain conceived as a tool, as the father of pleasure . . .); the enjoyment of all kinds of uncertainty, experimentalism, as a counterweight to . . . extreme fatalism."[4] Dinesen's lifework enacted this *Sprengung;* Schreiner's enacted the *Sprung,* the Benjaminian tiger's leap into the past.[5] The new women of Schreiner's fictions and her social writings catapult readers not into some utopian future, but into some distant past. In *Woman and Labour* she explicitly insists that the new woman is really the old woman—before she was made "parasitic" by capitalist divisions of labor. "The truth is," she says, "we are not new. We . . . are of that old, old Teutonic womanhood which twenty centuries ago plowed its march through European forests and morasses beside its male companions" (p. 147). In *An English South-African's View of the Situation* she constructs the entire British "race" in the same way (p. 13).

If as a pair these two women enact both the *Sprung* and the *Sprengung,* between them they also embody the two kinds of storytellers Benjamin describes in his essay of that title. People assume, he says, that the storyteller has come from afar. But there are really two kinds of storytellers. One has stayed at home and knows the local tales and traditions. The other tells tales inspired by travels in distant lands. Every storyteller descends from one of these tribes—is either peasant or mariner.[6] Schreiner is mostly peasant, admiring the staunch workaday Boer women, dressing as if she were a peasant herself. Her most autobiographical heroine, Rebekah in *From Man to Man,* in every way puts down roots in South Africa, husbanding vineyards, raising babies. But her short allegories that were so popular among feminists during her lifetime also make her a peculiar kind of mariner. Detailing the surprising joys that accrue to those who sacrifice themselves on the altar of some good larger than themselves, these storytellers speak as one who has recently returned from some perfect far-off land that never was but someday yet may be, and their tales are always narrated as if by one who has come back to tell them.

Dinesen was herself a tiller of the soil in Kenya, but her memoirs of Africa are written from Denmark and addressed to European and American audiences. These, then, really are stories brought back from a distant land, told as if by the sailor home from the sea. Repeatedly the storytellers of her tales explicitly insist that only the thing at a distance can be seen clearly. They rarely recount stories they have invented, but tell those they have heard and are recycling. Invariably they make a point of telling their readers and auditors so. This insistence makes Dinesen's tales what in Danish would be called *eventyr,* an untranslatable word used to describe early editions of Hans Christian Andersen's works or any fantastic or romantic story told by a similarly disembodied voice. It is such a voice that strikes the opening chords in the very first lines of *Out of Africa.* Beginning with a speaking *I,* the narrative here combines parallel constructions with gradual shifts in perspective from "I," to "you," to a strictly impersonal passive construction as Dinesen erases herself from her own memoir, as early as the end of its first two sentences: "I had a farm in Africa, at the foot of the Ngong Hills. . . . In the day-time you felt that you had got high up, near to the sun, but the early mornings and evenings were limpid and restful, and the nights were cold."

Her tales most often achieve this necessary distance from auditor and reader by being set either in an Italy of the seventeenth century or in a Denmark of some long-past era, and behind that disembodied storyteller is a Dinesen being quite explicit about what she is doing and why. "There is a firm conviction which, as an instinct, runs in the blood of seafaring families, that the final word as to what you are really worth, lies with the other sex," she tells us in "The Supper at Elsinore." This is true not because the other sex is "other," but because men and women in seafaring families are separated for long stretches of time and thus achieve the distance that is required for proper judgment and understanding:

> A sailor, or a sailor's daughter, judges a person of the other sex as quickly and surely as a hunter judges a horse; a farmer, a herd of cattle; a soldier, a rifle. In the families of clergymen and scribes, where the men sit in their houses all their days, people may judge each other extremely well individually; but no man knows what a woman is, and no woman what a man is; they cannot see the wood for trees.[7]

Just as to prepare for a future of awakening it is necessary to look closely at the past, seeing things only from a distance in space can provide the chance to see them closely, whole, and true.

Every European traveler or memoir writer reporting from or on an "Africa" has seen in it a representation of Europe's lost past, whether that "past" is construed to be an Edenic or a "savage" one. But wherever and whenever either Dinesen or Schreiner says in any part of her lifework "this is the way this place used to be," or "this is the way woman's condition used to be," or "this is the way Africa used to be," it is rarely an imperialist parading of a no longer available experience to which she and only she can claim to have had access. It is instead Benjamin's antinostalgic past that holds out a promise of the *Sprengung*. The Africa of Schreiner's writings is frequently described as past or passing, but it is invoked because reading its past closely reveals our own future. The land itself inspires this. The Karoo where she grew up "hums with that same intense resonance of a remembering emptiness, so that, as in the Sahara, one stands in the echo chamber seemingly of all existence, so palpable that one becomes convinced of seeing, by and by, in every shimmering mirage, the imminent past," says Mostert in *Frontiers* (p. 158), and that "imminent past" is what she bears witness to.

The storyteller's major function is to bear witness, and to do so the storyteller must be positioned at a distance too: be in every way detached from the tale being told—a position in which both Schreiner and Dinesen were psychically already quite comfortable. The stories they tell must also come from far away, because only the thing at a distance can be seen clearly; only the story coming from the past holds the kernel of truth the present needs to hear; only in hearing someone else's story can we recognize that it is our own we hear. This situation occurs so frequently in Dinesen's tales it hardly need be mentioned. Her noseless, earless storyteller Mira Jama is himself recycled in story after story, beginning tales only to be interrupted by an auditor who either takes up the story (because he discovers it is *his* story that is being told) or begins one of his own, to which Mira Jama invariably responds, "I know that story, I've told it before."[8]

The same narrative move is replicated over and over in Goethe's *Elective Affinities,* a novel Benjamin loved. Benjamin regarded this book as *novelle* rather than novel: whereas the novel pushes readers to consider "the meaning of life" and sets in motion their drive to interpret, a "story" like *Elective Affinities* inspires instead an open and attentive listening for the story's "moral" that bypasses consciousness and bypasses the drive to interpret. In his essay on Baudelaire Benjamin defines consciousness much as Freud does: as that which *blocks* experience, which serves as a screen between us and what we most need to know and experience. Emotions occur—fright, delight—only in those not expecting the experience: only in those, that is, who are not conscious. The function of the good storyteller is to be sure the reader or auditor is caught in an attitude of relaxed receptivity in which ideally all consciousness and all impulses to interpret remain asleep.[9]

No matter to what ostensible genre their writings belong, both Dinesen and Schreiner were in their own ways always working toward the production of story in this spirit and for this aim. Dinesen's fictions exist entirely in the space of once upon a time, as do her two memoirs of Africa. Whereas novels have individual characters whose psychological makeup we limn, stories are made up of representative types as much as is the author who produced them, types who carry no names but "the captain" or "the duke," as the characters in Dinesen's tales frequently do. Schreiner professed to be impatient with any fiction not realistic, but she discovered her own power as a storyteller as a fifteen-year-old, when the Orpen children for whom she served as governess were fascinated by her gift of improvising stories. These stories went on from day to day until their mother had to ask Olive to stop because the children were becoming too excitable.[10] The power accruing to the storyteller willing to lose her self in her stories was addictive. This storyteller had to have the right name, and it's probably no accident that at precisely this moment Schreiner asked to be called Olive rather than Emilie. From the Schopenhauer she was reading then, Schreiner no doubt acquired not just her belief in "will," or her formulations about woman's nature, but a more liberating affirmation of the importance of myth and allegory. "Naked truth does not belong before the eyes of the profane vulgar," Schopenhauer insists. "It must appear before them heavily veiled. Hence . . . myth and allegory are its proper element."[11] Undeniably, her fictional heroines are as mythic and abstract as Dinesen's. Gerald Monsman groups them efficiently: they are wicked stepmothers;

the excessively rich or excessively poor; the graceful and sensitive or the boorishly self-absorbed and sensual; the hopelessly guileless or the wily trickster; the philosophical naif or the brutal sensualist.[12] Like the "dukes" and "captains" of Dinesen's tales, characters in Schreiner's allegories in *Dreams* and *Dream Life and Real Life* have no names but "Life," "Love," "Joy," "the Woman," "the Man."

Like Dinesen's tales and Schreiner's allegories, Goethe's *novelle Elective Affinities* follows two deeply allegorical figures who have their origin in his speculations about what would happen if one entertained the idea that individual human beings, a man and a woman, say, behaved like chemical elements, coming together—"attracted" to one another—because of their oppositions, as are alkalis and acids (pp. 52–53), and Goethe's narrator is explicit about the aims of this kind of exploration. To be of any use, even to its creator, a story needs to be free of the messy particularities of individual human psychology and to be public in every sense of that word. "How beneficial it must have been for art," says Goethe's narrator, "when it was intended to be concerned almost exclusively with what was public property, and belonged to everybody, and therefore also to the artist!" (p. 170).

Embedded in Goethe's *novelle,* as in Dinesen's *Angelic Avengers* and her story "The Diver," are a number of other tales. All are made up exclusively of characters who discover themselves serving as auditors at a story that turns out to be their own. In both Goethe's and Dinesen's works it is paradox rather than personality that propels plot, something Benjamin finds always a part of the tragic order.[13] In Goethe's *novelle,* innocence turns out to be incapable of defeating evil because, incapable of comprehending it, it can muster no defense. Evil turns out to be an essential part of the world, because only the wily machinations of the evil and the cynic can bring about its vanquishing. Both Goethe's and Dinesen's *novelles* explore various versions of the idea that one must throw away or run from what one most loves in order not to lose it. Both works are propelled by the gradual unfolding of "fate," as characters, despite all intentions to the contrary, head toward what has been decided long ago: "In reality what fate is now doing is fulfilling my desire, my own intention, which I have thoughtlessly been trying to thwart." What readers of novels might take to be the actions, motivations, and desires of individual characters are revealed to be instead simply manifestations of historical time, working through them.[14]

Taken as a collective lifework, all of Dinesen's and Schreiner's aesthetic strategies can be seen as a working out of exactly this set of hypotheses and principles—and seen in this way, different ways of reading every part of it come into play. Dinesen's "Sorrow-acre," for instance, has been frequently read and reread by critics over the years. Read through a Benjaminian frame, however, different aspects of this tale come to prominence for perhaps the first time. Dinesen taps and recycles in this tale an old Danish folktale, "Det Schonbergske Forlag." Since her version begins "during a flood with high tidal waves," Donald Hannah places the story in 1634.[15] What is most fascinating in this tale, however, is not that Dinesen chooses a historical event, but *how* and *why* she does so in order to launch an exploration of a Nietzschean eternal recurrence. Recognizing in the flotsam this flood brings ashore near Ballum pieces that had belonged to his family, a young man begins to salvage them. When robbers try to steal these remnants the young man kills one of them, setting in motion a course of punishment and retribution that includes his mother's having to mow an entire field of barley between sunrise and sunset. She succeeds but dies in the process, and thus the land she harvests is forever after called the sorrow acre. Dinesen's story here is a very Benjaminian one. Speaking of the necessity to retrieve above all else what would appear to be merely the "flotsam" of one's past, this detritus of history turns out to be worth any price, even the life of the mother, because of the necessary history it will be found to reveal.

But like every story effective in Benjamin's terms, this is one from which we can learn *precisely because* it appears to be nothing more than a simple, timeless tale. Effectively evading consciousness and analysis, it allows us to experience the shock that comes as we access a reservoir of recollection of a past shared by all human beings of whatever race or gender: memory that creates a "chain of tradition which passes a happening on from generation to generation." The most important stories must begin, as this one does, with "one day" or "once upon a time" because they recount no particular history, no particular remembrance, tapping instead into some "data of pre-history"[16] where consciousness lurks only as what Benjamin calls "the hidden figure."[17]

In this respect the Africans Dinesen constructs, who are always running from consciousness, "longing for darkness," bear little similarity to the childlike creatures European missionaries believed they must enlighten. More advanced than Europeans, in her eyes they seem to demonstrate their recognition of the centrality of a mythic, distancing impersonal, of a running from individual consciousness—from "illumination." By contrast with the surrealist mythology Benjamin advocated, which "puts things at a distance," materialist mythology "*illuminates* the realm of dreams—the collective *Bildphantasie* or image-making capacity—in order to bring us to the verge (*Schwelle*) of awakening. Its aim is to sharpen our eye for 'the Next,' for the time and space of each present history."[18] "The Europeans have lost the faculty for building up myths or dogma," Dinesen says in *Out of Africa,* "but the mind of the African moves naturally and easily upon such deep and shadowy paths."[19] And in *Shadows on the Grass* she commends in particular those whites "in whose minds the past of their country, their name and blood or their home was naturally alive," because those whites might be able to "get on easier with the Africans . . . than others, to whom the world was created yesterday, or upon the day when they got their new car."[20]

Sounding very like Benjamin reading Baudelaire, Schreiner reads the entire African continent in this same way.

> Between the farthest star and the planet earth we live on, between the most distant planet and the ground we tread on . . . everywhere the close internetted lines of interaction stretch; nowhere are we able to draw a sharp dividing line, nowhere find an isolated existence. The prism I hold in my hand, rightly understood, may throw light on the structure of the farthest sun; the fossil I dug out of the mountain side this morning, rightly studied, may throw light on the structure and meaning of the hand that unearths it; between the life that moved in the creature that plowed in the mud of the lake shores three

> million years ago and the life which beats in my brain and moves in my eyes here in the sunshine today, I can see long unbroken lines of connection. Between spirit that beats within me and the body through which it acts, between . . . the life that has been and the life that is, I am able to see nowhere a sharp line of severance, but a great, pulsating, always interacting whole. So that at last it comes to be, that, when I hear my own heart beat, I actually hear in it nothing but one throb in that life which has been and is—in which we live and move and have our being and are continually sustained.[21]

Schreiner becomes here the storyteller recommended in Dinesen's "First Cardinal's Tale" in *Last Tales,* in one of the most frequently cited passages from Dinesen's works:

> Stories have been told as long as speech has existed, and *sans* stories the human race would have perished. . . . That is in the order of things. . . . But I see . . . today a new art of narration [that] . . . for the sake of the individual characters . . . will be ready to sacrifice the story itself. . . . A true story . . . has a heroine—a young woman who by the sole virtue of being so becomes the prize of the hero, and the reward for his every exploit and every vicissitude. But by the time when you have no more stories, your young women will be the prize and reward of nobody and nothing. . . . It will be, at the best, a poor time, a sad time, for a proud maiden, who will have no one to hold the stirrup for her, but will have to come down from her milk-white steed to trudge on a dusty road. And—Alas!—a poor and sad lover of hers will stand by to see his lady disrobed of her story or her epos and, all naked, turned into an individual. (pp. 23–25)

All naked, the individual has no importance or interest, since it is the story that both places people and moves—in the sense of motivates—them. "There is salvation," says Dinesen's storyteller, "in nothing else in the universe. . . . For within our whole universe the story only has authority to answer that cry of hearts of its characters, that one cry of heart of each of them: '*Who am I?*' " (p. 26).

To all of us post-Enlightenment people this sounds in truth like the very opposite of liberating—it sounds confining in the extreme. But the trick, as Nietzsche recognized, is to believe in our inevitable confinement in "fate" without becoming fatalists. Their identification with "Africa" helped Schreiner and Dinesen immensely in that project, not just because as European women they could answer the question Who am I? by describing their reflections in African eyes, but because Africa reflected back at them a mythic past that was *their* future. A "new means . . . against the fact of pain" to which Nietzsche refers, both Africa and Africans were in their formulations similarly engaged in acquiescences functioning as forms of resistance or transcendence. Dinesen admired what she called their "success [which] has nothing to do with freedom from pain or with finding happiness, but . . . with the richer sense of things that comes to those who learn to tolerate contradictions,"[22] and her admiration for what she called their "worldliness" can be seen in her construction of Africans as the quintessential enactors of Nietzsche's solution to the "problem" of man's "negative desire" to "control chance or escape necessity." They are, that is, *actors*. As she mimed "woman," she also imitated the imitations of the Africans of her construction, who were themselves actors. They knew how to "play," and how to live with the consequences of the dice's roll. To join in the play of the cosmos, as Nietzsche's Zarathustra says, is to play dice with the gods at the gods' table, which is the earth. In this game the bad player is the one who resorts to studies of causality, probability, and calculation, who uses effort to try for a desirable combination. But the good player affirms every possible chance the single throw might produce, "accepting each result as the desired" one. Affirming indiscriminately all possible chance outcomes fosters "an active love of fate that forces one to will whatever happens as the necessary manifestation of chance."[23] For the Nietzsche Gilles Deleuze constructs, it is this affirmation of whatever fate throws mankind that constitutes freedom itself. The endless, repetitive throw of the dice is not an affirmation of the same but an affirmation of difference: the dice always will be thrown, but the combinations resulting will always be different, always unexpected.

It may have been the appeal of this fateful embracing of the ever-the-same that promises endless difference that produced in these two women their attraction to modernism's aversion to the "finished" product. Schreiner failed to complete *From Man to Man* to her satisfaction, even though she worked on it for over thirty years and was still working on it at her death. Dinesen subtitled her tale "The Caryatids" "An Unfinished Tale," and nothing delighted her more than writing a tale that ended in a surprising, mythic recurrence: a repetition with a difference. If mythic eternal recurrence holds, then nothing—no action, no narrative—can ever come to a final end. Over and over Dinesen wrote about, and lived, the conviction that nothing was ever so fresh and new as what had always been; no freedom so great as that which could be gained only by accepting the inevitable headlong; nothing so imprisoning as trying to escape one's eternal destiny; nothing that could so clearly give us a cold, hard look at what is true better or more than the dream; no one so much in touch with the spirit of the age, especially with its fears, as the dreamer; no one more cut off from those same things than one who did not or could not dream; no one more alive than one who declined to flinch in the face of death; no one more dead than those afraid to contemplate death directly. If all of that sounds suspiciously like Walter Benjamin, Nietzsche, Adorno's Kierkegaard, or Deleuze's Nietzsche, that is no accident.

Virtually anywhere we tap into Dinesen's tales we can retrieve a vision that sounds remarkably like not only Kierkegaard, but Nietzsche and Benjamin—and at the same time like African art in its conviction that life is best seen as a series of eternal recurrences that one can either graciously accept (and be happy), or resist (and be forever restlessly unsatisfied); that nothing ever strikes the human being as so immediate and personal as what appears to be the abstractly universal; nothing more deadening than desire, which once sated can only rise again, leading to the undesirable kind of endless recurrence that ultimately leads only to ennui.

This is worked out especially clearly in "The Dreamers," and because in it one can find all of Benjamin, Nietzsche, and African art that has been invoked above, and because it prefigures what is to come about Schreiner's and Dinesen's debt to the techniques of the fauve painters, this reading might stand in synecdochically as an instance of the homeostatic, syncretic method characteristic of all Dinesen's works. Written in 1934 in Denmark and thus long after her sad departure from Africa, the story is set in 1863, on a dhow "on its way from Lamu to Zanzibar." Besides the cargo of ivory and rhino horn—which she reminds us is "highly valued as an aphrodisiac"—the dhow carries a more secret cargo "of which the slumbering countries which she passed did not dream."

> The still night was bewildering in its deep silence and peace, as if something had happened to the world; as if the soul of it had been, by some magic, turned upside down. The free monsoon came from far places, and the sea wandered on under its sway, on her long journey, in the face of the dim luminous moon. But the brightness of the moon upon the water was so clear that it seemed as if all the light in the world were in reality radiating from the sea, to be reflected in the skies. The waves looked solid, as if one might safely have walked upon them, while it was into the vertiginous sky that one might sink and fall, into the unfathomable depths of silvery worlds, of bright silver or dull and tarnished silver, forever silver reflected within silver, moving and changing, towering up, slowly and weightless. The two slaves in the prow were like statues, their bodies naked to the waist in the hot night iron-gray like the sea where the moon was not shining on it, so that only the clear dark shades running along their backs and limbs marked out their forms against the vast plane. The red cap of one of them glowed dull, like plum, in the moonlight. But one corner of the sail, catching the light, glinted like the white belly of a dead fish.[24]

In the visual collapsing of sea and sky here, distance becomes confused or obscured: the immediate seems far away, the distant near, exactly as in the poems of Baudelaire so much admired by Benjamin. The "upside-down" world here suggests one of Dinesen's debts to African cosmology, religion, and folktales. The verbal rendering of the landscape evokes fauve landscapes: one bright splash of color, or in this case two—the red cap of one slave, the bright white corner of a sail glinting against the otherwise monochromatic gray and silver of sea and sky. Meaning collapses here into dream, into the "core" of language itself, as does Baudelaire's poetry in Benjamin's readings, where even the stars become "the always-again-the-same in great masses."[25] The words Dinesen chooses here—a moon dim, bright, luminous (which is it?)—seem designed to support Benjamin's belief in the "ironic-allegorical character" of words that all and always "point toward . . . the figure of murmuring, of inarticulate and mummed speech, a figure of defiguration [which] can never be grasped in an entirely determined place and never in a completely determined sense."[26]

Susan Buck-Morss's discussion of Benjamin's attitude toward "the new" that can be deduced in his appreciative reading of Baudelaire's poems accurately represents the night sky and sea of "The Dreamers" as well:

> Benjamin speaks of "the inestimable value for Baudelaire of *nouveauté*. The new cannot be interpreted, or compared. It becomes the ultimate retrenchment of art." Making novelty "the highest value" [of art] . . . is "the quintessence of false consciousness, the tireless agent of which is fashion." It is the "appearance" of the new [that] is reflected like one mirror in another in the appearance of the "always-the-same."

Buck-Morss sees Benjamin as admiring Baudelaire's better self, the one that understood and wrote according to the "dialectic of temporality," a dialectic with no belief in progress, which he considered a phantasmagoria. In its place Benjamin saw Baudelaire expressing in his poetry "a strange sectioning of time," "shock-like segments of empty space," each of which is like a "warning signal."[27] "The Dreamers" begins in exactly such a space/time, which the fauves rendered visually as a time/space represented by color; a space/time of the before, the now, and the forever collapsing temporal as well as spatial distance, and of "meaning" collapsing in on experience. By invoking color, by collapsing sky and sea, by omitting stars from her sky, by choosing a language collapsing inward so that it means only itself, Dinesen renders the Benjaminian mythic space/time in which can be seen the *Immergleiche*, the only "truth" man is privileged to see. But this is not so fanciful or theoretical as my language might suggest. The *truth*

Dinesen tells in this mythic time/space is the true nature of desire. But predictably, it is told in a tale that thwarts the usual impulses to interpret and comes masquerading as a kind of fairy tale.

It begins as the story of the sultan's desire for a true virgin, whom he finds in an Amazon kingdom where the women had killed off all male children. But catching the virgin of his desiring looking longingly out the window at his water carrier, the sultan buries the virgin and the young man alive together "in a marble chest broad enough to make a marriage bed" (p. 274). He buries, that is, his desire. But the tale isn't well told. Mira Jama is unable to tell it well because, he says, sounding for all the world like Nietzsche, "I have lost the capacity of fear. When you know what things are really like, you can make no poems about them. . . . I have become too familiar with life; it can no longer delude me into believing that one thing is much worse than the other. The day and the dark, an enemy and a friend—I know them to be about the same" (p. 274). To lose one's capacity for fear, capacity for pain, and capacity to dream is really to lose just one thing, not three: "for really, dreaming is the well-mannered people's way of committing suicide" (p. 277). When the storyteller can no longer tell stories, his auditors step into the role of storyteller. The first, Lincoln Forsner, tells a story of his own desire: "To the world I looked a pretty, rich, and gay young man, on his way from one pleasure to another, and providing himself, on the way, with the best of everything. But in truth I was just being whirled about, forward and backward, by my aching heart, a poor fool out on a wild-goose chase after a woman" (p. 280). To chase desire is to engage in a repetition both deadly and deathless at the same time, and that repetition is of course the consequence of an inability to know his true desires. This failure in turn is seen as the result of his father's attempts to mold him into a creature of *his* own desires. And his father had occupied himself in that way because he suffered the only handicap that in Dinesen's tales can ever really impair a human being: he could not dream. "Now I felt that I was ever, as My Son Lincoln, being drawn, hammered and battered into all sorts of shapes, in order to be made useful, between one o'clock and three of the night" (p. 281).

Lincoln's tale will be about the one woman he has been able

to love, a woman in a brothel in Rome whom he loved precisely because she was the *Immergleiche* personified. She "sometimes seemed to me like a child, and then again old, like those aqueducts, built a thousand years ago, which stand over the *Campagna* and throw their long shadows on the ground, their majestic, ancient, and cracked walls shining like amber in the sun. I felt like a new, dull thing in the world, a silly little boy beside her then" (p. 286). The woman who is ancient and a child at the same time is in part Dinesen herself, described by Margaret Drabble in a eulogy after her death as a woman who had always been "both relic and pioneer." The storyteller here and the character whose tale she tells are both also versions of that mythic image in which are collapsed past, present, and future, and in which Benjamin sees "sedimented" the truths we most need to heed.

It takes many pages and at least three tales within tales to arrive at the *Immergleiche* embodied in the image of the "self-luminous" woman. First Lincoln loses the woman, Olalla the prostitute, and so we lose the end of that tale. We take up instead the tale of a new storyteller, Friederich Hohenemser, whom we come to know as "Pilot," because he, like the dog he has been named for, has no identity of his own but can only follow others: "Probably it was altogether his lack of imagination which prevented him from existing. For if you will create, as you know, Mira, you must first imagine, and as he could not imagine what Friederich Hohenemser was to be like, he failed to produce any Friederich Hohenemser at all" (pp. 293–94).

"Pilot" tells *his* tale to the trio of listeners, including Lincoln, Mira, and Baron Guildenstern of Sweden. The latter turns out to be not only an auditor, but another manifestation of the aridity of desire. He is full of endless tales of his sexual conquests, but except for the accident of differences of personality in the women he conquers, his stories are "an otherwise monotononous performance." Although in the beginning Mira the storyteller had been "highly impressed by such superabundance of appetite" (pp. 293–24), like Benjamin in his analysis of Baudelaire's poems he soon finds more than a little emptiness in all this libidinousness that "violates the scene of pleasure, ripping apart the myth of sexual love." For Benjamin, "tired out by their labors" the lovers of Baudelaire's poems become the image of self-alienation, the "hollowing out of inner life" that is "euphemistically called 'lived experience' [*Erlebnis*]. . . . The sex act itself stands under the sign of that joylessness."[28] As it continues, Dinesen's tale replicates over and over different versions of the same tale of joyless, repetitive desire, a desire that obliterates desire. The tale "Pilot" tells to the baron and Mira to pique their interest is predictably a tale of his *own* lady love. Her name is Madame Lola. A milliner-cum-revolutionary living in Lucerne who prompts him to join the street revolution, she disappears after Pilot is wounded, though not before producing around his bed an array of beautiful bonnets that had been ordered by all of Pilot's friends.

In response to the second aborted tale in "The Dreamers" the baron tells his own tale of lost love, the lady loved by the baron's friend Nat-og-Dag ("night and day"). Nat-og-Dag falls in love with Madame Rosalba, the saintly and mysterious widow of General Zumala. "She is a swan in the lake of life everlasting. That is the white half of my shield. And at the same time there is death about her somewhere, and that is the black half of the Nat-og-Dag arms. This I can only explain to you by a metaphor, which presented itself to me as I was looking at her." There is about her "a flavor which there is about no other woman. It may be the true odor of sanctity, or it may be the noble putrefaction, the royal corrodent rust of a strong and rare wine. Or . . . my friend, it may be both, in a soul two-parted white and black, a Nat-og-Dag soul" (pp. 305–6). Evident here in the clear conviction that opposites contain one another is Dinesen's debt to African philosophy, plus the obvious possibility that Dinesen considers herself just such a two-parted soul, containing the African and the European, as *Out of Africa* and *Shadows on the Grass* so often contend.

But Madame Rosalba disappears as quickly as the two women in the earlier tales, and at the inn where the storytellers find themselves a mysterious woman in a black cloak enters "like a dream." It is Olalla, thinks one storyteller; it is Madame Lola, thinks the second; it is Madame Rosalba, thinks the third. But the innkeeper assures them it is "the wife of Herr Councillor Heerbrand, of Altdorf" (p. 314). Discovered, the lady sets off into the night in a snowstorm by carriage with the three storytellers in pursuit. Both her carriage and theirs get stuck in the drifts, and the chase continues on foot. When she is finally caught, the men all ask the predictable and fateful question: "Who are You?" Standing in the middle of the snowstorm, cloak blowing around her, she becomes a sort of shape shifter, and as the wind fills her clothes "so that she looked like an angry owl on a branch, her wings spread out, [and] at other times it screwed them up all around her, so that on her long legs she was like a crane when it runs along the ground to catch the wind and get on the wing," they persist in their repetitive posing of the same question: "*Who are You?*" With no escape left, "she did what I had always feared that she might do: she spread out her wings and flew away" (pp. 319, 322).

At this point in truth, Dinesen's tale clearly has catapulted its readers into the realm to which the Benjaminian storyteller always aspires, a realm where analysis and interpretation find no place. Thinking themselves in the realm of fairy tale, readers may accept the lady's flight into thin air. But she has not ascended at all: she has leaped off the cliff to escape her pursuers. Carried half dead back to the inn, she finally reveals her identity, the secret each of her pursuers has desired. She is the famous opera singer Pellegrina Leoni, who has been living incognita since a fire in the middle of her performance in *Don Giovanni* stole her voice. This figure of the woman who has lost her voice is encoded in any number of Dinesen's tales and will be encountered here in a later chapter in her evocation of Hans Christian Andersen's tale of the little mermaid. But Pellegrina Leoni in this tale is more than opera singer or even the figure for speechless woman; she is the mythic image of woman.

In his introduction to Benjamin's *Schriften,* Theodor Adorno suggests that what Benjamin had in mind in his *Pariser Passagen* was not so much presenting a theory or offering analysis as offering his readers a parade of concrete mythic images that could be studied minutely. In employing what Adorno calls this "micrological technique,"[29] Benjamin intended to force a concentrated attention that would allow us to see in each such mythic image a historical moment that has been frozen in time so it records, "sedimented" as it were, all of history. As such, then, these mythic figures represent neither simple fairy tale nor mythic, timeless, or unchanging universals, but an intensely concentrated form of history itself, containing all we have ever thought to be true, all the ways we have behaved, all that humans have most feared or dreamed. Carefully attended to, such images provide our best and maybe our only access to "truth," regarded in the most concrete way possible. This is what Dinesen has produced in her figure of "woman" in "The Dreamers": a mythic image that also contains, as Benjamin suggests such images always do, something of both the utopian and the cynical.

This same "micrological technique" can be applied to a study of Schreiner's "Africans," and indeed Schreiner's own rhetoric encourages her readers to do so. "It is ordained by the laws of human life," she says in *Closer Union,* "that a Nemesis should follow the subjection and use, purely for purposes of their own, of any race by another which lives among them. Spain fell before it in America; Rome felt it; it has dogged the feet of all conquering races. In the end the subjected peoples write their features on the face of the conquerers" (p. 53). She emphatically does *not* advocate close study of African faces but offers a micrological study of our own, where the attentively Benjaminian reader will see "African" history written in the faces of Europeans.

The truth sedimented in the mythic image of woman in Dinesen's tale is in part that expressed by her one friend and protector, and it could be said Schreiner anticipates that Europeans will "read" in their readings of their *own* faces, "You, who killed her now, as you have told me, by asking her who she was—when in your time you are asked, on the other side of the grave, 'Who are you?'—what will you have to answer?' " ("Dreamers," p. 345).

But Dinesen's mythic woman is hardly singular; she is as multiple as the woman of the story herself, who can survive only by being multiple: by being ultimately unknown to any and, paradoxically, by being all things to all. She can live, that is, only by dying as an individual. "The time has come for me to be that: a woman called one name or another. . . . I will not be one person again, I will be always many persons from now. Never again will I have my heart and my whole life bound up with one woman, to suffer so much" (p. 345). She is a Doña Quixote. "The phenomena of life [are] not great enough for her; they [are] not in proportion with her own heart. . . . She [is] badly hurt and disappointed because the world [is] not a much greater place than it is, and because nothing more colossal, more like the dramas of the stage, [takes] place in it." Having been disappointed by every one of her love affairs—disappointed by attaining all the objects of her desire—"she would then, I think, [like] to become a man, and [sees] no sense in being a woman. For in all this splendor of woman's beauty, . . . she [is] like a lady who has put on her richest attire to meet the prince at a great ball, only to find that what she has been invited to is a homely gathering in honor of the police magistrate, at which everyday clothes are worn." The past tense of the original has been changed to present here to highlight the "truth" of this mythic image of woman: too large for the world, too multiple to be snared in a name or an identity, she is "a python" that "kills by the force of [her] embrace" (pp. 336–37).

In her contribution to a collection of essays called *Women's Writing in Exile,* Susan Hardy Aiken takes up this story, pointing out that Pellegrina Leoni is a self-exiled woman. She serves then as a representation of Dinesen herself, who was also self-exiled. Aiken points out that the three roles Dinesen's heroine takes up are "whore, revolutionary, and saint," "the three most overdetermined roles for Western women," and as such, for the men who tell her tale she is "a moving signifier."[30] But beyond what can be uncovered by a Benjaminian reading of her, there are yet several additional significations coming from African and Scandinavian religion and folklore that can be layered onto Aiken's reading. As revolutionary, prostitute, diva, and milliner, among other things, Pellegrina Leoni as a character is a representative instance of the kind of fusion with other identities and other forces characterizing all African religions we have come to know as voodoo, whereby through "possession" the human "takes these forces into himself, intensifies his own nature, intensifies the force which he himself *is*."[31] This assertion might seem a bit of a stretch except that one interesting detail of "The Dreamers" has so far been left out. The lady at its center is described in each of her avatars by each of her storyteller-suitors as being followed by a shadow figure. In each story his absence seems to signal her absence and possible death. In Kinyaruanda there are three words meaning life: *bugingo, buzima,* and *magara*. The first simply designates the duration of life. The second, *buzima,* is characterized by the determinative *bu*. As an abstraction, this determinative means the union of a shadow with a body. Says Jahn, "As an abstraction the word *buzima* belongs to the category Kuntu, the category of way or manner. It is a principle which specifies *how* life originates and it 'operates' as a principle. This principle asserts: if a shadow unites with a body, life originates and lasts till shadow and body are separated—which is death."[32] As always, however, Dinesen's particular syncretic performance here includes debts to both African and European sources. In Scandinavian myth and folktale, for instance, a central figure is the *fylgje* (from the verb *fylgja,* "to follow"). The *fylgje* is a projection of the *hug* (soul) that, taking a shape sometimes human, sometimes animal, has as its function, especially in the Icelandic sagas, to follow and protect,[33] precisely as happens with the multiplicitous and mysterious heroine of "The Dreamers."

What is produced in Dinesen's rich fictional evocation of the mythic woman here, Schreiner produces explicitly and probably quite consciously in her short allegories. In "The Woman's Rose" from *Dream Life and Real Life,* for instance, she portrays two such mythic women, one fair, one dark. The fair woman "reigns alone. All the men worship her" (p. 52) until the dark-haired woman who functions as the storyteller in this allegory comes to town, and then the men abandon the fair woman in favor of the new one, whom they now all "worship." "I liked them to ask me to marry them and to say No. I despised them . . . I did not know all men were my children, as the large woman knows when her heart is grown. I was too small to be tender. I liked my power. I was like a child with a new whip, which it goes about cracking everywhere" (p. 55). The biographical parallels are hardly to be ignored, but Schreiner propels the woman in this tale to a more universal, more impersonal status. In the end the rejected fair woman meets the dark one, who removes the one rose in town from her hair and fastens it in the fair one's hair. "It looks much better there," she says. "You are so beautiful to me," the dark one responds. In its modernist impersonality, this strange and somewhat airless story manages to catch the Benjaminian dream, the *Sprung,* the tiger's leap into the future: "When my faith in woman grows dim, and it seems that for want of love and magnanimity she can play no part in any future heaven; then the scent of that small withered thing comes back: spring cannot fail us" (p. 62).

Like Benjamin's sedimented image, Schreiner's mythic woman here is surely not just a working out of her own psychic material—though she is surely that—nor is she just what Benjamin calls "a temporal function of knowledge." She is instead "bound to a time kernel [*Zeitkern*] that is planted in both the knower and the known." It is, says Benjamin "*so* true, that the 'eternal' is in any case more a frill on a dress than an idea." The woman in Schreiner's allegory freezes for an instant the *dynamis* of what is happening so we can see a "now" that contains within it a "then" and an "after," a now that contains "truth . . . loaded to the bursting point with time."[34]

This all sounds very fine, but after the Benjaminian dust settles, we seem to be left with two women who lived in a real space and time with terribly ambivalent feelings about women and about being women. How then does a Benjaminian mythic woman help? There can be no disputing that both Dinesen and Schreiner begin with a fatalistic construction of this mythic woman. Schreiner confides to Havelock Ellis her conception of woman:

> Once God Almighty said: "I will produce a self-working automatic machine for enduring suffering, which shall be capable of the largest amount of suffering in a given space"; and he made woman. But he wasn't satisfied that he [had] reached the highest point of perfection; so he made a man of genius. He was [not] satisfied yet. So he combined the two—and made a woman of genius—and he was satisfied! That's the real theory—but in the end he sold himself because the machine he'd constructed to endure suffering could enjoy bliss too."[35]

In "The Caryatids" Dinesen makes even more explicit this reference to woman as the classic sufferer, adding for good measure a conception of woman as caryatid holding up the world that is exactly like Schreiner's conception of woman as responsible for the moral improvement of everyone, both male and female: "Is it forever, then, the task of women to hold up the houses, like those stone figures which they call caryatids?" "What about you? . . .

You women of the great houses," her narrator asks, "who are holding up the houses upon your arms? You believe . . . that you are the finest things in all the world, but then it is, perhaps, easier to make fine things out of stone than in flesh and blood."[36]

But even as both produced mythic women in fiction and allegory while they resisted identification as women in their private lives, both also can be seen at times acquiescing and even actively participating in turning their own bodies and lives into representations of exactly this mythic female, and in so doing I believe they enact in yet one more way their belief in the liberating power of the Benjaminian mythic. But to unwrap what I mean by the potentially liberating effects of the mythic and the subversive overturning of "woman" it enabled them to enact requires distinguishing my own understanding of the word mythic from that of earlier critics, critics of Dinesen especially.

Anders Westenholz's 1982 study *The Power of Aries* is subtitled *Myth and Reality in Karen Blixen's Life,* and Westenholz uses the term *myth* in the most general way to denote largeness or grandness. Dinesen surrounds herself "by people of mythic dimension," elevating "the trivialities of her everyday life to a heroic or mythic sphere" (pp. 37, 43). The brief portrait of Dinesen's "habits of mythologizing imagination" and her production of a "myth of herself" in Patricia Meyer Spacks's *The Female Imagination* offers more complex analyses of Dinesen's relation to myth, one having to my mind the particular virtue of recognizing how far Dinesen's "womanhood seem[ed] largely irrelevant to her actual experience" at the same time as her *mythical* self-image remained "intensely that of a woman" (pp. 386–87). In his 1965 study of Isak Dinesen Robert Langbaum saw her art as mythic in four distinct ways. Like others of her generation writing after Nietzsche, Frazer, and Freud—writers like Rilke, Kafka, Mann, Joyce, and Eliot—Dinesen moves away from the nineteenth century's emphasis on individuality, leading literature instead back to a universal principle of the unconscious life of man and nature, which "well[s] up in the human consciousness as myth." The more chaotic modern life became, the more Dinesen's vision led the individual self "back to union . . . with the past . . . back . . . to a mood of acceptance like the old tragic fatalism." We work out our destinies, suggests Langbaum, "at the point where our desires meet with external forces," and though he doesn't use the word *myth* in this context, that point where desire meets external forces is surely the locus of myth. Finally, he sees her works about Africa as attempts to recreate Europe's mythic, lost Edenic past, differentiating her works from Hemingway's by suggesting that whereas his African stories see in Africa a state of nature we have lost, Dinesen's "sharper sense of the past" leads her to "see in Africa also a kind of civilization we have lost," our two roads parting "when the first steam engine was constructed . . . and we have never found one another since."[37]

Abdul JanMohamed calls his chapter on Dinesen in *Manichean Aesthetics* "The Generation of Mythic Consciousness," and he sees both Dinesen's sense of being at home in Africa and native Africans' acceptance of her presence there as a consequence of her sharing their spirit of surrender to the mysterious arbitrariness of existence that is simultaneously random and always the same. This is of course the Nietzschean Dinesen who admired Africans' "worldliness."

To all these earlier associations of Dinesen and myth one can contribute just a bit of close reading that suggests more particularly how well both she and Schreiner seem to have recognized the particularly subversive value of Benjamin's belief in the liberating power that might accrue to those who lose themselves in the mythic in order to experience its *Sprengung,* or blasting apart. Toward the end of *Out of Africa,* for instance, as Dinesen recounts the final days when she is about to lose Karen Coffee after her valiant seventeen-year struggle to keep it economically viable, she walks with her friend Ingrid Lindstrom, who has come from her own farm at Njoro to sympathize and support her:

> As we walked over the farm, I knew that she was thinking of her own farm, praising her luck that it was still hers, and holding on to it with all her might, and we got on very well on that. In spite of our old khaki coats and trousers, we were in reality a pair of mythical women, shrouded respectively in white and black, a unity, the Genii of the farmer's life in Africa. (p. 372)

The place and space of scenes like this, and that in which Schreiner's narratives frequently unfold, is the place and space of myth far more than it is any landscape of Africa. The last several chapters of Schreiner's *From Man to Man* take place in such a space and place, in an extended, dreamlike conversation on the function of art that goes on between Rebekah and the man who is referred to over and over as only "the man" or "Mrs. Drummond's husband." As Dinesen's characters in "The Dreamers" become storytellers retelling the eternal story, in *From Man to Man* "the man" recounts a story of a distant time and place in order to proffer a lesson that is immediate and urgent, a lesson about the place and function of the artist. "Though I've lived longer in so many countries, yet when anything comes to me, it's nearly always Africa,—Africa that sets it. I've a curious feeling for the country as if it had a personal connection with myself. . . . I never wrote about it while I was there; one doesn't about things that are present, you know," says "the man" (pp. 446–47). How is it, he and Rebekah wonder, that a man might portray so vividly the truth of a place he has never seen? Rebekah has the answer:

> "Is it not," she said, "because no individual is an isolated nomad? He may be one minute growth of the life of his race, of humanity, of living things on earth. Is an artist not simply a man in whom some of the accumulated life of his race, of the millions of human creatures who have been ancestors in the ages past, is stored?" . . . An artist sees that which his race has never seen. Take the matter of wings. Age after age the artists of every race have seen them on their winged gods and great spiritual beings. . . . It is useless for the superficial onlooker to say those wings wouldn't carry them, that their pectoral muscles are not strong enough to carry them. The artist says, "I see them." In after ages, men will have wings. . . . The creative artist does not so much recall the life of the race; he paints its future. (pp. 450–51)

The artist experiences three stages. In the first there is "the sudden flash," during which the artist "has no power to unmake it or to make it other than it is." The second is when "will comes into play . . . though only within certain limits" (p. 452). Finally comes the reception of the art, when the woman who "fingers" it feels the "throb" that was the artist's, "live, across all the centuries, as an actual throb in me" (pp. 455–56).

Every writer has a particular vocabulary, but part of what is intriguing in Schreiner's portrait of art's mythic and timeless connection between all things is her choice of words: "finger it" and "throb" hark back to her description of man's relation to woman in the letter to Havelock Ellis.[38] But by placing her sentiments in the realm of the timeless and the mythic, Schreiner both distances them from herself, makes them "universal," connecting herself to others—European men, perhaps, across the waters and across the centuries—and then *reconnects* herself, safely, mythically, with things male, things powerful.

This, as it turns out, is what both she and Dinesen accomplish each time they embrace and inhabit a mythic image of suffering woman. In doing so they seem to make it possible to experience their own suffering from the outside, thereby distancing themselves from their pain while aggrandizing it as a mythic representation of the suffering woman and themselves as its mythic representation. Schreiner's fictions exist in the space in which a narrator or heroine projects forward to some day eons hence, where a past long gone and a far distant future collaborate to swamp and overcome a present that is far from happy. As Baby Bertie and Rebekah sit and contemplate their lives in *From Man to Man,* for instance, Rebekah muses,

> Sometimes I think, if one should live to be ninety and all the sights and sounds of the world about become dim to one, that then, as one sits alone in the firelight dreaming, or out in the sunshine, the child sister who was young with us will come back and sit with us there. No one will see her; and we two shall sit there alone . . . and we will look out at life together with our young eager eyes that have known no mighty sorrow. (p. 59)

Here Schreiner's allegory produces mythic women exemplifying the Benjaminian *Sprung*. Dinesen's tales more often produce the *Sprengung,* or blasting apart. Like each of Dinesen's collections of stories, her *Seven Gothic Tales* is full of mythic images of the eternal feminine: innocent shepherdesses, adoring Italian countesses. But all of these might best be seen as Benjamin sees the images in Baudelaire's poetry: as having been "hollowed out" and refilled with a subversive power. In "The Ring," from *Anecdotes of Destiny,* a young shepherd marries one of those pretty young shepherdesses. When the story opens, the two have been married only three weeks, and a saccharine narrator describes their marriage: "They were wonderfully happy. . . . Sigismund . . . had promised himself that from now on there should be no stone in his bride's path, nor should any shadow fall across it. Lise felt that now, every day and for the first time in her young life, she moved and breathed in perfect freedom because she could never have any secret from her husband" (p. 235). Predictably and with a perfect Kierkegaardian or Nietzschean perversity, for the rest of her tale Dinesen's narrator systematically reveals those secrets Lise "could never" keep from her husband. They are as subversive as anyone might hope. Sigismund rambles through the sheepfold rambling on about his plans for expanding his flock. And the thoughts of his innocent young wife do their own rambling: "How clever he is, and what a lot of things he knows," she thinks. But in the next breath, "What an absurd person he is, with his sheep! What a baby he is! I am a hundred years older than he!" (p. 236).

"What is it about the absolutely new experience of modernity," asks Benjamin, "that makes its objects correspond to the allegorical form in which the pagan figures survived in the Baroque, so hollowed out of their original meaning that they become allegorical signs, this time of the poet's own melancholy memories?"[39] To break open the gothic image of the eternal feminine that Dinesen creates in the innocent shepherdess of her story is to discover that the image has been hollowed out—"blasted apart" in Benjamin's terms—and refilled with woman's anger, whimsy, and frustration, and that what Susan Buck-Morss says of Baudelaire's allegory is true of Dinesen's baroque figure here: it "has the mark of rage" and "bears the traces of violence,"[40] all of which makes it even more clear why Dinesen loved to dress as Pierrot. As Derrida reminds us in *Disseminations,* Pierrot kills Columbine by tickling the soles of her feet.

Benjamin would have us study dialectical images because, while they remain *rooted* in the mythical, what they promise is not only eternal recurrence of the same (woman need not in perpetuity remain the caryatid holding up the world or the young wife always secretly subverting her husband's dreams; she need not always respond to men's desire for "the new woman" as opposed to the New Woman), they promise to "fan the spark of hope in the past," to "wrest historical tradition anew . . . from a conformism that is about to overpower it."[41] By urging minute study of particular mythic images of the past and insisting that when we do we will find ourselves ambushed, as it were, by clear images of our present concerns, Benjamin's work challenges the notion of dialectic, progress, development—in a word, challenges all those things Westerners, at least, have historically taken to be the stuff with which and by which we think and understand our worlds at all. In its place Benjamin offers us "dialectic at a standstill," something Adorno suggests resembles a snapshot of an instant, allowing us to see the modern as "at once the new, the already past, and the ever-same."[42]

This realm of ever-the-same in which "everything becomes and recurs eternally" and from which "escape is impossible!" unless the image is blasted apart is not only that of Nietzsche's *Will to Power* but also the realm of the universal portrait or universal image Westerners have taken to be at the heart of African art. Janheinz Jahn, one of the Belgian missionaries who functioned as an "interpreter" of Africa for Westerners, saw in all African art four categories: *muntu* is the human being, plural *bantu; kintu* is any thing or object, animate or inanimate, plural *bintu; hantu* is place and time; and *kuntu* modality, quality, style, rhythm, beauty. All are activated by two basic principles: *ntu* or force, and *nommo,* the word or sound. Contrary to what Westerners have been led to believe, says Jahn, the African artist never carved a fetish believing the gods were "in" his carving. Similarly, the artist was never interested in portraits of individual human beings. Rather, in each new work of art the artist used *kuntu* components—style, choice of materials, mode of representation—as "determinants" to express a *category* of being, not an individual. Thus even the so-called portrait heads of Benin, Jahn suggests, were not portraits at all, and European scholars were in error when they assumed that what was behind the image was the individual rather than the universal. The individual artist's use of determiners does not individualize, but "position[s] the figure in the ontological system, in the hierarchy of the world of the living [*muzima*] or the non-living [*muzimu*]."[43]

V. Y. Mudimbe, Kwasi Wiredu, Paulin Hountondji, and others have all stressed the importance of recognizing that what African art meant to and for those who produced it is probably out of the range of knowing of Western observers, and I cite the work of Jahn here not to explain how African art functioned for those who produced it, but to point out that Dinesen's and Schreiner's own lifeworks seem to function for them exactly the way Jahn describes African art. Neither was especially interested in rendering the particular or individual. But to say this is obviously not to suggest that they aim to render the ahistorical. Each used artistic means (*kuntu*) to *place* the individual woman in an ontological category, helping both the artist producing and the person experiencing that art to begin to answer one of the most important questions that can be asked: the *position* of this category of subject in the ontological hierarchy, in this case the category woman, which is by definition a hierarchy produced by the specific social organization of their culture. Both shared a modernist attraction toward, and rejection of, the "past" of woman: with woman's "femininity" as it has been historically construed, in Dinesen's case; with woman's stalwart, stolid endurance as it is represented in Schreiner's Boer farm wives.

What happens in the modern is exactly what Benjamin describes in the mythic image: all things fall *together* rather than fall apart; past, present, and future collapse into one moment of psychological time, for instance in cubism's collapsing of perspective into a present moment of seeing in which the viewer "sees" around, beneath, beside, and behind an object in a single moment, all at once, rather than sequentially. More than multiple perspectivism in space, this is multiple perspectivism of *time* as well.

This same collapsing of space and time into one another has regularly been cited by Western interpreters as a defining characteristic of African art. In Jahn's four categories, *hantu* (place and time) is one in which space and time fall together: "Hantu is the force which localizes spatially and temporally every event and every 'motion,' for since all beings are force, everything is constantly in motion. To the question, '*Where* did you see it?' the answer may be, 'In the reign of King X.' That is, a question of place can be answered in terms of time. To the question '*When* did you see it?' the answer may be: 'In the boat under the liana bridge after Y.' " "This is not unusual," Jahn notes. "Everyone who looks at a clock reads time by the position of the hands."[44] Even those of us who have become comfortable separating time and space by wearing digital watches, giving the lie to Jahn's example, still habitually collapse time and space: "That was the time I was in Provence." Or to bring the argument closer, we mark the passage of time the way Schreiner and Dinesen marked the time of their lives by reference to the places where it was played out. Schreiner's letters mark out her life in reference to place: Cradock, Barkly East, or Leslie Kloof where she was put out as governess, all the various dusty South African towns where she passed from family to family to escape her asthma; De Aar or Kimberley, or London, or any of the various spas at which she stayed while in Europe. In her letter cited in the previous chapter marking the moment of her life when she still believed in one "ideal love," she refers to that "moment" as a *place:* "One would hardly believe how young it was there," she says.

Dinesen's life more dramatically marks itself off in her imagination in one grand oscillation—Rungstedlund, Africa, Rungstedlund again, collapsing time and space and chance and necessity. Collapsing time and space also because the "Rungstedlund" of her childhood cries out for some future time/place of escape—her "Africa" of the imagination—and the Rungstedlund to which she returned after seventeen years represented not only her future, but echoes, to use her own word, of her past in Africa.

The "Bushmen" Olive Schreiner created in both her fictional and her political and social writings seem to function as such "utopian and cynical" mythic creatures that she too has blasted apart and refilled with subversive content. Zulu fighters in the late nineteenth century confessed to feeling that the Bushmen left an impression out of all proportion to their modest stature. They seemed able to appear and vanish "as though materializing from or dissolving into sand or grass,"[45] and even the most enlightened white South African historians, who studiously avoid racial generalizing, seem compelled to confess that Bushmen elicit a powerful conviction of having made contact with the timeless and the mythic. "The 'Bushmen's' power to disturb was always great," says Noël Mostert. "They left something in the minds and emotions of everyone who came in contact with them. Being mysterious and elusive, they became part of the shades, of the unknown. Even their young looked very old. People were afraid of magic in their minds, of instincts which they themselves long since had lost and no longer could comprehend."[46] Schreiner describes Bushmen in the same way in *Thoughts on South Africa* (e.g., p. 107), and her insistence that the new woman is really the old, old Teutonic woman of twenty centuries ago is partly her attempt to ally "woman" with the same mythic stature with which she infuses the "Bushmen" of her writings. It's possible to see Schreiner's own unpredictable, and what to some seemed arrogant, demeanor as a metaleptic troping of the same kind and order as that adopted by Bushmen in the face of constructions of them held by white folks who encountered them in Africa.

In the end Dinesen's and Schreiner's carefully cultivated ability to remain stubbornly woman-though-not-woman was a version of the same "now you see 'em, now you don't" that Schreiner must have learned from the Bushmen of her own and others' imaginations. Like so much else, their self-styled alliances with the mythic, including mythic Africans, confirmed and gave importance to their own suffering by elevating it to the status of the mythic. Such alliances with mythic womanhood, mythic suffering, and a mythic Africa helped to ensure their eternal recurrence or, at the very least, their continued survival.

5

Sketching Landscapes, Stretching Genres

I have always had difficulty seeing how a landscape looked, if I had not first got the key to it from a great painter. I have experienced and recognized a land's particular character where a painter has interpreted it to me. Constable, Gainsborough and Turner showed me England.

Isak Dinesen, quoted in
Thurman, *Isak Dinesen*

Africa, as it appeared in that desolate and sand-smitten seaport was not the Africa of her memory. The old Africa with its great grass and karoo flats and rough rock-crowned mountains, unridden and un-man-defiled old Africa, was little like the sand-smothered town in which she stood, which might have been in any country in Europe but for the ragged niggers slouching about the streets and the dark, dirty half-clothed fish-boys who dragged their wares along with tails draggling in the sand.

Olive Schreiner, *Undine*

The passages above suggest a far from unmediated vision of African landscapes. But seeing African landscapes either as paintings or as evidence of the degradation colonialism had wrought plays only a small part in the complex relation between Schreiner and Dinesen and the landscapes of South Africa and Kenya they describe in their works, where each woman predictably oscillates between identification with and alterity from those landscapes. Whether a particular piece of writing figures one or the other depends in part on the genre in which each happens to be working and on whether personal and psychic or public and political work is being done in them. But in all cases, generic expectations tend to be confounded. Schreiner's political writings often turn out to be doing some of her most important psychic work, and a critique of the colonial order can frequently be read out of the sketches that make up Dinesen's two volumes of memoirs of her years in Africa. *In* Africa, Dinesen was a full participant in the everyday workings of the colonial order, and her letters are filled with reports of these workaday arrangements. There she produces and records a self who is a user of squatter labor and even at times that most archetypal of colonial administrators, a tax collector. But back in Denmark, her Africa became shrouded in the romantic mists of memory, its landscapes serving psychic rather than economic needs. The straight-ahead look at black African male subjugation, such as that in Schreiner's sketch of the environs of Kimberley above, comes to the reader embedded—smuggled in, as it were—in a novel that is largely an uncritiqued, romantic, and very "feminine" fiction of woman's self-abnegation.

At times both women's sketches of African landscapes resemble those produced by the Anglo-Indian women Sara Suleri discusses in *The Rhetoric of English India.* More than just a way to pass an idle hour or gratify an artistic impulse, these sketches occupied an important place in the political domain. Producing a "picturesque" that aestheticized rather than analyzed the colonial landscape in order to romanticize these women's "difficulty into the greater tolerability of mystery," in the process they transformed "a profoundly dynamic cultural confrontation . . . into still life."[1] But Schreiner's and Dinesen's sketchings of Africa are different from those produced by the women whose works Suleri analyzes, because unlike them Schreiner's and Dinesen's position in Africa was not primarily that of dependent wives, but of self-sufficient or at least apparently self-sufficient working women. Part of the tensions in the marriage between Schreiner and her husband in fact began in his conviction that she had reneged on the financial agreement underpinning their marriage: that he would surrender some of his own undertakings in order to support her as she devoted full time to her writings, with the royalties she earned going into their common coffers. Though Karen Coffee was an enterprise financed by the Blixen family fortune, which was by all accounts what prompted her to marry him in the first place, its everyday operations were overseen by Dinesen herself.

Suleri suggests that the sketches the woman colonial in India was required to produce necessarily enclosed her and the Indians she sketched within that same idiom into "a picturesque repose," producing a kind of hysteria at her "narcissistic failure to locate a cultural-image for her [own] oppression."[2] But emboldened by their conception of themselves as masculine, and freed in a way by their relative economic self-sufficiency, Schreiner and Dinesen managed to produce self-enclosures that functioned quite differently. In part the sheer variety of sites at which those sketches were produced—in photographic representations, in encirclings in the landscape their female characters draw, in letters in which they inscribe their own self-protective circles that control self-revelation—enabled them to produce collectively a kind of carnival of shuttings-in and shuttings-out that they quite masterfully manipulated to their own advantage and for their own psychic survival. To discern what these differences enabled that was by and large not possible for Suleri's Anglo amatuer sketchers requires training a lens on the nexus where this peculiarly female obligation to "sketch" is considered. This constitutes the intersection where the modern's privileging of the visual, the political, space-clearing work the modern was performing, the particular artistic choices made by the fauve painters, the requirements of different genres, and the particularly tangled places in which female modernist sketchers of exotic places find themselves when their modernist sketches are enlisted in *personal* efforts to create their own spaces all come together.

Since Schreiner's and Dinesen's Africans oscillate between figurations of identity and of alterity as well as between individuated portraits and sketches of African landscape that make Africans part of the scenery of the Rift Valley or the South African veld, it has been difficult to decide how best to structure a discussion of these fluid and shifting constructions, erasures, projections, identifications, and alterities and the role each plays in Dinesen's or Schreiner's psychic economy. My solution has been to consider their relations with African landscapes and African people *as figures in these landscapes* here and their relation to individual Africans, insofar as such existed, in a later chapter, "African Gossip"—though in removing African people from their landscape this division has the unfortunate effect of doing on paper what colonialism habitually did in fact.

Jean and John Comaroff's *Of Revolution and Revelation* suggests one reason why, in Schreiner's case at least, such a division may be unavoidable. Since a frontier marks a space of cultural engagement not yet marked "on the maps of sovereign politics," it operates as a space where people are necessarily working to construct "a common world—a world of apparently understandable practices, meaningful symbols, and power relations."[3] But even before its official onset in 1905, apartheid precluded the kind of one-on-one engagement that would have allowed blacks and whites living in South Africa to hammer out anything like a common world, or to portray one another's worlds sympathetically. This is a point frequently made by Nadine Gordimer.[4] Yet close physical contact between black and white had been common in the earliest years of European intrusion in South Africa—the Comaroffs quote numerous passages from missionary journals describing early encounters between Nonconformist missionaries and native Africans. Every one recounts a strong and shared desire to touch and experience the other—the stroking of one another's hair and skin, the trading of objects—but this kind of physical closeness was rapidly proscribed. Simple lack of occasion for close contact surely in part accounts for Schreiner's portraying Africans from a distance.

But even when her descriptions of the landscapes and cityscapes around Kimberley and Johannesburg portray Africans as part of the scenery, they nonetheless manage to be decidedly and powerfully antinostalgic. Each sketch that includes adult South African men in the landscape at all produces a dramatic portrait of men scarred by colonial interventions. *An English South-African's View of the Situation,* her unsuccessful attempt to persuade Britain not to initiate the Boer War, offers frequent anti-utopian descriptions of the environs of the gold mines of Johannesburg. "Here are found," she says, "that diverse and many-shaded body of humans, who appear wherever in the world gold is discovered." She refers explicitly to the "Chinaman with his pigtail, the Indian Coolie, the Manly Kaffir, and the Half-Caste," all of whom considerably outnumber the no less multifarious white population. "On first walking the streets, one has a strange sense," she says, "of having left South Africa, and being merely in some cosmopolitan centre, which might be anywhere where all nations and colours gather round the yellow king."[5]

Nonconformist missionaries coming to the South African frontier during the years *Undine* portrays encountered not "ethnicity," say the Comaroffs, but a rather different mode of collective self-representation: a social landscape "populated not by 'Bechuana' at all, but by *batho hela,* just human beings—save, that is, for some semihuman bushpeople not worth speaking about or consorting with." But during the times about which Schreiner writes, "from that undifferentiated humanity (*botho*), under the appropriate conditions, arose ethnicity. Embodied in *setswana,* the social and symbolic substance of things Tswana, it had begun to grow . . . into an ever more articulate consciousness in contrast to *sekgoa,* the ways of the whites (who . . . were not perceived as unambiguously 'human' either)."[6] The fictional landscapes of *Undine* insist on this ethnicity in emergence perhaps as much as do Schreiner's political writings or more so. At the same time, in one crucial way they and she explicitly decline to participate in the construction of a "South Africa" at all, and in so doing Schreiner avoids any exercise in nostalgia that would return Africans to their natural "tribal" setting. The landscapes in *Undine* insist instead upon the extent to which European intrusions have turned that landscape into a kind of no place. Ezekiel Mphahlele includes Schreiner on his shortlist of white writers sympathetic to blacks in South Africa, reading in those wraithlike and degraded African male presences—like those in the middle distance in *Story of an African Farm,* for instance—powerful representions of Africans' "mute response to suffering," where the "African and Hottentot servants on Tant' Sannie's farm move about like shadows, . . . their very reticence . . . laced with agony."[7]

Passages like these, in which Africans drift on the periphery of her novels or political writings, frequently serve purposes other than the political, however, even when they occur in explicitly political works. The passage above is rendered through the eyes of Undine who, returning to South Africa after a long absence, sees the scene much as Schreiner would have after one of her own returns. Undine's first impulse as she confronts the scene greeting her at Port Elizabeth is to move on: "One thing was certain, here she would not stay. . . . She was attracted, like all the others who were near enough to feel its influence, by the great magnet that draws to itself all who are good-for-nothing, vagabonds, wanderers, or homeless—the Diamond Fields."[8] The language put in Undine's mouth here bears a striking similarity to that of Afrikaans writers of Schreiner's time. Piet Retief's "Manifesto," published in the *Grahamstown Journal* before one of the dozens of trekking episodes to which Afrikaners were prone during this period, for instance, reveals much about the defiant, apocalyptic trekker temperament, about the putative reasons for such treks, and about the language with which Afrikaners were describing the populace: "We despair of saving the Colony from . . . the turbulent and dishonest conduct of vagrants."[9]

Wanting to escape from those "vagrants" or "vagabonds," Undine moves on away from them. But the squatter community in which she ends up on the outskirts of Kimberley is no better, and Edwin Wilmsen's *Land Filled with Flies: A Political Economy of the Kalahari* suggests why this might be so. Although in his biography Schreiner's husband suggests that *Undine* was written in large part about 1872 or 1874, existing in manuscript by the time Schreiner was eighteen and perhaps begun even a year or two earlier, the scene and spirit portrayed seem to conflate several historical moments, all of which confirm her later biographers' speculations that she continued to work on that book much later. The scene, for instance, is an accurate portrait of the environs of Kimberley between 1900 and 1905, even while Wilmsen's work suggests that the Snappercaps family of the novel, who offer to share the long, dusty wagon ride to Kimberley with Undine, represent instead an accurate historical portrait of the Dorstland (Thirstland) trekkers crisscrossing the veld between 1875 and 1881,[10] most of whom finally settled in kraals among the Zhu. The more one reads histories of Afrikaners, the more one must conclude that Schreiner's landscapes might best be read as a generic representation standing in for any one of the dozens of trekking episodes that took place over many years in South Africa. The "ragged niggers slouching about the streets" in Kimberley are likely "Bushmen" or San. Doubly dispossessed by colonial policies, few found work in the diamond mines; most fell into foraging as a way of life. Pushed farther and farther into the bush, they came to be seen in a very short time as "traditionally" landless, though they had not in fact been landless at all until colonial policies made them so. To the extent that Schreiner's story depicts a landscape during the time of one of the later treks, it would have been a moment in which South Africa was in the throes of a great depression following the war. As hard times continued to erode most economic distinctions between Afrikaners and black Africans so they were no longer in a clearly defined boss/laborer relationship, the two groups increasingly found themselves living side by side in the same slums, exactly as Undine finds herself living in a dusty tent city, eking out a bare survival doing ironing for white folks, side by side with African women.

But the terrain Undine walks once she settles at DuToit's Pan, a suburb of Kimberley, provides Schreiner with numerous opportunities to produce verbal sketches of this cityscape:

> Though the street was so thronged with the streaming crowd of niggers and diggers returning home from the work that they kicked up the red sand into a lurid cloud over their heads—stark naked savages from the interior, with their bent spindle legs and their big-jawed foreheadless monkey-faces, who, though they were going home to fire and meals, could hardly get out of their habitual crawl—colonial niggers half-dressed, not half-civilized and with some hundred percent more of evil in their black countenances than in those of their wilder brethren, great muscular fellows, almost taller and stronger than their masters, the white diggers, who formed a thin sprinkling in the crowd and who, in spite of the thick dust that enveloped them, might be distinguished by their more quick and energetic movements.

Teeming with human beings, this street inspires Undine to feel "it [was] glorious to be alone" there.[11]

Here the sketching of landscape makes visible the effects of European policies on African laborers, rendered more powerful by Schreiner's insistence on Undine's blindness to what she insists her readers must see. But the same strategy that produces political critique does psychic work for Schreiner at the same time. Gerald Monsman notes the frequency with which Schreiner's metaphors and the adjectives she uses to describe Africa are intertwined with her own psychic material. Each time she refers to a South Africa in danger of being "crushed" or "smothered," the safe assumption is that those fears are Schreiner's own, projected onto a landscape that she first identifies with and then clears. "There is a certain colossal plenitude, a certain freedom in all its natural proportions . . . truly characteristic of South Africa," she says in *Thoughts on South Africa,*[12] allying herself with Africa's power, and allaying her own claustrophobia at the same time.

Despite its later revisions, *Undine* remains in some ways a piece of Schreiner's juvenilia, and this partly accounts for her callow heroine's lack of fellow feeling with Africans. Undine has never shown herself particularly sympathetic to anybody, European or African, and the eyes through which we see—or in this case *fail* to see—Africans here are hers and not Schreiner's. But the novel was worked on for many years, and a further triangulation between Schreiner's biography and South African and British social and economic history uncovers other strong traces of Schreiner's psychic concerns working themselves out in characteristic ways.

In their rampage through the Transvaal in 1901 during the Boer War the British became convinced that the only way to subdue the rural and guerilla Boers was by systematically ransacking and burning their homes. The home of Schreiner and Cronwright-Schreiner was one of the casualties of that policy, and with it, the manuscript of *Woman and Labour.* After its destruction, Schreiner chose to rewrite only those sections in which she had explored the harmful consequences of what she called woman's economic "parasitism," so it is safe to assume that she found this topic of particular concern. Economic comfort, she says in this reconstructed manuscript, has a "debilitating effect" on women, and the "female labor movement . . . in its ultimate essence, [is] an endeavor on the part of a section of the race to save itself from inactivity and degeneration."[13] If economic considerations are a prime factor in any group of women's rising up, how then do we account for the fact that it is not the poorest women who revolt first? Her answer is that it is only as women achieve a certain level of creature comfort purchased for them by their husbands' work that they are brought face-to-face with the debility or languor inevitably produced by lack of engagement with a kind of labor that would give point and bring respect to their lives. As far back as 1848 Elizabeth Gaskell was asking the same question in *Mary Barton* and arriving at the same conclusions. Assessing in an aside the causes for the constant headaches experienced by the wife of the local foundry owner in Manchester, Gaskell concludes they are "the natural consequence of the state of mental and bodily idleness in which she is placed." Mrs. Carson's real problem is that she is "without education enough to value the resources of [her] wealth and leisure," and by way of commentary Gaskell adds, "It would have done her more good than all the aether and sal-volatile she was daily in the habit of swallowing, if she might have taken the work of one of her housemaids for a week; made beds, rubbed tables, shaken carpets, and gone out into the fresh morning air, without all the paraphernalia of shawl, cloak, boa, fur boots, bonnet, and veil, in which she was equipped before setting out for an 'airing,' in the closely shut-up carriage."[14]

Twenty-four or even fifty years later, depending on when this section of *Undine* was completed, Schreiner is still convinced that languor and restlessness rather than economic hardship prompt women to rise up, that the real enemy to be resisted is neither sexism nor the economic order, but enervation. As always crossing generic boundaries and conflating psychic and political concerns, her *Closer Union* (an extended letter written to the editor of the *Transvaal Leader* in 1908) makes the same argument the cornerstone of her choice to favor a federation of small states over a unified South Africa. A collection of smaller states will be better able to inspire "general intellectual vigour and initiative," whereas turning South Africa into one large state would ensure that it would become "torpid and retrogressive," its people "almost as moribund as those in China."[15]

In making the risk of enervation a major piece of her argument for the necessity of both meaningful labor for women and a federation in South Africa, she is also very much a creature of her times. In *The Human Motor,* Anson Rabinbach details extensively how new discoveries in physics and new understandings of human physiology exacerbated the late nineteenth century's fear of enervation and entropy. Gillian Beer makes a similar argument in "The Death of the Sun: Victorian Solar Physics and Solar Myth," where she suggests that because astronomy was teaching Victorians that the sun was cooling and physics explained that all bodies in motion eventually slow down and come to rest, Victorians had difficulty reconciling that narrative of inevitable decline with the more Darwinian narrative of inevitable progress.

Whatever its cultural, historical, and psychic origins, this conviction that meaningful labor staves off enervation might be expected to get a more personalized treatment in *Undine* and to be generalized there into a statement about how meaningful work is necessary not just for Undine but for everyone else in the South African landscape. Authorial interventions suggest that in what are probably later revisions inserted by a more mature Schreiner she may well have been exploring the value of individual labor and the necessity for women to resist economic "parasitism." "Is not all work, if it be earnestly done, noble and ennobling?" she asks, and a narrative voice—Schreiner's—immediately intrudes: "No longer would [Undine] be bound by prejudice, but, leading a life based on reason, she would enjoy the greatness of the man who labours."[16] The quintessential Enlightenment rhetoric could hardly be more explicit here. But occurring only eight pages after her less than sympathetic description of the hardened laborers of the diamond mines at Kimberley, it seems to suggest Schreiner was not able or willing to extend labor's ennobling and vitalizing benefits to native Africans, and here any critical perspective or distance between her heroine and Schreiner herself evident in her descriptions of African workers wandering DuToit's Pan dissolves. In that cityscape white workers remain distinguishable not by the color of their skin—Schreiner doesn't mention that at all—but "by their more quick and energetic movements."

Although Schreiner's sketches of Africans in the landscape do emphatically resist the imperial nostalgia for unspoiled natives characteristic of so much writing by nineteenth-century male travelers, they nonetheless remain entirely consistent with rhetoric produced by male contributors to the late nineteenth-century discourses of social Darwinism and eugenics. For the latter, Africans were seen as noble as long as they were rural, living in their "tribes" in harmony with the land. Once part of the city and its business, this less evolved form of humanity could not help but become degraded, could no longer be romanticized. This is a position having political consequences, but it is considered here because it is a passage that, like so many in Schreiner's political and social writings, is doing more personal and psychic work. Amid all the voices being raised in favor of or against British initiation of what became the Boer War in 1899, Schreiner had written and spoken out strongly against it. She begins *An English South-African's View of the Situation* by positioning herself explicitly: "Amid all this chorus of opinion" about British involvement, "there is one voice which . . . has not yet been heard" fully. That voice is "the voice of the African-born Englishman who loves England, the man who, born in South Africa, and loving it as all men, who are men, love their birth-land. . . . *Our* position," she says, "is unique." Even making every allowance for the fact that her references here are to a non-gender-specific "mankind," the insistence in her repetitions is remarkable. She is "the man who . . . as all men, who are men." "Let us consider what exactly our position is," she proposes. "Born in South Africa, our eyes first opened on these African hills and plains; around us, of other parentage, but born with us in the land, our birth-fellows, were men of another white race [Afrikaners]." All African-born Englishmen get homesick for England: "We still keep fastened in memory of the past the old oar with which we won our first boating victory on Cam or Thames."[17]

The series of memories Schreiner's invokes, memories that are said to bind all South African–born Englishmen, goes on for many lines. They are all explicitly and exclusively male. Even after years of absence, this African-born Englishman who returns to South Africa will experience something that must have been very like Schreiner's experience as she returned after one of her own long absences: "Joy [as] our ship has cast its anchor in sight of Table Bay . . . when we saw the black men with their shining skins unloading in the docks, and the rugged faces of South Africans browned with our African sun, we put our foot on the dear old earth again, and our hearts have cried: 'We are South Africans! We have come back again to our land and to our people.' Is it strange that when we are in other lands, and we fear that death approaches us, we say: 'Take us back! We may live away from her, but when we are dead we must lie on her breast'?"[18]

Here African landscape produces none of the textual apartheid erasing indigenous people from colonial landscapes that is characteristic of the male travel writing Mary Louise Pratt discusses in *Imperial Eyes*.[19] Indigenous Africans figure prominently in the scene welcoming the long-absent Englishman approaching

Table Bay and home, but just as the South African–born English of her prose are all male, the Africans greeting that English "man" as he arrives are explicitly and only black *men*. Schreiner's textual apartheid clears the landscape of any sign of the female except for the African continent itself, upon whose breast she and all "other" African-born English *men* will lie when they die. England is female too; she is "stepmother to this South African people," because "we English are a virile race."[20] Despite her portraits in which South Africa becomes a great and powerful woman, her political writings seem designed to allow her to maneuver rhetorically into exactly the same place she produces for herself in her correspondence with male intellectual friends in Europe: she becomes one of the guys.

Isak Dinesen produced two volumes of memoirs but few explicitly political writings. Schreiner produced political writings but no memoirs per se. Of all Schreiner's writings, *Thoughts on South Africa* comes closest to memoir, but what private revelation there is in it is largely directed toward making a political case for a South African federation. Whereas Schreiner's novels are set mostly in South Africa, Dinesen produced no novels set in Kenya, and no fiction aiming to be realistic in any case. Neither woman produced travel literature, since neither ever was a traveler in Africa. Having had the good fortune to read many of Schreiner's shorter works in their original editions, in handling those now fragile little books I have been struck by the number of publisher's advertisements that surround her own text as it appeared in first editions published by Hodder and Stoughton in 1899, by Fifield in 1909, and especially by T. Fisher Unwin. In Unwin's edition of her 1896 *Political Situation* and her 1891 *Dreams* Schreiner's text is sandwiched between pages of advertisements for other books: European "captivity narratives," books promising a look at the lives of "three famous Metebeleland chiefs" in "darkest Africa," which must have fed an appetite so large that Schreiner showed considerable restraint in resisting writing to and for that audience, especially considering the constant financial pressure she felt all her life.

Though neither woman wrote travel literature, a contrastive analysis setting Schreiner's African landscapes against those produced by men who did write travel literature about Africa and Schreiner's Africa against that in Dinesen's letters and memoirs proves useful. Contrasting what happens in their writings with what happens in their artfully constructed lives, and contrasting their writings with those of Europeans producing travel literature, especially as that has been considered by Mary Louise Pratt in *Imperial Eyes* and by Sara Suleri in *The Rhetoric of English India,* also yields some interesting discoveries.

A very much earlier avatar of this book set out to compare memoirs and personal letters written by British men in colonial outposts of the empire with their fiction set in those same outposts: Norman Douglas's in Tunisia; E. M. Forster's in India; Leonard Woolf's in Ceylon; Somerset Maugham's in Malaya and elsewhere; Graham Greene's in West Africa; W. H. Hudson's and Aldous Huxley's in miscellaneous outposts of empire. But that story turned out to be far too easy to tell. Almost without exception, the self produced in letters sent home to family members or manufactured in memoirs for European readers was excessively fictionalized, the tropes in both entirely predictable, repetitive, and self-contradictory at the same time. On the one hand "I am utterly changed," "I am utterly alone," and "you would not understand" get obsessively reiterated. Here, for instance, is Leonard Woolf in *Growing,* the volume of his memoirs covering his tenure as a colonial administrator in Ceylon, now Sri Lanka: "I have no connection with yesterday: I do not recognize it nor myself of it. I am of and in today moulded and marked by innumerable things which have never touched you and when I come back and find you all the same, someone will say quite truly . . . 'Really they seem to be interested in none of these things.' "[21] This is one of Schreiner's and Dinesen's tropes too. The more self-aware and honest male travelers openly confessed, as Paul Gauguin does in his *Intimate Journal,* to having gone away "to find a setting to give the dream a local habitation."[22] Or as does Maugham, confessing that in going to the South Seas "I wanted to recover my peace of mind shattered through my own foolishness . . . I went looking for beauty and romance, . . . but I also found something I never expected. I found a new self."[23] In some cases these male travel and memoir writers produced what Pratt calls utopias of the anticonquest: stories of reciprocity and romance rather than the dystopias of exploitation and neglect typical of male explorers who saw foreign landscapes as "empty" or containing nothing but "raw materials" that could be turned into capital.[24]

These categories are helpful; the former explains Gauguin, the latter the writings of people like Henry Stanley. But there were other reasons the male traveler traveled, and other stories he told. The male colonial traveling at the end of the nineteenth century and the beginning of the twentieth exhibited a strong need to go to some distant place in order to produce a hardier and more virile self for family and friends back home who were the consumers of those letters and memoirs. Rudyard Kipling's bad eyes, Robert Louis Stevenson's tuberculosis, Maugham's physical smallness and weakness, his stammer and his shyness, even the groin rash Leonard Woolf perpetually suffers in the heat of Ceylon, all disappear behind the manly swagger adopted in letters or memoirs. Or those physical weaknesses transmogrify through the medium of memoir into a virility gained by passing for native. Kipling poses proudly in photographs as just another Indian; Huxley produces a more virile subjectivity for himself in his essays in *Jesting Pilate;* Maugham brags in *The Summing Up* that he was able to "pass for a Pathan. Born in India of Afghan parents, who had settled in the country, educated at Rangoon, and sent out to wander"; Sir Richard Burton urges readers to look at the frontispiece of his *Personal Narrative of a Pilgrimage to Al-Madinah and Meccah* to see how much like an Arab he looks.

But while their letters and memoirs endlessly recycled the fiction of their virility and power, the forgiving fictionality of fiction seems to have freed these male traveler/administrators to tell more of the truth about their relation to the landscapes in which they had put themselves. Writing fiction invariably enabled the late nineteenth-century and early twentieth-century male traveler to confess his insecure and insignificant place in the same colonial landscapes in which he figured so largely in letters home. Written for public consumption, fiction serves readers who expect it to say nothing particularly revelatory about the psyche of its writer. Exactly that understanding seems to have enabled confessions of private fears and insufficiencies by allowing the male traveler to enter his own narrative—so long as that is disguised as a story about someone or something else. In the face of the expectation that letter or memoir will provide something like personal honesty about the private self, the usually less than virile European male traveler seems able to enter that genre's discursive sphere only under the protection of various kinds of public masking, or after assuming one of the postures acceptable for British males in the outpost. The insecure, bookish, house-bred man, as T. E. Lawrence describes himself in his "Translator's Note" to the *Odyssey,* could become a tiger in his letters home.

In *Imperial Eyes* Pratt provides rich close readings of male travel writings that first empty out African landscapes and then proceed to fill them up again with statistics, scientific cataloging of species, or metaphors that transform African landscapes into more familiar European ones.[25] Jean and John Comaroff suggest that white missionaries described the Karoo as a "vast desert"—which it is not—because, accustomed to particularly European contours, colors, flora and fauna, their eyes simply could not *see* that landscape; for them it "lacked definition." Insofar as its features could not easily be discerned and they therefore could not comfortably place themselves in that landscape, it also defied surveillance,[26] leading to accelerated attempts in their writings to contain, confine, and domesticate it. It may be that Undine's passage down the teeming streets of Kimberley, a journey in which she feels it was "glorious to be alone," stems in part from similar impulses.

But if male travel literature habitually described African landscapes as empty, waiting to be filled—among other things, by the metaphors, meaning, and significance provided by the European writer—it is also often described by male Europeans as teeming with raw materials to be turned into cash. The chapter called "What Is Rhodesia" from Henry Stanley's *Through South Africa,* which would have been written at about the same moment as Schreiner's *Thoughts on South Africa,* quickly devolves into a consideration of the most crucial question Stanley has about the country: "What are its prospects?" His chapter titles give the game away: "Enormous Possibilities in View"; "An Embryo State Fairly Started into Existence"; "Rhodesia Has a Great Agricultural Future before It"; "The Opening of the Bulawayo Railway—

Few Events of the Century Surpass It in Interest and Importance"; and "What Water Storage Would Do." Distant as Schreiner is from any *particular* Africans she sketches in her writings, hers is nothing compared to Stanley's textual apartheid, which clears the land of humans of any kind:

> Cape Colony possesses three valuable assets which seem to me to have received scant attention. . . . What fortunes might be made of the waste land, the rainfall and the glorious climate. . . . The land is unworthily despised. The rainfall is allowed to waste itself in thirsty sands deep down beneath the level of hungry plains, while the climate does not seem to have suggested to any capitalist that a revenue superior to that obtained from the Main Reef of Johannesburg might be drawn.[27]

What inspires this enthusiastic rhapsody on South African landscape and climate is Stanley's plan to irrigate the Karoo, and turn it into health spas for sick Europeans.[28] Not entirely uncontaminated by this temptation to see Africa as raw material, in *Closer Union* Schreiner refers to "Bantu" quite explicitly as "a great material" that needs to be "wisely handled,"[29] though as always it would be hard to know whether her rhetoric here is an attempt to speak for African interests in terms Europeans might be more likely to accept or is yet one more attempt at male bonding.

Schreiner's relation to African landscape is readable also in her positioning of female characters, and here, exactly like the fiction produced by European male travelers in or about colonial settings, Schreiner's enables her to carry out some private revelation that becomes possible precisely because the discursive field she enters is presumed to be public. This work of private revelation stands out in boldest relief if it is set off against the male travel writings Mary Louise Pratt considers and against the amateur sketches produced by the Anglo-Indian colonial wives Sara Suleri talks about. In the African landscapes of Schreiner's novels "Kaffir" children gambol everywhere, the adjective *naked* attaching to them like a second skin. Far different from the Karoo European missionaries and other early visitors described as empty or barren, Schreiner's is seen with the eye of one whose home it has always been, one who can see its contours. It is filled with a lavish array of flora and fauna: angora goats, mimosa, love-grass, chick-week, black-widow burrs that stick to one's skirts, willows, lilies, *avondbloem* (evening flowers), orange trees, meerkats, and once in a while, though not often, even the occasional cluster of Kaffir huts where "long curls of blue smoke" rising from chimneys mark the only sign of native Africans in any numbers.[30] One of the best things about Noël Mostert's generous *Frontiers: The Epic of South Africa's Creation and the Tragedy of the Xhosa People* is his frequent detailed and affectionate descriptions of the landscapes where he grew up. In his largely favorable review of Mostert's book, J. M. Coetzee takes issue with these affectionate portraits, seeing them as the product of someone "clearly liberal, idealistic, secular," whose portraits are "colored by a somewhat mystical nostalgia for his lost African childhood."[31] Mostert's loving evocations of the Karoo, however, are quite similar to those of Schreiner who, clearly liberal, idealistic, and secular herself, saw South African landscapes through the same eyes. *Karoo* is the Khoikhoi word for "dry country." But the Great Karoo, especially around Cape Colony where Schreiner and he grew up, has sudden green pockets. Overall "a brooding master presence," it nonetheless possesses "an ability to resurrect a full and astonishing life after a shadow of rain has passed inland."[32]

If landscape affects temperament, Schreiner's can certainly be read in this landscape. She and her husband retreated to Hanover in Cape Colony to sit out the Boer War they had so vehemently protested in *Closer Union* and elsewhere, and Lyndall Gregg often makes reference to her aunt's loneliness there. "Anyone who knows the Karoo, and those ironstone kopjes at sunset," she says, "can well understand the deep depression they will induce."[33] Schreiner's propensity to flare up unexpectedly is well known and well documented. Her friend Mary Brown reports walking in on Olive as she was writing her allegory "I Thought I Stood before God's Throne." She found Olive in her nightclothes, wild-eyed, hair flying, with pages of manuscript scattered around her. When asked what she was writing, she reports, "Olive closed the fist of her right hand and struck it violently against the palm of her left. . . . She had, she said, 'been at one of those infernal gatherings of women. I did not know what I was going to. I hate to be asked out and then find out I am *expected to talk*."[34] Cronwright-Schreiner, Havelock Ellis, and everyone else who knew Schreiner all give similar accounts. Rebekah in *From Man to Man* behaves in the same way: pacing the floor of her study, "striking the palm of one hand now and then with the doubled-up fist of the other."[35] Her heroines also tend to crumple, chew, and swallow paper, especially in moments of exasperation or distraction. Her nephew Willie received his first telegram on his sixth birthday, and it seems to have quickly disappeared. Looking for it everywhere, Schreiner finally confessed to him, "Oh my darling boy! I am so sorry, but I must have eaten it!"[36] an anecdote adding a certain concreteness to the discourse of writing and the body. Schreiner's emotional landscapes, characterized by railing, flailing, and eating paper at one moment and by a calm confidence and sunny sense of peace with the universe at the next, replicate the landscapes of the Karoo and the South African veld.

But fostering a certain generic indeterminacy allows both Schreiner and Dinesen to smuggle into their narratives not just some of their own private psychic work but, often at the same time, a living history of colonized Africa under the guise of personal memoir or novel. Schreiner's *Thoughts on South Africa* finds its power because of her insistence that what she has produced is "a purely personal document."[37] But this "purely personal document" contains not so much a specific history of British policies in the Cape Colony as portraits of the *effects* of those policies. Whereas Dinesen painted her self at the center of her writings and Africans only on the periphery, as "shadows on the grass"—herself and Lord Delamere, Berkeley Cole, and Denys Finch Hatton as "the people who, wherever we went, were followed, at a distance of five feet, by these noble, vigilant and mysterious shadows"[38]—that portrait was as politically astute as it was psychically efficacious. The British set slaves free in South Africa in 1834, twenty-one years before Schreiner's birth there. But during her childhood policies in force still declared African children born on farms where their parents had worked "apprentices" who were required to work on those farms until age eighteen.[39] Although fathers of such children may have been legally free, they nonetheless understandably often remained attached to those farms by family ties. Not infrequently they simply hovered around them where it must be presumed that their own children's unpaid labor only made it more difficult for them to find paying work there themselves had they wanted it. Those men hovering on the periphery of Afrikaner farms may also have been in peonage. The Glen Grey Act against which Schreiner and Cronwright-Schreiner protest in *The Political Situation* required African men to work for European farmers in Africa for a certain amount of time every year whether they wanted to or not, and even though their going out to labor for white farmers entailed neglect of their own cultivated lands.[40] African men in South Africa were often forced to accept being "hired" for a tenure of "their lifetime."[41]

After the Anglo-Boer War, in 1913 the act variously referred to as the Natives Land Act or the Natives Land Bill set aside no more than about 8 percent of South African land for occupation by the 4 million native Africans, reserving unlimited access to the other 92 percent for the 1.5 million white settlers. Other South African historians estimate this act restricted Zulu, Xhosa, Shangane, and Basuto ownership to no more than 13 percent of their own country's land. But whether 8 percent or 13 percent remained theirs, the immediate result was that between the 1890s and 1910 unregulated squatter shanties sprang up on mining land all along the Rand.[42] South African historians are not in complete agreement on how rigidly this Natives Land Act was enforced in the Cape Colony. Noël Mostert suggests it was ineffectively enforced, a position the landscapes in Schreiner's novels seem to contradict. At the same time, what was called "sowing on the halves" became the law. Replacing the requirement that Africans pay one-half of their produce to white settlers in exchange for the "right" to farm on white-held lands with a requirement that this right to farm be purchased with labor rather than produce, this law transformed Africans from peasants into laborers and South Africa itself into a version of a feudal state.

The African men hovering as "shadows" in the middle distance of Schreiner's South African landscapes no doubt recognized how much in danger they were of becoming subject to Haarhoff's Curfew Bill, which would have made any native African, "whether domestic servant, householder, newspaper editor or clergyman," caught "walking the pavements in our town" subject to arrest, something the Cronwright-Schreiners protested vehemently in their collaboratively written *Political Situation.*[43]

In 1918, during the time Dinesen resided in Kenya, the Resident Native Labourers Ordinance was passed by colonial authorities. It imposed new labor obligations on the native squatter, reduced possibilities for native ownership of livestock (prompting Africans to refer to the ordinance as *kifagio,* or "the sweeping out"), and imposed more extensive obligations on them to serve as laborers for European farmers.[44] Each woman was, then, exposed to visible daily embodiments of exile in the person of Africans displaced by the Resident Native Labourers Ordinance in Kenya or the Natives Land Act in South Africa. A writer may exile himself or herself from a home that feels insufficiently like home. But after such self-exile, the writer inevitably keeps trying to return to that place that's been left. It may have felt like a prison, but it's now a prison she's locked out of, says Sara Suleri.[45] Dinesen's own confessions bear out this observation. As she writes *Out of Africa,* sitting in Rungstedlund, she says, "Out there I longed for Denmark. Now I suffer homesickness for Africa."[46] Like everyone else since, Schreiner's husband recognized that her characters were parcelings-out of herself. In *Story of an African Farm,* "Lyndall and Waldo are in large part two sides of Olive herself and are so meant to be, though," he adds, "there were more than two sides to her complex personality."[47] As a British woman in South Africa she was somewhat distrusted by both Boers and black Africans. As a South African woman she was not quite trusted by her European counterparts, and as a woman prone to exasperated fulminations at "women," she cannot have been quite trusted by fellow feminists. Hungering for Africa while she was in Europe, she returned to South Africa each time feeling no more at home, in part because she felt she had no one with whom she could "talk impersonally." The other sides of her personality not portrayed in characters like Lyndall and Waldo, then, are surely those embodied in the "Kaffirs" and "niggers" hovering on the periphery of the landscapes of *Undine:* people not welcome or able to join in a community, yet not psychically or economically free to walk away. But if the working out of Schreiner's plot in *Undine* enables her to smuggle in a critique of the colonial order and its policies, the reverse is also true. The critique of the colonial order allows her to smuggle in psychic work of her own, and that work is frequently far more retrograde than the political.

It's a chastened and humbled Undine who walks the landscapes of DuToit's Pan described so well in the later portions of Schreiner's novel, providing readers with vivid portrayals of the devastation wrought by European intervention on the bodies of native Africans. She exhibits for the first time a gentle, maternal manner with the Snappercaps children and displays a self-effacement and abasement that grows daily as she settles in to earn her way and purify her soul. But what exactly it is that has required this growing self-effacement, abasement, and need for purification is explicable only by reference to a psychic landscape rather than a colonial one. Above all, Undine is one more Schreiner heroine who suffers for her erotic attraction to men who have mastered the art of mastery, something Schreiner seemed to recognize was a personal danger. Its most explicit articulation can be found in a letter to Havelock Ellis, written just after she had received the proposal of marriage from Dr. Brian Donkin. She confesses to Ellis that "more and more I feel that marriage is not and cannot be a right thing for a nature like mine. If I am to live I must be free, and under existing circumstances I feel more and more that no kind of sex relationship can be good and pure but marriage." Recognizing that the man who has proposed to her is "tender and sweet and reverent to me," she recognizes at the same time that it is precisely *because* of this that her "heart aches when I think I can never marry him." "When I find a man as much stronger than I am [stronger] than a child, then I will marry him, no one before. I do not mean physically strong, I mean mentally, emotionally, practically." She concludes, "I do not think there is such a man."[48]

Like Schreiner, Undine has come back to South Africa from Europe where, also like her, she had declined the overtures of the sensitive, intelligent man and yielded instead to a magnetic attraction to one who is cruel and generally disdainful of females. Schreiner makes a point of highlighting the brutality of the man to whom Undine is attracted by emphasizing his cavalier cruelty toward his dog, the same sign George Eliot uses to signal Grandcourt's potential for cruelty to Gwendolen Harleth in *Daniel Deronda.* The same exploration of the attraction to the hypermasculine male, and the exploration of the penalties women suffer for such an attraction, occurs in *From Man to Man,* where, during some serious pillowtalk between Rebekah's mother and father, the suffering their daughter endures as a result of her similar choice of the muscular and hypermasculine Frank as a mate is explored. Why, her father wonders, had Rebekah rejected the sensitive and intellectual John-Ferdinand? Her mother's response is so offhand it can only confirm Schreiner's uncritical belief that *all* women would of course make the same choice: "After all, I should have chosen Frank! He's so big and strong."[49] Her heroine and her heroine's mother would without hesitation make precisely the same life choice Schreiner and *her* mother have made. Each marries the man with the great forearms, figuratively or actually, and then cultivates a compensatory intellectual friendship: Schreiner with the apparently impotent Havelock Ellis, Rebekah with the androgynous, cross-dressing Gregory Rose.

But these compensatory arrangements fail, as Undine and *Undine* both end in an orgy of self-sacrificial expiation. The novel's rendering in film could hardly avoid being saccharine in the extreme: a dusty, exhausted Undine, presumably to atone for the sin of having married a rich man in order to get money to give to the cruel young man she really loves, gives away her dead husband's fortune, and in an instance of the perverse workings of fate of which Kierkegaard would be proud and by which Dinesen would be amused, she finds herself ironing shirts for this same cruel young man, who has come to South Africa where he and his wife live in a big white house that Undine regularly visits, gazing at it from a distance, until she learns of his death. After his death she secretly keeps watch over his body all night in a shed, slipping away at daybreak.

The reader stepping back from the emotional landscape being sketched here would have to conclude that in the end Undine needs to humble herself and atone not for the sin of having chosen the cruel and brutish man, but for some more retrograde sin that is nowhere explicitly articulated. That is the sin of not having been sufficiently self-sacrificing soon enough, or successfully enough. Havelock Ellis thought very highly of *Undine,* and what he appreciated was the self-abasement embodied in its heroine. He thought the heroines of Thomas Hardy were to be admired most because they were all "Undines of the earth . . . driven always by native instinct."[50] Both, in other words, exemplify those features of woman's "instinctive nature" that Schreiner's more modernist impulses inspired her to try to clear away, the same ones her Schopenhauerian inclinations and her desire for approval from male sexologist friends prompted her to embrace. Although modern readers might want to regard Undine's degradation as a consequence of her uncritical surrender to an ideology of female self-sacrifice that would prescribe self-denial as a necessary antidote to desire for the brute male, every rhetorical gesture of the novel suggests that Undine's falls into various kinds of economic and spiritual degradation, her renunciation of fortune and happiness, and her acts of self-denial and self-flagellation are to be regarded as redemptive.

Dinesen's sketches of Kenyan landscapes produce the same complex mix. There is in them the same subtle critique of the colonial order, perhaps more effective for the modestness of its claims: "The Colony is changing and has already changed since I lived there," she says early in *Out of Africa.* "When I write down as accurately as possible my experiences on the farm, with the country and with some of the inhabitants of the plains and woods, it may have a sort of historical interest."[51] But what is proffered as a personal memoir with some modest gestures toward critique also allows a corollary to the compensatory psychic work the African landscapes of Schreiner's writings provide for her. Judith Lee a few years ago pointed out, for instance, the two dramatically different versions of her self in Kenya that Isak Dinesen produces as she tells and retells the same story in different genres: in a personal letter and in the more public memoir *Out of Africa.* When some Kikuyu children get hold of a gun left lying outside at Karen Coffee, one child is killed and several are wounded, one severely. In the letter to her mother back in Denmark recounting this event, Dinesen produces the kind of anecdotal, amateur sketch Suleri would identify as an instance of the feminine picturesque: "I was in my bath before dinner when I heard a shot,—which I always hate to hear, especially at night."[52] This scenario will be familiar to the reader of late nineteenth- and early twentieth-century colonial memoirs or travel literature. Though her convenience and comfort have been disturbed, the composed European woman nonetheless behaves effectively and with dispatch. She drives the two badly wounded children to the hospital, where one child dies as he is lifted out of the car and the other "would certainly have died if we had not taken him [to the hospital]." Given no particular emphasis, this becomes simply one event in the life of the European women in Africa, reproducing even, probably for her mother's comfort rather than her own, the trope of the native who doesn't really feel pain: She "doesn't think" Maturri suffered, "the shock [having] no doubt been too great." The child dies en route to the hospital, bouncing along in her antiquated auto, but he "cannot have felt anything at all," for he was, she says, "moaning but . . . unconscious."[53] A class as well as a racial trope, this is one Dickens satirizes in *David Copperfield,* as Rosa Dartle owns to Steerforth how reassuring it is to learn that when the poor are hurt they don't feel pain.

Dinesen's letter to her mother also makes full use of the colonial idiom Fanon describes in *Black Skin, White Masks:* "If it were not for me they would be worse off." At the same time, Dinesen takes care to ensure that her account slides off immediately into the more mundane business of running Karen Coffee. In the epistolary account, Dinesen's trip to the hospital is followed immediately by a reference to a meeting she has the next morning in Nairobi in which she tries to arrange "to get some money for my white people before Christmas."[54] This report in turn is rapidly displaced by some speculations on whether she will be receiving guests at Ngong during the upcoming Christmas holidays, and those speculations are displaced in turn by some quick reviews of her reading: Strindberg, *The Forsyte Saga.* The letter ends with an assessment of the literary conventions of English fiction.

Considered in its entirety this apparently miscellaneous letter, taking up and then dropping one topic after another, is in fact a carefully if perhaps unconsciously crafted effort at colonial self-construction. First the languid colonial lady whose bath is rudely interrupted, Dinesen next becomes the efficient colonial administrator taking care of natives who cannot do so for themselves, a construction extended as the letter progresses, as she recounts the financial negotiations she undertakes for her workers. But since her audience is her mother, these "masculine" constructions need in turn to be displaced by a final set of reinscriptions of herself within the feminine. The account ends, then, with accounts of hostessing and with aesthetic analyses of the conventions of reading European fiction. In the end, that is to say, she reinscribes herself in the aesthetic Suleri identifies as the position of the female colonial.

But this same incident becomes the frame or container for a very different and more extensive kind of work when it is recounted in a seventy-page section of *Out of Africa*. In that version Dinesen is not in the bathtub when she hears the shot but is "standing before my house" when a "shot fell, not far off. One shot. Then again the stillness of the night closed in on all sides." Here, adrift in a vast world like a female Marlowe trying to figure out the meaning of the mysterious woman on the shore crying out with her arms raised skyward, Dinesen confesses, "There is something strangely determinate and fatal about a single shot in the night. It is as if someone had cried a message to you in one word, and would not repeat it." As in her letter to her mother, Dinesen's first response in this version, after standing for a moment wondering what it meant, is to go to bed and read a book: "In Africa, when you pick up a book . . . [carried] all the way from Europe. . . . Your mind runs, transported, upon a fresh deep green track."[55]

But mercifully, in *Out of Africa* the attempt to tuck away the incident as just one colonial hardship is a maneuver that fails. Dinesen had arrived in British East Africa in 1913, the same year Leonard Woolf published *The Village in the Jungle,* a novel inspired by and set in Ceylon, where he lived from 1904 to 1911. Of that time Woolf says, "For seven years, excited and yet slightly and cynically amused, I watched myself playing a part in an exciting play on a brightly coloured stage or dreaming a wonderfully vivid and exciting dream."[56] Dinesen watched herself doing the same in Kenya. They each wrote themselves into different scenarios, producing different versions of the self as they rendered the same experience differently in different genres. The different positionalities Woolf allows himself as colonial administrator echo Dinesen's exactly. A comparison between his novel and his memoirs reveals the same predictable inversions. In both *The Village in the Jungle* and *Growing,* the volume of Woolf's memoirs recounting his years as a colonial administrator, colonized landscapes are turned into vast, mythic ones in which he figures mostly as a small creature overwhelmed by the power of the landscape, constantly under threat of its encroachments on *his* territory:

> The village was called Beddagama, which means the village in the jungle. It lay in the low country or plains, midway between the sea and the great mountains which seem, far away to the north, to rise like a long wall straight up from the sea of trees. It was in, and of, the jungle; the air and smell of the jungle lay heavy upon it—the smell of hot air, of dust, and of dry and powdered leaves and sticks. Its beginning and its end was in the jungle. . . . The jungle surrounded it, overhung it, continually pressed in upon it. It stood at the door of houses, always ready to press in upon the compounds and open spaces, to break through the mud huts, and to choke up the tracks and paths. It was only by yearly clearing with axe and katty that it could be kept out. It was a living wall about the village, a wall which, if the axe were spared, would creep in and smother and blot out the village itself.[57]

In *Growing* Woolf describes having drinks with a colonial couple: "As the Duttons and I talked we were embedded in, overwhelmed by this starry magnificence. . . . The conversation was curious, uneasy, and I felt—I could not say why—that every now and then it became tense and sinister. It was partly that the cosmic surroundings of the Tangalla Rest House . . . as upon the Jaffna plain, made the Duttons—and of course myself—appear minute, helpless, infinitely insignificant, almost tragically ridiculous." Woolf's description makes "an enormous sky meet an enormous sea"; the "palms . . . so lusciously magnificent . . . that Nature seemed to tremble on the verge—I don't think she ever actually fell over the verge—of vulgarity."[58]

Descriptions of "choking" or "threatening" landscapes like this one suffuse memoirs and novels such as Somerset Maugham's *The Summing Up* and are everywhere in "The Desert" section of *Tomorrow and Tomorrow and Tomorrow,* in which Aldous Huxley finds himself "gasping for breath in a world where all the windows are shut." The European male's conviction that the natural world he intrudes on is intruding on *him* is still being compulsively reproduced. Posed against the jungles of Iquitos in South America in *Burden of Dreams,* the documentary film about the filming of *Fitzcarraldo,* director Warner Herzog hisses, "Here, nature is unfinished: obscene. Even the stars are a mess!" Like Herzog, or like Woolf, Huxley, and Maugham, Dinesen portrays herself in *Out of Africa* as the small colonial lost in a vast sea, sky, and landscape that alternately awe and threaten to overwhelm her. But her careful self-positioning in that book also places her in yet one more way on Rosalind Krauss's deictical/deixical axis. She is not quite male/not *not*-male; not quite a colonial/not quite *not* a colonial either—complicit in and resistant to the colonial order, both at home and not at home in the colonized landscape. Although the narrative of the accidental shooting of African children in its *Out of Africa* version *begins* with the familiar small me in a large landscape posture, for instance, the shot ringing out sets in motion extensive meditations on the damage done to Africa by colonial policies that would be quite uncharacteristic of a Leonard Woolf; extensive comparative discussions of the differences between European and African systems of justice, between and among Maasai, Somali, and Kikuyu.[59] "From the farm," she says, "the tragic fate of the disappearing Masai tribe on the other side of the river could be followed from year to year. They were fighters who had been stopped fighting, a dying lion with his claws clipped, a castrated nation."[60] After becoming a British protectorate in 1886, Kenya rapidly came to be seen as a kind of expansive winter resort for those Europeans rich enough to make the trip. "The Highlands of British East Africa as a winter home for aristocrats has become a fashion," crows a pre–World War I publicity poster.[61] This rhetoric, like that of male colonials' memoirs and letters, hardly leaves room for any consideration of the tragic fate of the Maasai, and one might entertain the idea that Schreiner and Dinesen in their best moments resist what Suleri calls the "privacy of the picturesque," with its emphasis on the anecdotal rather than the historical. Insofar as they do, each manages a "breakdown of the boundaries between official and intimate language,"[62] in which the political is introduced by way of personal anecdote.

In the midst of her report about the shooting of Wanyangerri and Wamai (who seems to become Maturri in the letter to her mother), history edges its way in twice: as metaphor and as aside. The first is rhetorically a not uncomplicated move, since her critique relies on an allegorizing tendency that bestializes and hypersexualizes Africans. "Once, on the farm, I had three young bulls transmuted into peaceful bullocks for my ploughs and waggons, and afterwards shut up in the factory yard. There in the night the Hyenas smelled the blood and came up and killed them. This, I thought, was the fate of the Masai." A few pages later, critique enters as aside: "The Government had . . . introduced the *Kipanda,* the registration of each individual Native, in the country, so we would now have to call a Police Officer out from Nairobi to make a lawful inhabitant of the farm out of Kabero."[63]

The "Isak Dinesen" produced in *Out of Africa* is, then, a very different one from the portrait of the colonial lady interrupted in her bath that is produced in the letter to her mother. The former gives public articulation to some clear-headed exposition and honest exasperation with the social, medical, and legal systems she encounters in trying to help those children, as the consequences set in motion by their injury and death reveal some of the injustices of the colonial order. But this is not to elide the fact that this same account offers a more personal, psychic payoff for her as much as do Schreiner's African landscapes. In the *Out of Africa* account it is not just white male colonial administrators or hospital doctors in Nairobi who are less efficient than they might be. African chiefs are too. The latter squabble and quibble as they negotiate what should be paid by the family of the child wielding the gun to compensate the family of the child who has lost his life. The ineffectualities and small-mindedness of *all* males, European and African as well, allow Dinesen to portray herself as the patient go-between in these negotiations. In the space her exasperation clears for her between these two groups, *she* resides: the efficient, competent, powerful one who gets things done.

Olive Schreiner in time came to recognize that her arguing for the rights of the Boer republics over the rights of native Africans during the war had not been the right choice, and she worked hard in the years following the war to find a way to identify herself more with African interests. But her alliance with those interests very much resembles Dinesen's. "If, uninstructed in the highest forms of labour, without the rights of citizenship, his own social organization broken up, without our having aided him to participate in our own; if, unbound to us by gratitude and sympathy, and alien to us in blood and color, we reduce this vast mass to the condition of a great seething, ignorant proletariat—then I would rather draw a veil over the future of this land," Schreiner says. In part the way she frames her argument here should be understood as another strategic attempt to speak for African interests in terms Europeans might be able to accept; as such, it is politically blemished by expectations of "gratitude" from labor and couched in patronizing tones suggesting the writer saw Africans as objects of rather than makers of policy. Writing to Jan Smuts's wife Isie, Schreiner asks her to "tell Jan . . . when I die . . . he will have to take care of all my black people for me. I shall leave them to him in my will."[64] But in speaking of Africans as a "vast mass," Schreiner constructs here a position functionally the exact equivalent of the one Dinesen constructs for herself in her discourse of East Africa. This is not just a *political* posture, and the Africans being sketched are no residents of an African landscape at all but a "mass of black people" who serve as the raw material necessary for Dinesen's and Schreiner's own pschic self-production. Cleared of African inhabitants, African landscapes frequently served this function as well. These landscapes will be surveyed in the next chapter.

6

African Landscapes, Fauve Painters

"You think we ought to begin things fresh. . . . But I don't see precisely—conquer a territory? They're all conquered already, aren't they?" "It's not any territory in particular. . . . It's the idea, don't you see?"

Virginia Woolf,
The Voyage Out

So far is he from having any desire for a more accurate knowledge of the earth's surface that he said he should prefer not to know the sources of the Nile and that there should be some unknown regions preserved as hunting grounds for the poetic imagination.

George Eliot, *Middlemarch*

Besides serving as backdrop for psychic and political work, African landscapes become for Dinesen and Schreiner the subject of a kind of verbal still life, and this respect that their prose is rendering African landscapes can be seen to be as incidental as for the still life painter, for whom the subject is not apples and a bowl so much as line, light, brush stroke, and the emotional evocations that accrue as a consequence of particular uses of color, line, contour, and contrast. In *Vision and Painting* Norman Bryson suggests that Western painting overall is predicated on exactly this kind of disavowal of deictic reference. Absent is information about a particular "here," "there," "then," or "now," and absent also is any self-reflexive gesture that might point back to "its own *spatial* position relative to" such content or information.[1] Dinesen's and Schreiner's verbal paintings of African landscapes are marked by these same absences and are often distinctly fauvist in the rendering.

When Louis Vauxcelles coined the term "fauves" or "wild beasts" in 1905 to name the group of painters who were experimenting with wild, nonrepresentational uses of color to evoke the emotional experience rather than the actual look of the landscapes of Paris, the Mediterranean coast, and later the environs of the Thames,[2] he could hardly have imagined that the methods of those painters, Henri Matisse and André Derain in particular, would become a part of the verbal palette Isak Dinesen would use to describe the lions, giraffes, and rhinos of the Kenyan plains or to portray those plains themselves. He would have been surprised to discover how frequently Olive Schreiner's descriptions of the South African veld rely on the same muted gray blues interrupted only by a solitary splash of brilliant red characteristic of numerous paintings appearing during the middle period of fauvist experimentation. During the brief moment of the fauves, from 1902 to 1908, Olive Schreiner's attention was on surviving the aftermath of the Boer War, including tending a husband who was one victim of an epidemic of typhoid that followed. Carrying her own water and baking her own bread, she would describe herself during this period as just another "backveld *tante*"—a version of Tant' Sannie in *Story of an African Farm*.[3] Up to her elbows in pickle brine, as she said, she was hardly browsing among fauve paintings at the Salon d'Automne in Paris.

Isak Dinesen had begun studying at the Royal Academy of Art in Copenhagen in January 1904. She came to Paris to continue those studies, but she did not arrive until March 1910, after the three major exhibitions of fauve work that had taken place in spring 1902 and 1903 at the Salon des Indépendents, showing work done in the previous winters, and at the Salon d'Automne, for work done that summer. In coming to Paris Dinesen was following in the steps of many aspiring young Scandinavian artists during this time. In Denmark she had studied drawing in 1902 at Misses Sode and Meldahl's private art studio, where she found herself more than a little frustrated because she was not allowed to draw from live figures and was required to have a chaperone even to sketch marble torsos. It might be presumed that her studies at the Royal Academy of Fine Arts in Copenhagen would have prepared her technically for more serious study, but once in Paris she never made contact with the vital circles where experimentation was most alive—most notably at the Académie Julian, where Matisse was training Derain and some Norwegian pupils as well. While Matisse was busy teaching her young compatriots there, Dinesen was studying, if her desultory efforts can be dignified with that word, at the far more bourgeois Académie de Simon et Ménard. Biographers' accounts of her year in Paris present a somewhat embarrassing portrait of a young woman more interested in social life and dresses than in art, and more occupied with finding ways to balance out the highs and lows of the manic-depressive nature she may have inherited from her father than in learning to balance colors on canvas.

Since there is no particular evidence she saw fauve works or the works of Scandinavian artists influenced by them,[4] and no evidence Olive Schreiner saw fauve paintings, no direct influence or source is being asserted here. But that there should be some strong shared predispositions is not particularly surprising. Because the fauve painters were young, between twenty and thirty years of age during their fauve period, Dinesen shared a certain generational kinship with them. Like her, they admired Nietzsche for his

Figure 7. Henri Matisse, *Le bonheur de vivre*, 1906. Photograph courtesy of the Barnes Foundation.

antirationalist and anti-individualist leanings, a passion Schreiner absorbed through Nietzsche's precursor Schopenhauer.

Many of these young painters going through a fauvist period of experimentation were obsessed in particular with finding ways to create space around the figure, often by using the boldest polarities of red and green to effect decisive boundaries between figure and ground, or by outlining the figures with a heavy line that separated them from the landscape or background. Critics of these paintings were not always kind. Critiquing one of Matisse's earliest fauve experiments, *Le bonheur de vivre,* exhibited in the 1906 Salon des Indépendants (see fig. 7), Paul Signac sniffed, "Matisse, whose attempts I have liked up to now, seems to have gone to the dogs. Upon a canvas of two and a half metres, he has surrounded some strange characters with a line as thick as your thumb."[5]

By studying closely not only paintings from the later nineteenth and early twentieth centuries like *Bonheur,* with a vexed critical history, but also and especially paintings of lesser reputation that have been relegated to attics and museum storerooms, Bram Dijkstra in *Idols of Perversity* is able to consider how it is often precisely the exaggerated presentation in these "bad" or lesser paintings that most dramatically reveals male fears of "feminine evil" in operation during this period. Dijkstra does not concern himself with whether Matisse's painting is good or bad. He considers *Bonheur* instead as one representative instance of a whole genre of paintings and poems during this historical moment that were representing obsessively and with equal amounts of fascination and abhorrence groups of females dancing to delirium.[6] Dijkstra sees the bold outlining separating the female figures in *Bonheur* from their landscape as a means of protecting the viewer from those dancing women. The cultural history Dijkstra uncovers in these paintings suggests different ways to read not only paintings like Matisse's *Bonheur,* but Dinesen's photographic portrait, discussed earlier, as well. It suggests different ways of reading Dinesen's fondness for staging *ngoma*s for her European visitors too. In *The Wretched of the Earth* Frantz Fanon suggests that any study of the colonized world needs to consider the centrality of the *ngoma* in the psychic economy of the colonized. Regarding the *ngoma* as a kind of exorcism in which emotional sensibility is able to "exhaust itself in dances which are more or less ecstatic," he sees the dance as a permissive circle that "protects and permits, . . . [is] a huge effort of a community to liberate itself, to explain itself." There are, he says, "no limits inside the circle," a circle that functions as a space and an occasion in which "the most acute aggressivity and the most impelling violence" can be "analyzed, transformed, and conjured away."[7]

From the perspective of the male fauve painter or his critics, then, the strong borders in Matisse's *Bonheur,* like those in innumerable paintings from this period such as Othon Friesz's *Spring* of 1906, protect both landscape and viewers from the wild, dancing women so clearly separated from the landscape by the bold outlines around their bodies. But produced by the woman writer or painter, these same boundaries might best be seen as operating in the other direction, protecting woman from landscape and from intrusion or chastisement from those outside the circle: as producing a space where the women's "acute aggressivity" can be safely exorcised. With all her bouts of head banging and fist slamming, Schreiner seems to have been far more capable than Dinesen of open release of frustration. Dinesen for her part had recourse to some of the forms of release characteristic of other European colonials. She killed lions. But since the ecstatic exorcism available to participants in the *ngoma* was denied to her, she approximated its charmed, protective circle by becoming after her fashion its ringmaster and spectator, and she produced protective circles keeping herself in and everybody else out by producing verbal paintings of Africa that are frequently fauvist in intention and effect. She also replicates fauvist emphasis on the emotional impact rather than the "look" of her African landscapes, always favoring the lyrical over the literal. One particularly dramatic instance that might stand for hundreds occurs in *Out of Africa* as she describes Denys Finch Hatton's burial site in the Ngong Hills:

> The great country of the hills opened up reluctantly round me, and closed again, the day was like a rainy day in a Northern country. . . . The things close by, that suddenly appeared just before us, looked fantastically big. The leaves of the grey wild-olive bush, and the long grass, higher than ourselves, were dripping wet and smelled strongly,— . . . It was very still here in the hills, only at times when the rain came down stronger, there was a whisper to all sides. Once the mist parted, and I saw a stretch of indigo blue land before me and beyond me, like a slate,—it must have been one of the tall peaks far away,—a moment after it was again covered by the drifting grey rain and mist. . . . I smoked a cigarette. Just as I was throwing it away, the mist spread a little, and a pale cold clarity began to fill the world. In ten minutes we could see where we were. The plains lay below us, and I could follow the road by which we had come, as it wound in and out along the slopes, climbed towards us, and, winding, went on. To the South, far away, below the changing clouds, lay the broken, dark blue foot-hills of Kilimanjaro. As we turned to the North the light increased, pale rays for a moment slanted in the sky and a streak of shining silver drew up the shoulder of Mount Kenya. Suddenly, much closer, to the East below us, was a little red spot in the grey and green, the only red there was, the tiled roof of my house on its cleared place in the forest.[8]

Cleared of all inhabitants, this is a psychic, not an African, landscape. It is landscape as consolation, and in it color defines perspective, represents distance, and represents emotional experience: all blues, grays, gray greens, the entire landscape shrouded in mist. The pale cold clarity described in the landscape also describes Dinesen's prose, which renders superbly what fauve painters referred to as the "color space." In that color space her own sadness is projected onto the African landscape, where the breathtaking beauty not so much of the landscape as of her verbal painting itself becomes a kind of palliative for her pain in trying to accept the untimely death of Denys Finch Hatton in a plane crash. Any writer attempting to produce a verbal painting like the one Dinesen achieves here struggles mightily, because inevitably as the scene is being painted time passes, things happen, things move—if only the glint of light slanting across the sky. Tableaus threaten to become events instead; and as they do, description constantly threatens to slide into narration. Narration would require telling the story: of the failed relationship, perhaps; of Denys's death, of his burial. But by force of will and skill Dinesen wards off that threat even as she invokes the more powerful and positive aspects of the relationship that is now gone. Dinesen loved flying with Denys Finch Hatton, and in her description she couples the fauve attention to color and perspective with their characteristic experimentation with new modes of rendering the visual. This coupling produces the astonishing effect of allowing Dinesen to experience the memory (and consequent pain) of flying while she gains the consolation provided by the art of description itself.

The red tile roof of Dinesen's house abruptly interrupts an otherwise misty blue gray scene, in a verbal equivalent of such fauve paintings as Albert Marquet's *Pont-Neuf* of 1906, reproduced here (fig. 8). Were this painting shown in color, we could see that the muted blues, grays, and violets of bridge, water, and road are broken only by three small splashes of unexplained orange red: one perhaps the signage on a passing truck. In a painting similar in spirit and color, the *Parlement de Londres* of 1906, André Derain interrupts the muted colors of sea, boats, and a preponderantly blue and gray skyline with nothing but two splashes of orange red, unexplained except perhaps as someone's shirt or hat lying in the

Figure 8. Albert Marquet, *Le Pont-Neuf,* 1906. Courtesy of the Chester Dale Foundation. Photograph © 1994, the National Gallery of Art, Washington, D.C.

bottom of a small rowboat in the foreground. The muted grays, blues, browns, and violets in both paintings recall the abstract masses of a Turner painting.[9]

These same muted colors suggest the near monochromatic landscapes Noël Mostert remembers from his childhood on the Karoo in *Frontiers,* the same ones Schreiner's niece Lyndall Gregg describes in her memoir of her aunt. The same muted grays, blues, and violets punctuated by small spots of an especially bright yellow or ocher predominate in descriptions of landscape throughout *From Man to Man* and *The Story of an African Farm.* To this monochrome palette of the African Karoo both Lyndall Gregg and Noël Mostert attribute the repressed melancholy the landscape is said to inspire. Schreiner's relationship to this landscape was psychically and aesthetically one of love/hate. Staying in Hanover, for instance, she was fond of telling people that God had made it at night. And "when he saw it in the morning, . . . was so angry that He threw stones at it. Anyone who knows the Karoo, and those ironstone kopjes at sunset," as Lyndall Gregg says, "can well understand the deep depression they will induce."[10] Mostert's *Frontiers* is in many ways as valuable for its vivid and affectionate portrayals of South African landscapes that confirm Schreiner's as for its history of the Xhosa. Part of what is remarkable about his descriptions of the area around Algoa Bay and the colors around the coastal cape and the Great Karoo is that his African landscapes are as melancholy as Schreiner's and that they too suggest that the colors of nature here are identical to the color use of the fauves both early and late. In what he calls this "brooding master presence," the monochrome of the veld is broken by a sudden spot of color, exactly as in a fauve painting: "Sometimes, out amidst the ochre grit of the veld, one came across a nest of [ostrich's] big white beautiful eggs, . . . luminous, sudden, miraculous, alien," he says, replicating exactly any number of early fauve paintings in which color abruptly stops or runs off into pure white canvas. In his South African landscapes as in Schreiner's, "aloes, flame red, flare among the rocks and on the ledges." The same Great Karoo that is the setting for most of Schreiner's novels Mostert describes as an "arid emptiness" where the fossils of creatures that walked two hundred million years ago "are embedded now in pale outline in the reddish, bluish and green shales of its mesas,"[11] suggesting again that her descriptions in novels and most especially in some sections of *Thoughts on South Africa* are fauvist in their representation.[12]

Whether in the more characteristic fauve paintings where pure primary colors vibrate against one another or in those where muted tones contrast with single bright splashes of color, the central feature remains oscillation itself. Henri-Edmond Cross, one of the lesser-known fauve experimenters, recounted for one correspondent his eagerness to get to his palette to experiment "in order to prove to myself that I still know how to put a green next to a red. . . . This garden is all red—the flames of the geraniums which overstimulate the blue-green of the mimosas." "It is in the midst of these ardors," he insisted, "that I find calm."[13] This space of deliberate disharmonies where calm is sought in the midst of ardors is of course the place of psychic oscillation where Dinesen and Schreiner felt most at home. As the red flame of geraniums overstimulating the blue of mimosa brought calm to Cross, the red tiled roof of her African home juxtaposed with the gray blue mists of Denys's grave site produces a similar calm in Isak Dinesen as she describes the landscape where his body is laid to rest.

It is one thing to suggest that the African landscapes in Schreiner's novels and Dinesen's memoirs are fauvist because the predominant colors of Kenya and South Africa lend themselves to the same palette. But walking through the Fauve Landscape exhibition at the Metropolitan Museum in New York, a man standing beside me studying the colors in the paintings done at L'Estaque and Collioure in southern France exclaimed over the same thing that had impressed earlier critics of their work: how much the "blond, golden light that suppresses the shadows of the Mediterranean coast" where Vlaminck and Matisse painted in the summer of 1905 [14] resembled the light of Africa. But this Africa of Schreiner's and Dinesen's verbal paintings remains far more an Africa of the imagination than an actual place and space. One need only note that their descriptions tend to be the same whether it is Africa they describe or some *other* landscape entirely to recognize how true this is. Here, for instance, is a description from *From Man to Man,* in a chapter titled "How the Rain Rains in London," where the fauve landscape is that of England, not Africa.

> There were a few bushes and small trees growing below. Near by, a few yards from where they stood was a great building which was closed and seemed unused; it had a red roof covered over with a fine yellow lichen that stained it everywhere. Far off were more houses. . . . On the slope about them everywhere were the marks of cows' feet, which had sunk deep into the soft, soaked turf. Some of the footprints were full of clear water, in some blue flowers had been growing which raised themselves stooping and half crushed. She looked round at the gray sky, at the bushes, at the barn a few hundred feet off with its red roof, damp with yellow lichens, and at the mud and grass at their feet.[15]

Similarly, there is little difference between Dinesen's African landscapes in *Shadows on the Grass* and what she describes in that book as her dreamscapes. The same "vastness . . . [and] quality of infinite space" characterizes both:

> I move in mighty landscapes, among tremendous heights, depths and expanses and with unlimited views to all sides. The loftiness and airiness of the dream come out again in its colour scheme of rare, luminous blues and violets, and mystically transparent browns. . . . Long perspectives stretch before me, distance is the password of the scenery, at times I feel that the fourth dimension is within reach. I fly, in dream, to any altitude, I dive into bottomless, clear, bottle-green waters. It is a weightless world. Its very atmosphere is joy, its crowning happiness, unreasonably or against reason, is that of triumph.[16]

Here adaptation of the fauve palette renders a psychic landscape, one of infinite, uninhabited—and thereby liberating—space around her own figure. Collapsing earth, sky, and sea, she also taps African cosmologies as well as invoking again the fascination with flight that Denys Finch Hatton personified. Juxtaposing bright colors and muted ones, she creates perspective as a fauve painter does, and all elements combine to produce the conviction, made explicit in Dinesen's dream *langscape,* that triumph—which as always is synonymous with solitude—is a matter of exactly these acts of the imagination that are characterized by an aesthetic distancing and an amalgamative troping that transport the reader to an entirely nongeographical or placeless place of the imagination neither African nor European: to a weightless world.

Olive Schreiner's use of color and perspective in her novels produces similar African landscapes: grand, static places in which the writer-recorder is but a small impersonal voice in a vast enveloping scene where the deliberate actions of the protagonist can have little or no effect on landscape or history:

> Babie-Bertie leaned her head back against the door; a rich fragrant odor rose from the fresh earth; she drew the white shawl she had thrown over her head closer round her face, and sat watching the wet world. The sun was setting at the end of the great valley below the farmhouse; all the west was a bloody pall of crimson, all the east a faint reflection of its redness.

> On the water of the great dam by the willows, in the windows of the farmhouse, in the puddles by the roadway, on the wet leaves of the thorntrees, even there it was reflected; and the little flat and the lower hills on the other side of the valley and the tall mountains were all touched with its redness. A curious feeling came over her as she sat there watching it; it was as though a strong great hand were put out and took fast hold of her heart, that trembled and was so heavy, and held it fast.[17]

African influences reached the fauve painters through various channels. By 1905 Gauguin was introducing the fauves to non-Western art forms, and since the "'Primitivism' in Twentieth Century Art" exhibition at the Museum of Modern Art in New York in 1984 their productions have been purported to explore "affinities" between modern art and tribal art. If the word *appropriation* is substituted for the word *affinities,* Western artists' debt to things African becomes obvious and traceable here. Their tendency to suppress specific time and place in the interest of representing the timeless and the mythic was often adopted in direct imitation of what these European painters believed Africans were doing in their art. Fauve landscapes and the figures in them were both rendered as abstractions rather than as particular sites or people. Marcel Giry notes, for instance, that Matisse tried hard "to express the permanent, true essential character of beings and objects, at the expense of charm," and he cites Matisse's own expression of his intentions: "I'll condense the meaning of this body, in seeking the essential lines. At first sight its charm will be less obvious, but it must eventually emanate from the new image I have obtained, which will have a wider, more fully human meaning."[18] Works like his *Bonheur de vivre,* with their flat representations of the human figure, reveal how well he accomplished those aims.

The grand, abstract rhetoric of *Story of an African Farm* makes it a difficult work to love. But its flat prose makes it the verbal equivalent of Matisse's painting, and its aim reveals the same drive for a new image with a wider meaning, often exactly as Giry says of Matisse's *Bonheur,* at the expense of charm. Schreiner's characters' dialogue is often the anguished language of some universal female Diogenes looking for truth or happiness:

I stayed in my situation four months after that, but I was not happy. I had no rest. The people about me pressed on me and made me dissatisfied. I could not forget them. Even when I did not see them they pressed on me, and made me miserable. I did not love books; I wanted people. When I walked home under the shady trees in the street I could not be happy for when I passed the houses I heard music, and saw faces between the curtains. I did not want any of them, but I wanted some one for mine, for me. I could not help it. I wanted a finer life. (p. 257)

When the narrator steps in, the voice heard is that of an equally restless everywoman speculating on great and abstract themes:

We do not yet know that in the soul's search for truth the bitterness lies here, the striving cannot always hide itself among the thoughts; sooner or later it will clothe itself in outward action; then it steps in and divides between the soul and what it loves. All things on earth have their price and for truth we pay the dearest. We barter it for love and sympathy. The road to honour is paved with thorns; but on the path to truth, at every step you set your foot down on your own heart. (p. 126)

To produce prose like this is to position the writer as a kind of disembodied voice looking out on a vast, otherworldly landscape in which the painter/writer is invisible, inconsequential, or very small. It is to produce a spiritual landscape at the intersection of the modernist impersonal and the Benjaminian mythic and timeless, one of the places where Dinesen and Schreiner habitually set up residence and felt most at home. Formal decisions to erase the storyteller behind the story and place the describer above and isolated from the landscape described do of course buy a certain psychic comfort for the writer. But such formal decisions nonetheless have consequences beyond what Gatsby refers to as the "merely personal." Those consequences can be discerned most easily by looking at one of the numerous accounts of lion hunting in Dinesen's two memoirs. Though the most celebrated of those from *Out of Africa* has generally been read as Dinesen's hymn to the erotic relation between Finch Hatton and herself, looked at in terms of her painterly technique it reveals much else as well:

> We walked a little again and the deep growling was repeated, this time straight to the right. "Put on the light," Denys said. It was not altogether an easy job, for he was much taller than I, and I had to get the light over his shoulder on to his rifle and further on. As I lighted the torch the whole world changed into a brilliantly lighted stage, the wet leaves of the coffee-trees shone, the clods of the ground showed up quite clearly.
>
> First the circle of light struck a little wide-eyed jackal, like a small fox; I moved it on, and there was the lion. He stood facing us straight, and he looked very light, with all the black African night behind him. When the shot fell, close to me, I was unprepared for it, even without comprehension of what it meant, as if it had been thunder, as if I had been myself shifted into the place of the lion. He went down like a stone. "Move on, move on," Denys cried to me. I turned the torch further on, but my hand shook so badly that the circle of light, which held all the world, and which I commanded, danced a dance. I heard Denys laugh beside me in the dark.—"The torch-work on the second lion," he said to me later, "was a little shaky."—But in the centre of the dance was the second lion, going away from us and half hidden by a coffee-tree. As the light reached him he turned his head and Denys shot. He fell out of the circle, but got up and into it again, he swung round towards us, and just as the second shot fell, he gave one long irascible groan.
>
> Africa, in a second, grew endlessly big, and Denys and I, standing upon it, infinitely small. Outside our torchlight there was nothing but darkness, in the darkness in two directions there were lions, and from the sky rain. But when the deep roar died out, there was no movement anywhere, and the lion lay still, his head turned away on to his side, as in a gesture of disgust. There were two big dead animals in the coffee-field, and the silence of night all around. (pp. 235–36)

In this verbal painting there is the characteristic clearing of a space around the main object, and consequent framing: "outside our torchlight, nothing but darkness." Here can be seen also the superimposition of several perspectives: "as if I myself had been shifted into the place of the lion." The same sharp angles of perception creating multiple profiles that characterize cubist painting characterize Dinesen's prose here: "straight to the right," "the lion . . . half hidden by a coffee-tree . . . turn[s] his head . . . swung round towards us." This cubist perspective is characteristic of any number of Dinesen's descriptions of Africa: "Seen from this vantage point, it looked like X; but from another, it looked like Y." Or "at night it looked like X, but by day . . ." Or "In the rain it was . . . but in dry season, it was . . ." In this particular verbal painting there is the characteristic bold, pure color chosen for emotional rather than representational fidelity: "the whole world changed into a brilliantly lighted stage." And perspective is chosen for emotionally rather than mathematically accurate perspective: "Africa, in a second, grew endlessly big, and Denys and I, standing upon it, infinitely small."

At times *Out of Africa* presents almost nothing but such horizontal and vertical planes and the shifting, multiple perspectives those planes produce:

> The hills from the farm changed their character many times in the course of the day, and sometimes looked quite close, and at other times very far away. In the evening, when it was getting dark, it would first look, as you gazed at them, as if in the sky a thin silver line was drawn all along the silhouette of the dark mountain; then, as night fell, the four peaks seemed to be flattened and smoothened out, as if the mountain was stretching and spreading itself. (p. 5)

Beautiful as they are, these last two descriptions and others like them cry out for more than an appreciation of their brilliance, as Dinesen's adaptation of fauve techniques to render distance and perspective achieves other than purely aesthetic ends. At least during her earlier years in Kenya, Dinesen was obsessed with bagging at least one of everything that walked the land. In reading the first passage describing a lion hunt one would expect the primary response would contain at least some revulsion at this instance of European violence turning Africa into a slaughterhouse. But this does not seem to have been the reaction of most people reading her accounts, and it is her skillful aestheticizing and painterly brilliance that make the difference. One is surprised to discover, for instance, that what one might expect to be a narrative account leaves as its afterglow the impression of something purely descriptive; another painterly tableau: "there was no movement anywhere." Partly Dinesen achieves this by making the scene not so much a narrative of an action as a succession of mini-tableaus. Technically this is accomplished by leading the reader's eye, by way of the lantern, from one static scene framed in its "circle of light" to another as her arm moves the lantern and therefore the circle of light moves from one thing to another. All the while, what is described each time as within this circle of light is largely static. There is no connection between one circle of light and the next, and certainly none between the arm that holds the gun and the static lion lying on the ground. There is no connection either, causal or physical, between the lion that stood "facing us straight" and the "shot which fell." The passive construction, of course, ensures that this is so. This shot is not reported as having come from a gun held in a European hand so much as it is simply presented as an emanation from the natural world, "as if it had been thunder." Far from an accessory after the fact, Dinesen paints herself as victim, "shift[ed] into the place of the lion." In this tableau drained of volition and action, Dinesen hears the shot not only "unprepared for it, [but] even without comprehension of what it meant." The act is carried out in the absence of *any* context. "The circle of light," she says quite explicitly, "held all the world." Even more curiously, her painterly technique here manages to smuggle in a critique of the hunt while absolving the hunter. "There were two big dead animals in the coffee-field," she says—a deflation of her own romantic rhetoric to be sure. But abstract constructions—"*There were* two big dead animals"—absent her and Denys from the scene and pointedly absolve them of responsibility for the deaths.

Susan Stewart's analyses of tableaus in *On Longing* offer additional ways to explain how and why Dinesen's scene works the way it does. The writer creating a tableau creates a world of things defined in spatial relation only to one another, and drained of relation to anything beyond. Should any action be introduced, the description of the world of things making up the tableau would "become 'mere' context," and description only "supplemental to the description of narrative events." It is a problem found over and over again, she notes, "in pastoral and ethnographic writing."[19] Dinesen's lion hunts exist in works that are hybrids of exactly these two kinds of writing.

One would think nothing could transform tableau into narrative event more quickly than a lion hunt, no matter which genre it occurs in. But a comparison of her tableaus with the lion hunt in "Brothers Are the Same," a short story from Beryl Markham's collection of African stories *The Splendid Outcast,*[20] is instructive. Given the vexed relationship between these two women in Africa, one that among other things found them competitors for the affections of Denys Finch Hatton, there is a certain piquancy in such a comparison. No easy person to get along with, Markham named one of her dogs Tania, which was one of Dinesen's nicknames, because the dog was, she said, "a little bitch with short legs."[21] The lion hunt in Markham's story bears some similarity to Dinesen's account in *Out of Africa*. In her introduction to Markham's story, Mary Lovell reports that although when first read it appears to have been "written out of her deep knowledge of African culture," Markham's husband reports that "he had been obliged to comb a reference library for information on Masai tribal customs which Beryl was not able to provide."[22] Written long after she had left the British protectorate of Kenya, while she was living on a ranch in southern California after World War II, just as Dinesen's account of her lion hunt was written while she lived back at Rungstedlund in her family home, Markham's story is like Dinesen's a retrospective, and both have the intensity that characteristically comes about only when the event recounted and its "exotic" setting have acquired the enhancing haze memory produces.

The backdrop to "Brothers Are the Same" is a childhood encounter in which Markham herself had been attacked by a lion kept by a family friend. In the story she draws on this early experience to portray Temas, who is undergoing the traditional test of courage and strength required of the young Maasai aspiring to be a moran.

> Suddenly he lay as still as sleep and watched only the ravine and listened as to the tone of some familiar silence. It was the

> silence of a waking lion, for morning light had breached the thicket, and within his lair the lion was roused.
>
> Within his lair the lion sought wakefulness as suspicion came to him on the cool, unmoving air. Under the bars of sunlight that latticed his flanks and belly, his coat was short and shining. His mane was black and evenly grown. The muscles of his forelegs were not corded, but flat, and the muscles of his shoulders were laminated like sheaths of steel.
>
> Now he smelled men. Now as the sunlight fell in streams upon the sorrel coat and warmed his flanks, his suspicion and then his anger came alive. He had no fear. Whatever lived he judged by strength—or lack of it—and men were puny. And yet the scent of them kindled fire in his brooding eyes and made him contemplate his massive paws.
>
> He arose slowly, without sound—almost without motion—and peered outward through the wall of thorns. The earth was mute, expectant, and he did not break the spell. He only breathed. . . . The silence held. The interminable instant hung like a drop that would not fall, and Temas remembered many of the rules, the laws that governed combat with a lion—but not enough, for stubbornly, wastefully, foolishly, his mind nagged as young Temas confronts the lion, fearing he will not be brave enough to kill it. His hand trembles, he does not lift his spear; he loses his moment.

While Temas pauses, apparently frozen immobile by and in his own mental operations, ten other young warriors "spring like flames" and hurl their spears at the lion. Markham's narrator remarks, "Suddenly the world was small and inescapable. It was an arena whose walls were tall young men that shone like worn gold in the sun, and in this shrunken world there were Temas and the lion."[23]

In one crucial way this scene replicates, as Dinesen's frequently do, the familiar perspective characteristic of so much European writing from the colonies: "The world is very small/I am very large" or, alternatively, "The world is very large/I am very small." But the lion hunts that Dinesen recounts exhibit far less of what might be thought of as mental colonization. Markham details minutely not only what is in the young moran's head but what is in the lion's. In fact her pronoun "he" in the first line of the passage registers for a while as indeterminate: Is it the lion or is it Temas who "lay as still as sleep and watched"? In a sense the question is irrelevant, for her spectacle lays inner and outer of both man and beast equally bare for full inspection. If Dinesen's tableau cuts the scene off from any context, thereby cutting off the hunted and the hunters from intrusion or surveillance, one side effect is that it at least preserves the privacy of the players, even the lion. Perhaps when critique enters her tableau it is the more powerful for its spareness, for the dramatic disjunction between it and the static, framed—and inviolate—character of the rest of the scene she paints. Unlike Markham, who tells us what the lion smelled, what he felt, what he thought of men, what he experienced of the natural world around him, and much else besides, Dinesen reveals only one thing about the lion's interior, and even that she indicates is only speculative. In death, she reports, the lion's head lies to one side not "*in* a gesture of disgust," but "*as* in a gesture of disgust." As so often, Dinesen's prose oscillates between evasion and critique.

Whether it is done in painting or in prose, in fiction or in memoir, describing nature is of course always a social practice, as T. J. Clark in *The Painting of Modern Life* and Paul Carter in *The Road to Botany Bay* have made abundantly clear, each one considering the specific ways socioeconomic and political contexts reveal themselves in visual (in the first instance) and verbal (in the second) representations of landscape. Clark insists that the very *terms* of modernism are all themselves constructs: high aesthetic self-conscious attention to form and arrangement, rejection of the past and of naturalistic representation, the cultivation of a synchronicity in which past, present, and future are collapsed into the present as in cubism and futurism, in which one sees things from several places or times at once, as well as the turn from realism to style ("No artist tolerates reality," said Nietzsche). "The circumstances in which they first crystallized out . . . [in] a sort of sealing and congealing as well as a simple assumption of order . . . [serve as] a closure against consciousness of their *being* terms, and therefore against an awareness of modernism having circumstances."[24]

Dinesen's, Markham's, or Schreiner's verbal representations of an African landscape, like modernism itself, all do have circumstances. First, quite as much as the painter, the writer needs to spend at least *some* time in *plein air* to render landscape at all, and "out there" inevitably encounters other people. Will the landscape be rendered with or without those others? And if it is peopled, will those people be rendered from a great distance, walking solitary against the horizon, or up close? Rendered in masses, in the abstract, or with each person and body in all its individual particularity and circumstance? Will the writer or painter include his or her *self* in that landscape? Will it reflect the changes wrought by the introduction of roads, machines, or factories or, in the case of the East Africa of Dinesen's time there and of South Africa during Schreiner's, the changes wrought by laws changing the nature of landownership for African people? Will artists succumb instead to the temptation to portray a prelapsarian, nostalgic landscape untouched by human hands?

These same decisions were being made by the fauves working in France between 1903 and 1908. T. J. Clark suggests, for instance, that to look closely at Van Gogh's paintings is to admire his relentless honesty in rendering the smokestacks on the horizon of his paintings, just beyond the sylvan hayricks and fields of poppies. Argenteuil is one of the villages artists throughout the centuries have loved to paint. Painting there in the 1870s, Monet appreciated the railroad passing through the town because it enabled him to stay in touch with Paris. But for Maurice Vlaminck, the most left-leaning of the fauve painters, that same railway was a mixed blessing: "For a little village," he remarked, "a railway is what a wound is for a human being—a gaping sore which admits infection."[25]

In her catalog for the 1990–91 fauve exhibition Judi Freeman notes that the fauves inherited the enduring tradition of mythological figures situated in lush landscapes that had been a feature of European painting at least from the seventeenth century to the nineteenth: from Nicolas Poussin and Claude Lorrain, following as heirs to the Venetians Giorgione, Titian, and Correggio of the fifteenth and sixteenth centuries through the eighteenth-century French painters such as François Boucher, Jean-Honoré Fragonard, and Jean-Antoine Watteau. They all placed the human figure in the landscape, either contemplating it or frolicking in it, and though at first the fauves continued that pastoral tradition, somewhere it gave way to the picturesque: to the painting of charming, unpopulated scenes of nature. The fauves painted bridges, roads, and seascapes, but as they sat at their easels they most often carefully left out most or all of the people that must have been passing by as they worked. Braque's *Paysage à La Ciotat,* painted in the summer of 1907, was an uninhabited countryside; Dufy's *La Tuilerie Saint-Henri—The Saint-Henri Tileworks*—was a factory with no workers: there were bridges and beaches, but few strollers on either.[26]

As white women colonials writing in and of the African landscape, both Dinesen and Schreiner had to make certain choices not only about how to render that landscape (in their fictions), but about whether and how to situate themselves in it (in their letters or memoirs). As women with a great deal of psychic ambivalence about that urge to merge, oscillating between desires for evasion and invasion, they faced constant decisions about how much they would allow themselves to figure in or merge with the landscape, how much to remain isolated, and how much to create protective boundaries around themselves. Implicated as they were by blood, by ethnic or national origin, and by association with the colonial order changing the landscape of Africa at the turn of the century, they also faced a different set of choices that had both aesthetic and psychosociosexual political dimensions. Would they portray the landscapes of Africa as they were becoming before their eyes, or would they portray them nostalgically, muting those changes that had to have been very visible to them and showing them, if at all, through the kind of retrospective decolonization that Said sees as part of a colonized people's "heroic effort to win back control over their own territory"?[27] They made choices about whether to present the landscape as seen by privileged colonizers/tourists in a world not their own—"taking the view" as tourists habitually do, "buying" momentary ownership of a place not their own—or, conversely, as seen by residents taking "legitimate" possession of the landscape in which they lived and worked.

Underneath Schreiner's portrait of the site of European mining interests in South Africa, in the gash of Kimberley Hole, there is a portrait of Schreiner herself. Similar self-portraits lurk beneath Dinesen's landscapes and still lifes—behind the elegaically traced contours of the drastically shrinking territory available to the Maasai, Kikuyu, and Somali during the seventeen-year span when she lived there. Both women faced the same "burning question" confronting the fauves: what to depict and how.[28]

In *The Painting of Modern Life* Clark identifies the desire to escape the encroachments of the industrial world (and the petite bourgeoisie that industrialization produced) as one of the major defining circumstances of modern art, resulting in the production of an art "characterized by its desire to take its distance from the petite bourgeoisie and the world of entertainments it ushered in." But even so, the modernist artist remained interested in those entertainments as subjects for his paintings. One might recall in particular Matisse's *Luxe, calme et volupté,* but there are parades of other fauve and nabi canvases that catch figures in the same way, in the act of enjoying their bourgeois leisure pursuits: bathing, picnicking, or promenading on the boulevards. It is a narrative that has become familiar to all who read Marxist critique: leisure becomes performance and, as Veblen suggested, what gets performed is *class.* Clark's assessment is that "the implication of leisure in class struggle goes some way to explain the series of transformations undergone by the subject in painting from 1860 to 1914, shedding light in particular on the painters' changes of mind about how leisure should be depicted: the way, for example, styles of spontaneity are repeatedly displaced by styles of analysis—grandly individualistic modes of handling." In this context Clark finds interesting the speed with which the fauvist style, "which had appeared for a moment to open nature again to the free play of fantasy—collapsed into its cubist opposite. By the time of fauvism, one could say, the myth of recreation could be stated only in mythical terms: the dream of freedom and self-consciousness, of crepuscular boating and *Le bonheur de vivre,* is adjourned to the golden age."[29]

This quick summary of the possible origins of the modernist emphasis on technique and the place of leisure in the subject matter of painting between 1860 and 1914 sets the stage for a different kind of understanding of exactly *why* Isak Dinesen's verbal paintings of Africa were, and *remain*, so popular, and the descriptions of African landscape in Schreiner's novels so appealing. We can ask of their works the same questions Clark asks about the artist's choices of subject matter and ways of rendering that material: What needs was this art serving for its viewers? What forms of visibility were provided by their art? How in their description of landscape, of countryside, was the countryside "kept at a distance, brought into view, produced as a single human thing, a prospect or a panorama?"[30]

Dinesen's descriptions of lion hunts on the Kenyan plains, for instance, are from one crucial perspective nothing but artful representations of bourgeois leisure, portraits of white Europeans wealthy enough to purchase a piece of prelapsarian Eden where they might play at being self-sufficient creatures hunting their own food. In the lush descriptions of the hunt with their frissons of danger juxtaposed with the inevitable champagne lunches on the lawn, we experience all the comforts of the "civilized" world and the challenge and romance of the uncivilized in rapid oscillation. As surely as a rapid oscillation between blue and yellow produces an afterimage of green, the afterimage produced by *that* rapid oscillation is of a world in which one can have it all, with application of enough will, imagination—and cash. If as critics suggest the modern was being born at exactly the moment when everyday life was being colonized and commercialized and pleasure was being transformed into leisure, Dinesen's landscapes of Africa, when they are painted through the mists of nostalgia, oscillate between nostalgic depictions of the "exotic" (Chris Bongie defines exoticism as any discursive practice intent on recovering "elsewhere" values "lost" with the modernization of European society)[31] and far more straightforward looks at those altered landscapes *and* at her own imbrication in the undesired transformations going on in the African landscape:

> There had been big stretches of Native forest on the farm in the old days, but it had been sold to the Indians for cutting down, before I took over the farm; it was a sad thing. I myself in the hard years had had to cut down the wood on my land

> round the factory for the steam engine, and this forest, with the tall stems and the live green shadows on it had haunted me, I have not felt more sorry for anything I have done in my life, than for cutting it down.[32]

The position of the European or European American reader enjoying this writing today surely has to be extraordinarily complex. Dinesen has produced a rather comfortable place for her readers to inhabit as they "take the view" with her, *prise de vue* being a leisuretime activity since the eighteenth century, feeling virtuous that we recognize our own involvement in the erasure of the natural world she depicts for us as vividly as do the fauve painters. In the same moment we both enjoy the spectacular pleasure of "consuming" this landscape and do penance for our consumption by confessing our own guilt. So too, even my own analysis here of Dinesen's aestheticizing of the African landscape, and my own dutiful and regretful acknowledgment of her implication in its passing, both function to carry off my own guilt at my pleasure in reading her words. A sensitive consumer is her/my best product.

7

African Gossip and the Two-Way Street

How do we negotiate between my history and yours? How would it be possible for us to recover our commonality, not the ambiguous imperial-humanist myth of our shared human attributes . . . but, more significantly, the imbrication of our various pasts and presents?

S. P. Mohanty,
"Us and Them"

I was a fairly famous doctor to the squatters of the farm. . . . I had been, in the beginning of my career, miraculously lucky in a few cures, which had made my name echo in the manyattas. Later I had made some very grave mistakes, of which I still cannot think without dismay, but they did not seem to affect my prestige; at times I felt that the people liked me better for not being infallible. This trait in the Africans comes out in other of their relations with the Europeans.

Isak Dinesen,
Shadows on the Grass

As D. H Lawrence writes to accept Mabel Dodge Luhan's invitation to visit her in Taos, he ends up sounding exactly like Leonard Woolf in Ceylon, or for that matter like any other late nineteenth- or early twentieth-century traveler who has spent time in other cultures and landscapes. Fresh from five weeks in Ceylon followed by a stay in Australia where he had holed up to write *Kangaroo,* Lawrence writes to Luhan to confess that he needs to get away both from what he calls the "boneless suavity" of the East—presumably Ceylon—and from "the thick, choky feel of tropical forest, . . . the metallic sense of palms and horrid noises of the birds and creatures" who "hammer and clang and rattle and cackle and explode" as well, the latter presumably his representation of the landscape of Australia. But Lawrence isn't sure he'll be much more comfortable around the Native Americans in Taos. The ease with which Tony Luhan wore his own masculinity may go a long way toward accounting for Lawrence's discomfort, but he is quick to generalize and displace it. "All dark people have a fixed desire to jeer at us," he insists. Convinced they are always secretly laughing at white folks' foibles, he's sure dark people also deliberately resist attempts to see their own: "They seem," he says, "to be built round a gap, a hollow pit."[1]

After twenty-two years in Africa "Konga Vantu," otherwise known as Dr. D. Crawford, FRGS, refers obsessively to what he calls "that hard, impersonal stare of those bottomless-eyed natives, not the intense, penetrating thing of Europe. You might be something worked on tapestry or painted on a china cup," he thinks, "so impersonally does he look at you."[2] Passages like these suggest how much the European subject becomes real to itself by seeing its reflection in the eyes of another,[3] a phenomenon W. J. T. Mitchell discusses at length in his *Iconography: Image, Text, Ideology*. This is a phenomenon prefigured explicitly in earlier nineteenth-century writings like Thomas Carlyle's *Sartor Resartus*, in which a main symptom signaling Herr Teufelsdröck's dark night of the soul is his recognition that he has become a kind of reflection junkie: "How could I believe in my strength, when there was as yet no mirror to see it in?"[4] Dinesen's rhapsodic, appreciative descriptions of Maasai, Kikuyu, and Somali such as that in the epigraph above from *Shadows on the Grass* are often not so much descriptions of Africans as reports of Africans' responses to *her*.

When she is away on business, "the Natives would take such periods of distraction of mine meekly," she says, "as if I had been in reality lifted from their existence into another plane, afterwards they referred to them as to times when I had been away. 'That big tree fell down,' they said. 'My child died, while you were with the white people.' "[5] Like all good writings from the colonies describing the contact zone, hers imply also that her social relations with Africans are entirely voluntarist. It is the magnetism of her personality, her superior skill as a negotiator, her prestige, her good sense, her warmth, her humor, her skill as a physician, and not economic necessity, that accounts for Africans' attention to her. Becoming real to herself by seeing her reflection in their eyes, Dinesen becomes real and important to European and American audiences by reporting those reflections.

Middle-class white women sit in kitchens and dish; black teenagers stand on street corners and dis. Walter Benjamin would recognize the two as analogous forms of discourse in the sense that each has as its project assuring a community's cohesion and stasis. "Dissing" and "dishing" arise, as all gossip does for Benjamin, "because people do not wish to be misunderstood."[6] Intramural dissing or dishing bonds like with like. Gossip about others also binds like with like, not infrequently by insisting—hoping and fearing in equal quantities—that *they* are gossiping about *us*. I want here to hold Schreiner's and Dinesen's "gossip" about "Africans," like Lawrence's about "dark people," up against Africans' gossip about white folks as the latter gets represented in Schreiner's and Dinesen's "gossip" about Africans.

In the process I of course implicate myself in this gossip, since even to posit ways that Dinesen's and Schreiner's representations of Africans are misrepresentations presupposes a knowledge of real Africans that I cannot have. Neither making a trip to Africa nor being African myself would rectify that problem, since the Africans whom Schreiner and Dinesen lived and worked among can exist for me only as communities of interpretation to which I have no direct access.[7] But how these representations of Africans figure *structurally* in their system of self-production can be considered. This is the best any of us can do whenever we speak about people or texts from another place or time—as when any of us, whatever our ethnic or racial makeup, speak or write about Shakespeare.

My inspiration here comes from the writings of Rainer Nägele, Avital Ronell, and others who in recent years have produced a Benjamin who is a version of Benjamin's own eponymous hero, the destructive character. His virtues are many. Believing the paths our everyday thinking takes have become far too well worn and therefore barren, the destructive character works mightily to kick up some dust on them. He does this partly by cultivating oppositions whenever and however he can, because oscillation between absolutes allows us to "see double" or "with a double clarity." He is fond of intersections and crossroads, especially those "between the public and private zones that commingle demonically in prattle."[8] The destructive character can't be bothered worrying that his gossip will be overheard or that the object of his gossip objects to the stories he tells. That is a possibility he cultivates and even welcomes.

Dinesen constantly reminds her readers that she told her tales to while away the time during her long evenings in Africa and to entertain Denys Finch Hatton. Back in Denmark years later, writing them down became a means of consoling herself for having to leave Africa. She offers at every opportunity, in other words, extremely *personal* reasons for writing her two memoirs of Africa.

But she did make them public, even reciting portions aloud from memory to large audiences. In doing so she produces memoirs that are hybrids and places her works at the crossroads where prattle or gossip exists. Under Schreiner's hand the "public" discourse of the novel became a hybrid one too, her novels part of an autobiographical, even confessional, mode.

No one reading late nineteenth-century travel literature, anthropology, memoirs and journals of colonial administrators, or any of the discourses of the pseudosciences of sexology or eugenics produced during that time can fail to be struck by the extent to which *all* of it is gossip. Consider this passage, written by Havelock Ellis:

> While the men among primitive peoples are fitted for work involving violent and brief muscular effort, the women are usually much better able than the men to undergo prolonged and more passive exertion, and they are the universal primitive carriers. Thus, among the Andombies on the Congo, according to Sir H. H. Johnston, the women, though working very hard as carriers, and as labourers in general, lead an entirely happy existence; they are often stronger than the men and more finely developed, some of them, he tells us, having really splendid figures. And Parke, speaking of the Manyuema of the Arruwimi in the same region, says that they are fine animals, and the women very handsome; "they carry loads as heavy as those of the men, and they do it quite well."[9]

Ellis reproduces innumerable reports of happy African "tribes" like the Andombies and the Manyeuma, lifting his material from T. H. Parke's 1891 *Experiences in Equatorial Africa* and various other gossipy reports produced by earlier travelers to other continents and cultures. His raw materials also include letters from unnamed respondents, confessions from people with whom he's had conversations about their sexual practices, summaries of articles from medical and psychiatric journals, and stories from Freud frequently commingled with what can only be called found stories from unnamed sources. All of this material gets woven remarkably uncritically into the texture of his own gossip in his books on sexology.

Olive Schreiner was an active participant in this same gossip.

When the Africans in her political writings are abstract or mythic, they are idealized portraits: picturesque, noble, long-suffering, misunderstood, hardworking. But there is her other gossip as well, gossip designed to allay European fears over the threat of miscegenation. In her political writings, Africans tend to be either noble beyond belief (when her project is arguing for universal suffrage and self-determination for black South Africans) or debased beyond belief (when her project is consolidating personal relationships with her male sexologist, eugenicist friends). In the latter cases no European female, at least none of high intellect, could possibly be attracted to a male from any outpost of the empire:

> Were it possible to place a company of the most highly evolved human females—George Sands, Sophia Kovalevskaya—or even the average cultured females of a highly evolved race—on an island where the only males were savages of the Fuegan type who should meet them on the shores with matted hair and prognathous jaws, brandishing their instruments of death, to greet or welcome them, it is an undoubted fact, that, so great would be the horror felt by the females towards them, that not only would the race become extinct, but if it depended for its continuance on any approach to sex affection on the part of the women, death would certainly be accepted by all, as the lesser of two evils.

Nor could a European male of any discrimination possibly be attracted by any of the African females of South Africa. "A Darwin, a Schiller, a Keats . . . would probably be untouched by any emotion but horror," she assures readers of *Woman and Labour,* should they find themselves by any chance "cast into the company of a circle of Bushmen females with greased bodies and twinkling eyes, devouring the raw entrails of slaughtered beasts."[10]

One issue Schreiner's prose raises at points like these is how a woman so concerned to keep space between herself and everybody else could at the same time be so interested in close observation of others. Another question is how a woman who was publicly such a staunch defender of African self-determination, a fierce opponent of the Boer War for its impact on both native Africans and Afrikaners, an adamant feminist who resigned from feminist groups over suffrage for African women, could produce what Fanon calls a discourse of the bestiary.[11] The answer to the latter question is that working fiercely for African rights did not preclude Schreiner's working just as fiercely on her own psychic project, and that involved trying to forge personal and psychic alliances that would nourish her. And since the people with whom she tried to forge such alliances were notorious eugenicists and sexologists, her various discourses necessarily oscillate between dramatically opposed constructions of Africans. She can produce a gossip of "Africans" rivaling that of Havelock Ellis, Karl Pearson, or Edward Carpenter, who was writing things like *Intermediate Types among Primitive Folk* (1911) and *The Intermediate Sex*. When she does, hers becomes a contribution to the familiar discourse of social Darwinism: "The development of distinct branches of humanity has already brought about . . . a severance between races and classes which are in totally distinct stages of evolution."

> Where any two peoples inhabiting one country are so physically related that they have a powerful sexual attraction for each other, and that individuals brought face to face are unconscious of racial difference, the problem of union can be one of great moment, but cannot be one of permanent difficulty. Wait, do nothing, and in time, literally and not figuratively, love finds out the way, smooths away difficulties, and makes of the two races one. Where races are so far removed that they are more or less sexually repellant to one another that not difference of speech and training divide them, but marked differences of physical and mental conformation, of colour and build, then, if these two races are obliged to inhabit the same territory, the difficulty of arranging for their happy and useful interaction becomes steadily greater as time passes, *and does not tend to solve itself* [my italics].[12]

The passive construction, in which racial relations become formulated as a problem that is supposed to "solve itself," is telling. In *From Man to Man* the nadir in the relationship between Rebekah and her husband Frank comes not just because he's had one more affair, but because the last has been with a "Kaffir" woman. And everywhere either in her fiction or in her political writings that a potential for close contact between the races is considered, her sentences become so excessively long—sometimes one sentence takes up an entire page—that sorting out subject from verb becomes impossible, her syntax so involuted it cannot be followed. Sentences are introduced with phrases like "ignorant persons may suppose . . ." that confound all efforts to determine exactly whose thoughts are being represented and where she stands in relation to them. Only once does she make her position quite clear:

> This one thing at least is certain—that the conviction that it is undesirable that any two distinct human breeds should mingle does not necessarily imply superiority or inferiority in either. In my kennels I may have greyhounds and mastiffs, poodles and lap-dogs, St. Bernards. Because I desire to keep them distinct I do not therefore hold one breed superior to the other . . . if I refuse to mingle them recklessly, it is not because I value any so little, but all so much.[13]

But for all her pains to ensure careful separation of the "races" here as well as in her fictional sketches of African landscapes, where an Undine rubbing shoulders with Africans on the streets of DuToit's Pan can feel it is "glorious to be alone," Schreiner did manage after all to cohabit with Africans, and she did so by becoming one of Ellis's unnamed sources. Although she insisted in private letters that neither he nor anyone else could "ever possibly understand her," and though she drew all kinds of private enclosures around herself to ensure her privacy, at the same time she saw to it that gossip about her own sexuality got inserted into the gossip that makes up Ellis's writings on sexology. Biographers and critics have long known that Schreiner used Ellis as a kind of receptacle for her most private confessions about her own sexual inclinations and fantasies. Theirs was a perfect symbiotic relation meshing her need to tell and his to hear. But knowing this in the abstract hardly prepares one for a read through works like that compendium of hearsay, Ellis's two-volume *Studies in the Psychology of Sex*. Some of his work is made up of secondhand reports of others' "research" into things like "sexual periodicity" or the male menstrual cycle, "sexual inversion" and "the mechanism of detumescence." But much of it is no more than gossip at second, third, or even fourth hand. Unnamed sources testify to their own sexual practices or give accounts of others' sexual practices they claim to have observed. Whole rooms full of young women are said to reach orgasm as they experience the vibration from the sewing machines in the sweatshops, and we learn of it by way of Ellis's report of a "lady's" report of a supervisor's account of the young women's orgasms. We learn about the male's monthly menstrual cycle from Ellis's report of one man's wife's report of it. The closest we get to firsthand is in the letters Ellis reproduces from unnamed sources, as in the following, from the same section titled "Auto-Eroticism":

> As an example, I may mention the case of a man of 57, a somewhat eccentric preacher, etc., who writes: "My whole nature goes out so to some persons, and thrill and stir me so that I have an emission with no thought of sex, only the gladness of soul found its way out thus, and a glow of health suffused the whole body. There was no spasmodic conclusion, but a pleasing gentle sensation as the few drops of semen passed."[14]

Ellis adds parenthetically, "In reality, no doubt, not semen, but urethral fluid."

I gossip about this gossip because, reading Ellis's volumes on sexuality with the knowledge that Schreiner was both a close friend and a confidante who offered up her own experiences to Ellis, one cannot *not* presume that some of the reports in Ellis's works are accounts of Schreiner's own sexuality:

> A typical case known to me is that of a lady of 28, brought up on a farm. She is a handsome woman, of very large and fine proportions, active and healthy and intelligent, with, however, no marked sexual attraction to the opposite sex; at the same time she is not inverted, though she would like to be a man, and has a considerable contempt for women. She has an intense admiration for her own person, especially her limbs; she is never so happy as when alone and naked in her own bedroom, and, so far as possible, she cultivates nakedness.

> She knows by heart the various measurements of her body, is proud of the fact that they are strictly in accordance with the canons of proportion, and she laughs proudly at the thought that her thigh is larger than many a woman's waist. She is frank and assured in her manners, without sexual shyness, and, while willing to receive the attention and admiration of others, she makes no attempt to gain it, and seems never to have experienced any emotions stronger than her own pleasure in herself.[15]

Schreiner would have been a lady of twenty-eight in 1883. Ellis and Schreiner formally met less than a year later, in England in May 1884. Ellis reports being immediately impressed by her "short vigorous body in loose shapeless clothes, sitting on the couch, with hands spread on thighs."[16] Yvonne Kapp reports that on an early trip Schreiner took with Ellis, Eleanor Marx, and Edward Aveling, Schreiner once got so caught by a particular idea occurring to her that she burst out of her bedroom to share it with Ellis, appearing before him obliviously and unabashedly naked. Ellis told Hugh de Selincourt he had received nearly two thousand letters from Schreiner during the course of her life.[17] Many of those letters contain quite private confessions. In how many other passages in Ellis's works might Schreiner have managed to make the "hard, reserved stuff" of the inner self she insisted she could reveal to no one visible to all the world? Most interesting of all is the way the Africans who remain on the peripheries of her fictional worlds and who exist largely as abstractions in her political writings commingle with her in the pages of Ellis's treatises on sexuality, where her own sexual practices cohabit with reports of those of "Kavirondo," "Hamites," "Baganda," "Nilotic Ja-luo," "Bongo," "Mittoo," and "Niam-Niam," "Awemba," "Angondi," "Azimba," and "Wa-Yao."[18]

If Ellis, Schreiner, Dinesen, and the European communities of which they were a part were engaged in a kind of gossip about Africans that produced both a flattering positionality for themselves and a kind of safe commingling, it's pretty safe to assume Africans were gossiping back. What the Comaroffs call the riposte of the ruled can always be recognized behind the assertion of the ruler,[19] and particular instances are easier to recognize if we think of gossip in the spirit Benjamin's work makes possible. It's possible, for instance, to appreciate Thurman's account of Africans' calling Bror Blixen "Waddler" as evidence of a kind of proleptic African postmodernism dripping with irony, a postmodernism neither Bror Blixen nor most biographers recognize. Unfamiliar with the kind of self and other ironizing with which Africans were quite comfortable, Bror assumes that the Wahoga Africans called him means the far more flattering "wild duck." Schreiner's frequent references in her novels to giggling, eye-rolling house "Bushmen" give some opening onto this counterdiscourse of South Africans, especially that of the Tswana. "The sight of white men threw them into fits of laughter," say the Comaroffs, and they would with little ceremony "pronounce our customs clumsy, awkward, troublesome, and laugh extravagantly at them."[20] One constant presence in *From Man to Man* is Griet, "with her small, yellow-brown, Bushman face, with its touch of Hottentot." Always giving "pretended orders to the Kaffir maids," she "tumbl[es] in and out of the wagon over the heads of others, doing nothing and glorying in the confusion" (p. 77). There are also portraits of myriad unnamed and undifferentiated Africans in the kitchens, parlors, and kraals of the families of Lyndall, Rebekah, and Undine who are frequently caught giggling at the foibles of white folks.

When the trekker Snappercaps family stops its wagon for the night while carrying Undine to the diamond fields of Kimberley, readers' eyes are often directed off into the middle distance, where "among the bushes" we see "the driver, a great heavy Basuto," and "the leader, a sprightly little Hottentot . . . watching the meat on the roaster with . . . wicked little black eyes" and "a more than usually apish appearance" (pp. 258–59). If discomfort doesn't tempt us to slide right by such descriptions, we can recognize evidence of African gossip, and evidence as well of some of the serious compensatory work to which the white South African writer was apparently compelled. The confusions that inspire Schreiner's Bushmen to double up in glee and Europeans to regard their eyes as wicked usually grow out of white folks' naive misapprehensions. The whites keep thinking they are in control: of landscape, people, farm animals, even household routines. The

Bushmen's commanding knowledge of terrain and ability to travel soundlessly through landscape and appear suddenly, almost magically, has always unnerved white observers because it suggests the commanding knowledge these native Africans have that whites can't begin to approximate.

Although Noël Mostert, for instance, puts the word Bushman in quotation marks for the first thirty pages of his 1992 study *Frontiers,* he never replaces it with !Kung as might be expected. Several pages into his study, he instead owns that "Bushman" has so many "affectionate associations" for him and is so "intensely evocative" that rather than abandoning the term he chooses to abandon the quotation marks instead (p. 34). "The 'Bushman's' power to disturb was always great," he says. "They left something in the minds and emotions of everyone who came in contact with them. Being mysterious and elusive, they became part of the shades, of the unknown. Even their young," he says, "looked very old. People were afraid of magic in their minds, of instincts which they themselves long since had lost and no longer could comprehend." Exceedingly competent people, they "relish their own superiority over whites, and over other blacks." He notes that even the most conservative nineteenth-century South African historians like George McCall Theal grudgingly recognized their comfortable sense of competence and superiority to others living in the dry, unforgiving climate of the Karoo. In dry seasons, Mostert suggests, they would wait until Afrikaners and other blacks were "almost speechless from thirst," at which point they would nonchalantly lead the thirsty to where water could be found. A Bushman might wait with patient bemusement until others tried unsuccessfully to kindle a fire in the open air, then "look on with a smile of contempt until they desist, when he will produce his fire sticks and accomplish what they could not do" (p. 31).

Like everyone else of her acquaintance, Schreiner is prone to racial generalizing. Hottentots possess particularly artistic imaginations, are acute in their perceptions, have a complex language, but lack intellectual stamina. Bushmen are childlike and culturally unsophisticated. They are also dirty, and they smell.[21] Bantu possess great moral, physical, and intellectual strength and a spirit of proud independence and reserve. She admired the resourcefulness, strong sense of personal honor, and self-reliance of those other native Africans she referred to collectively as Kaffirs, though the word *lazy* tends to get attached to them in her prose. But the largely paternalistic posture evident in the rhetoric of teaching, training, and bringing up to standard the "backward" African that Schreiner adopts in even her most sympathetic political writings is seriously jeopardized by the actuality of Africans more competent than their white countrymen.

"In the long valleys of the African plains," Dinesen says in her essay "On Mottoes of My Life," "I have been surrounded and followed by sweet echoes, as from a sounding board. My daily life out there was filled with answering voices; I never spoke without getting a response; . . . The natives of Africa . . . came into my life as a kind of answer to some call in my own nature." She wrote frequently of those echoes of her own nature she recognized in Africans: "From the very first day [in Africa] an understanding sprang up between them and me, so that I may say that my love of them, of both sexes and all ages, as of all tribes—above all with the Masai, the warrior-tribe who were my neighbors when I rode across the river—was as strong a passion as I have ever known." The only unpardonable sin in her universe seems to have been cultivating the kind of nature that drew out no such answering echoes in others: a person for whom "conversation or correspondence . . . is nothing but a double monologue."[22] She believed that especially the "nature" of Somali and Maasai echoed her own, and she admired their proud resignation to the whims of fate that provided her with a model for the kind of resignation she believed was required of her in the face of a lifetime of physical pain caused by her syphilis, the emotional pain of a failed marriage, the early and untimely death of her lover, the loss of her farm in Kenya, the return to live out her life in her mother's home in Denmark. "Out of the blackest part of my soul, across the zebra striping of my mind, surges this desire to be suddenly *white,*" says Fanon,[23] and Dinesen and Schreiner could have said the reverse. Schreiner's Khoikhoi tend to "weep a lot" and are prone to "emotional storms."[24] As is Schreiner. Xhosa have a "severe, disciplined cultural reserve." As does she. Their questionings—"Why didn't god just *destroy* the evil spirit?" they wondered when missionaries talked about

Satan—frustrated and largely defeated efforts to convert them.[25] As Schreiner's heroines' relentless questioning defeats Christian belief in them, and nearly defeats her readers too.

The two women's gossip about Africans in some measure serves a function analogous to that of their identifications with European men. Their attraction to white men who have mastered the art of mastery was an identification with mastery itself: with the mastery they projected onto those men and to which they then found themselves attracted. This desire for a mastery already very much their own is glaringly obvious in their relations with other white women. Yvonne Kapp's observation, for instance, that Schreiner didn't so much take or have women friends as "capture" them becomes relevant again. This desire for mastery is obvious also in their relations with white men, where their belief in the ideal would necessarily have produced attempts to master—that is, to direct and dictate—the terms of intimate relationships. Each woman's literary and extraliterary writings speak resoundingly of her need to have mastery not only over the erotic relationship itself, but even over what the erotic relationship *meant* spiritually and philosophically. Even Dinesen's and Finch Hatton's lion hunt had to be made to demonstrate some universal truth of male-female relations the two of them were enacting. If their attraction to white men is an attraction to mastery, their attraction to African men is an attraction to stoicism coupled with a thinly disguised arrogance and a secret jeering in the face of mastery.

In the end, if Lacanian terms are adopted, dividing colonialist writers' representations of Africans into the imaginary and the symbolic, the African men constructed in Schreiner's and Dinesen's writings would have to be judged to be sometimes imaginary and sometimes symbolic; sometimes expressions of alterity, at other times of identity. Abdul JanMohamed, for instance, at the beginning of his essay on colonialist discourse, classifies Dinesen's writings with other "imaginary" colonialist texts that fetishize the other but acknowledges that they approach the "symbolic" by his essay's end. To the extent that Dinesen habitually distills all of Africa—"natives" as well as wildlife and lanscape—into what he sees as a fetishizing that transmutes "all specificity and difference into a magical essence," her Africans speak to her own narcissistic needs. But at times her texts seem aimed at finding syncretic solutions to the Manichaean oppositions—black/white, civilized/savage, adult/childlike—that colonial writers so often produce.[26] JanMohamed recognizes that resorting to such a rigorous system of binaries thwarts a fully nuanced understanding of the fluid process of alternating identity and alterity with which Dinesen constructed "Africans." A fully nuanced assessment of the two women's relationship with Africans can be uncovered only by close analysis of the minutiae of their everyday lives. As Lacan tells us, "The question of [the subject's] existence bathes the subject, supports him, invades him, tears him apart even." The exact outlines of this "subject" can be traced only by studying carefully all "the tensions, the lapses, the phantasies" produced "always by means of elements of the particular discourse in which the question is articulated in the Other."[27] When either woman lapses into imaginary portrayals of Africans, it is precisely because it is the African's *otherness*—that is, that he is black, not white; male, not female—that constitutes his allure and prompts Dinesen's and Schreiner's urge to merge. The logic is straightforward enough: If as woman I feel woman is other, if black African male personifies the most radical alterity, and if I identify myself as other personified, then that other—black African male—*c'est moi.*

But whether theirs are imaginary or symbolic Africans, their constructions need to be read also as a bit of history in the making. This is necessary even though uncovering their history making is difficult, especially in Schreiner's case, because the only point on which Afrikaans, indigenous African, and white South African historians seem to agree is the undecidability of certain crucial issues: When was it, exactly, that capitalism entered South Africa, and how long did the country retain feudal relations?[28] The question whether white-black relations in South Africa were capitalist or feudal during Schreiner's time there is not unimportant, since Schreiner, for instance, oscillates between a self-conception that involves seeing herself as a kind of noblesse oblige defender of native interests (which posits for her an identity as separate from them) and a self-conception as a fellow squatter/exile from her own land (which posits a strong identification with the black Africans among whom she lived, including to some extent the Bushmen whose portrait she paints so ambivalently). Determining this requires accepting the accuracy of a particular material analysis of South African history that is in crucial respects not verifiable.

But some things are. The bulk of Dinesen's and Schreiner's self-construction was being carried out between 1880 and 1930, making it coterminous with the height of colonialism in both countries, meaning their lifeworks necessarily are entangled in the nexus of racial relations in operation during that time. These relations were being worked out and worked over, presented and represented, as theirs were, in art and in psychology. Hal Foster is writing the "history" of that moment now. In psychoanalysis, he notes, primitivism and racialism were very much bound up together, as Freud began to associate instinct with the racial other. For the white European that racial other represented both free oral desire (through the cannibalism Europeans were convinced Africans practiced) and free genital desire (through the incest European propaganda suggested they practiced). This projection and sublimation constituting the prime project of imperialism was the project of modernist art as well. Freud recognized both cannibalism and incest as versions of a desire to merge with the other or turn other into same.

Dinesen and Schreiner demonstrate exactly such an urge, sharing with other modernists a fascination with the primitive as the origin of vitality and sexuality. That vibratory hum of alternating attraction and repulsion evident in Schreiner's descriptions of black Africans is evidence of her own process of projection and sublimation, alterity and identity in these terms.[29] As for Dinesen, JanMohamed believes that though she sympathizes with the plight of Africans under colonialism and makes genuine and significant efforts to improve their situation, she thinks of them frequently as primitive children.[30]

I would like to push beyond JanMohamed's analysis and that of Robert Langbaum as well. Langbaum regards Dinesen's elegaic tone in describing Africa and Africans as prompted by Africa's representing in Europeans' minds their own lost natural Eden as well as the more gentle *civilization* lost to their own continent. This is surely true. But Dinesen's tone is prompted also by far more immediate and concrete events occurring between 1918 and 1937.

In the earliest years of the British "protectorate" of Kenya, Kikuyu and European settlers could and did work together in substantial ways, evolving working relations that at least approximated collaboration and companionship. During these earlier years the Kikuyu were by and large more prosperous and successful farmers than were European settlers. But as a consequence of colonial policies conditions for Kikuyu worsened, and during her time there Dinesen would have experienced a gradual but profound constriction of her own relations with the Kikuyu laboring on her coffee plantation as colonial administrators passed a stream of laws designed to force them into ever more subservient labor relations with European settlers. One of the laws passed during this time was referred to by the Kikuyu as *kifagio,* Swahili for "sweeping out," since it enforced a systematic reduction in size of livestock herds they were allowed to own.[31]

If Dinesen passionately believed in the ideal, as she surely did in all areas of existence, that ideal included a vision of native African and colonial settler working side by side in harmony in some comfortable or comforting simulacrum of mutuality. In part the elegaic tone of her descriptions of her relations with Farah, with Kamante, or indeed with Africa itself was a product of her first-hand, day-to-day experiencing of the transformation, and loss, as a consequence of colonial policies, of that ideal relation between herself and the Africans she worked with. The "get ahead" spirit of the Kikuyu who provided much of the labor for Karen Coffee that she so much admired and emulated was being betrayed by the colonial system, by the Resident Native Labor Ordinance of 1927, which made that getting ahead impossible and was beginning to transform the Kikuyu into "Mau Mau" who would attack European-"owned" property by 1950.

In *Shadows on the Grass* and *Out of Africa* elegy alternates, then, with regular and palpable articulations of exasperation at colonial administrators. Just as palpable is her closest African workers' genuine appreciation of her efforts—by definition always small, local, and doomed to be ineffective—at fighting on their behalf, with the district commissioner in particular. In my earliest readings of Dinesen's two memoirs her constant references to the esteem in which the Africans held her—calling her "Lioness

Blixen"—seemed nothing more than the usual colonial writer's self-aggrandizing accounts of the adulation of a "simple" people for a "greater" person of the sort that can be found in all colonial writings, such as the "Jaffna" chapter of Leonard Woolf's *Growing*. But *behind* Dinesen's pseudomodest accounts of the admiration with which Africans regarded her, and behind her palpable exasperation at not being able to "help" the Kikuyu, are not only her reports of genuine Kikuyu appreciation of her efforts in their behalf—fighting for schooling for the *watoto* that would extend beyond the meager five and a half hours a week they were allowed by law[32]—but evidence of *her* distress at the gradual worsening of Kikuyu prospects during the years she was in Kenya.

Whether Dinesen's Africans are imaginary or symbolic depends also, however, on which culture she is representing and which position in her own self-production she allots to particular people at any particular time. The positionality she allows herself most often in her African writings is predictably that of protector, adviser, guide, good parent, the familiar discursive domain of the colonizer Fanon describes: "If [I] leave, all is lost."[33] Herself precariously balanced between emotional and financial independence and dependence, the reasons she produced Africans in this way should be obvious. Producing a secure home for herself required producing Africans who reflected back her own self-sufficiency and power. Her "Kikuyu" do this.

But she actually produces multiple versions of them. If in her personal relations with European men like Bror Blixen and Denys Finch Hatton the male was equated with unpredictability and rakishness, necessitating her production of herself as their seductress, a storytelling Scheherazade who worked to keep their attention and interest, in the Somali Farah and the Kikuyu Kamante in particular Dinesen found the men her own psychic homeostasis required: men who took her seriously as a person and worker and who would *be there* for and with her. They had to. Their livelihood and that of their families required it. And in order for her *own* self to be enhanced because these men took her seriously, they had of course themselves to be serious men. And so she produced them.

In substantial ways Dinesen's relationships with African men more closely approximated the ideal of marriage articulated in *On*

Modern Marriage than did any of her relationships with European men. In holding up one exemplary marriage in that book, she notes that "the relationship between the spouses was no personal one, and strictly speaking, they could not personally or directly bring happiness to or disappoint each other, but must mutually provide the greatest significance to each other through the relationship they occupied and the importance they had for their mutual task in life" (p. 67). The same is true for Schreiner, whose narrator (indistinguishable from Schreiner herself) in *From Man to Man* pronounces,

> Some women with complex, many-sided natures, if love fails them and one half of their nature dies, can still draw a kind of broken life through the other. The world of the impersonal is left them: they can still turn fiercely to it, and through the intellect draw in a kind of life—a poor, unbroken, half asphyxiated life, not what it might have been, like the life of a man with one lung eaten out by disease—who has to live through the other alone—but still life. (pp. 92–93)

It would be difficult to determine exactly when the passage above was composed, given Schreiner's work on the novel from 1874 to 1920, but in its heavy reliance on metaphors of disease and infection it seems to be an instance of the kind of prose Samuel Hynes identifies as particularly prevalent around the time of World War I in a great many writers, including Virginia Woolf and D. H. Lawrence, who tended to rely regularly on such metaphors of infection.[34] They can be found in Schreiner's political prose as well, most notably in a speech on the Boer War given July 9, 1900, in Cape Town, in which she insisted that even if the war was successful it would result in a body politic that had healed itself outside while "deep within the body . . . [a] foreign irritating substance [would] produce disease and putrefaction." Annexing the Free State and the Transvaal was "an attempt to introduce into the body social of South Africa . . . an irritating and extraneous substance."[35]

These metaphors may have their origin in the social and political moment when they were constructed, as do her characteristically high modernist references to the impersonal in the passage above. But if the impersonal was a term very much in the air during the time she was writing, the terms in which Schreiner frames the value she sees in the impersonal—bluntly, as a kind of booby prize—are hardly destined to produce much happiness or satisfaction with whatever successes each gained as a result of her impersonal efforts. The ideal marriage Dinesen describes in *On Modern Marriage,* based on mutuality, impersonality, and a shared belief in the importance of a mutual task, is in no small measure also psychically compensatory. The more success Schreiner may have achieved in the impersonal world of political and social activism, the more those very successes must necessarily figure as evidence of her exactly proportional failures in the realm of the personal.

In this respect at least Dinesen was more efficaciously balanced, largely because the African fellow workers her writings produced enabled her in turn to produce a particular identity for herself. Schreiner's African men, largely distant abstractions, dots on the distant veld, tumbling, grinning, and lazy or degraded and demoralized by colonial policies, leave no place for her own construction as a competent partner in any endeavor with them. She cannot work the fields with them as Dinesen does, nor does she work with (rather than *for*) them for their political self-determination. The space she so desperately needs to alleviate her psychic claustrophobia eludes her because of her entanglement with European rather than African men. Possessing not only inherited power of place, position, and rhetoric but all the other privileges and entitlements accruing to white European males, Havelock Ellis and Karl Pearson could—and did—actively resist her productions of them, leaving her without the more comfortable and comforting homeostasis Dinesen's productions of African men provided her.

Dinesen's productions of Kikuyu men may have frequently been respectful and admiring but she was also capable of producing representations bearing out Fanon's harshest interpretation of colonials' productions of Africans: "torpid creatures, wasted by fevers, obsessed by ancestral customs."[36] African men are too silly and frightened to get themselves to doctors when they ought, too petty to resolve simple quarrels without her intervention.

Her constructions of African women can unfortunately be even harsher. African women exist in Schreiner's and Dinesen's lifeworks in three forms and three only. "African woman" is a large, highly abstract category holding a particular place in their philosophic schema about what woman is. Seen up close, African women are servants in the house, efficient or incompetent, but in either case those over whom Schreiner and Dinesen are masters—as honorary males. But in Dinesen's memoirs African woman also predictably represents the eternal feminine in two avatars. She is earthy, long-suffering, capable of stoically enduring great pain, or she is an entirely imaginary creature, in the Lacanian sense: a "dusky dove," a "giraffe," and much else that succeeds in painting African women into the background of a mystical landscape in which they become indistinguishable from the flora and fauna of the African continent.

The coquetry Dinesen so often attributes to African women is of course what she herself felt the need to practice to keep the attention of Denys Finch Hatton, and Somali women in particular bear that symbolic weight. They are "coquettish, wily, covetous beyond belief, and sweetly merciful at the core."[37] When African women are represented as radical alterity it is most frequently when their emotional lives are *least* different from her own. Her extraordinary interest in their domestic arrangements can be explained by her own unorthodox position in that regard. For many of her years in Africa she was a woman separated from her husband, geographically or psychically or both, and a mistress engaged in a relationship with a fickle and easily distracted man. "I had read the old Nordic Sagas as a child," Dinesen says, "and now in my intercourse with the Somali I was struck by their likeness to the ancient Icelanders. I was therefore pleased to find Professor Östrup . . . making use of a common term to characterize Arabs and Icelanders: he calls them 'attitudinizers.'"[38] Here her maneuver is a simple production neither of alterity nor of identity. Dinesen's constructions of Somali women as dusky doves, though it seems to place African women into the kind of picturesque Sara Suleri describes for the Anglo woman, places European women in the same place in an apparent gesture of interracial and intercontinental sisterhood. But it simultaneously *removes* Dinesen from membership in that expanded sisterhood.

Suleri suggests that the Anglo-Indian woman writing about

the Indian woman produced "a body transcribed but not read,"[39] because to read the body of the Indian woman would be to read her own history there as well. But Dinesen's memoirs scatter readings of African bodies on every page, and this occurs because she sees those bodies from the perspective of one who constructs herself as not woman. This makes her readings largely indistinguishable from those of the male colonial. Her subject position is the familiar one of the privileged possessor of the masculine gaze. It is the gaze of the connoisseur. "Most Somali women have a certain dignity that is attractive; this one is not beautiful, but they are finely formed with beautiful hands and feet, and carry themselves well."[40] African women become here the other of her desires, exactly as Native Americans did for her father. She is discriminating consumer and assessor of their comparative beauty; avid participant in the mystification and mythologizing of African femininity; impatient and critical judge of their superstition, self-centeredness, or ineffectiveness in times of crisis; admirer of their stoicism in times of pain. In her anger that no one of his wives had taken the sick Juma to the hospital, she almost hisses: "Beastly hags, [they] could not be bothered to send for me; native women are revolting, quite without feeling."[41] Somali women have a "ravenous ambition to distinguish themselves before all others and at any cost to immortalize themselves through a word or gesture."[42] Whether she paints them affectionately, "seated, like large flowers, on the grass,"[43] or as beastly hags, they are bodies transcribed directly from the male colonial's book. The only way they are different is that her African women often tend to be attempts to exorcise her own most discomfiting "stuff": *her* ravenous ambition, *her* wily, covetous nature.

From the point of view of her own psychic health, what is sorriest about these constructions of African women is that they cut Dinesen off from precisely that group of people with whom, as a dawn-to-dusk farmer, she might far more happily have identified. In Kenya's Kisumi district African women—those dusky doves in her memoirs—were spending an average of two hours before sunrise and from 12 to 2 P.M. and 6 to 10 P.M. each day on domestic labor. In addition they spent five to ten hours a week gathering wood and another 10.8 to 14.1 hours on food and cash crop farming. Carrying water took up 1.9 hours of their week during the wet season and 3.6 hours during the dry.[44] They were good farmers.

Partly Dinesen just didn't let herself get close enough to identify with these African women: her myth of Africa got in the way, just as preapartheid conditions in South Africa interfered with Schreiner's representation of the contact zone between white and black women there. Although it was partly also each woman's identification as male that got in the way, the discreet distance from which Dinesen describes African women may have been her way of allowing them the freedom from surveillance that she as white woman lacked, a lack she responded to in part by constructing the complicated image evident in her photographs. "I have a fear of being an object," she tells her brother Thomas. But her response to that fear, unfortunately, is to produce African women as just that: they sit, watching the *ngoma,* like large flowers on the grass.

This is not to suggest, however, that the psychic payoffs Dinesen's gossip about African men *or* women generates necessarily preclude their doing other kinds of work at the same time, a consequence perhaps of the generic hybrid her works seem to be. Typical of this hybridity is the passage here from *Shadows on the Grass:*

> Farah was a Somali, which means that he was no Native of Kenya but an immigrant to the country from Somaliland further north. In my day there were a large number of Somali in Kenya. They were greatly superior to the Native population in intelligence and culture. They were of Arab blood and looked upon themselves as pure-blood Arabs, in some cases even as descendants of the Prophet. On the whole they thought very highly of themselves. . . . The Natives of the land, the Kikuyu, Wakamba, Kawirondo and Masai, have got their own old mysterious and simple cultural traditions, which seem to lose themselves in the darkness of very ancient days. We ourselves have carried European light to the country quite lately, but we have had the means to spread and establish it quickly. In between, an oriental civilization, violent, cruel and very picturesque, gained a foothold in the Highlands through the slave and ivory trade. . . . From here slaves were freighted east-

> ward to Arabia, Persia, India and China . . . you will see little black Negro pages in old Venetian pictures. From here came the forty black slaves who, together with forty white, carried Aladdin's jewels to the Sultan on their heads. . . . The Sultan of Zanzibar, I was told when I was there in 1916, was still paid an appanage of £5,000 as compensation for his loss of income from the slave trade. I have seen, at Zanzibar, the market-place and the platform where slaves were put up for sale.[45]

I have quoted at length here because few passages in all her works are so richly suggestive. What art is being produced here, and what history being written in this curious mix of gossip, myth, fairy tale, history, and spectacle? In it Dinesen is partly the quintessential Benjaminian storyteller in the best sense, bearing witness to a particularly important history. At the same time and to no less a degree, however, she speaks to the accuracy of Jean-Loup Amselle's deconstruction of the concept of ethnicity as she constructs "ethnic" groups in order to divide and conquer.[46] Might hers not be regarded as the aesthetic and ethic of the consumer, revealing the consumer's instinct to choose and recommend one "product" over another—Somali are better than Kikuyu—in the way a travel writer recommends the amenities of one hotel over those of another, or a man the figure of one woman over that of another?

The same hybrid writing produces similar mixed results wherever it is found in Dinesen's writings, and it is of course found everywhere. "The Kikuyu, Kawirondo and Wakamba, the people who worked for me on the farm," she says of her fellow workers, "in early childhood were far ahead of white children at the same age, but they stopped quite suddenly at a stage corresponding to that of a European child of nine."[47] What is not visible here in her consumer's assessment of her workers is how far the *watoto*'s arrested development was the result of systematic sacrificing of the education of these children to the labor needs of European settlers in Kenya. Tabitha Kanogo's "Self-Help among Squatters" fills in the silent spaces in Dinesen's African gossip here. Some white settlers began creating makeshift schools for squatter children, having discovered that the promise of schooling for their children would lure more Kikuyu workers to their farms. But not only was there no clearly defined curriculum in these schools, the settlers who instituted them often set strict limits on the number of hours per day a child could attend, it being clearly understood that the teaching was in no way to interfere with the farmwork.[48]

To be fair, it must be said that Dinesen was genuinely interested in the education of squatter children, and several incidents reported in *Shadows on the Grass* are devoted to that concern. But predictably, that concern takes the form of individual attention to particular people rather than any systematic addressing of the educational needs of these workers and their children, who were of course also working for her at Karen Coffee. Abdullahi was a Somali, Farah's younger brother. Dinesen's gossip about him reveals the same maddening mix of concern, paternalism and maternalism, whimsy, sentimentality, sensitivity and insensitivity that characterizes so much of her African gossip. It reveals the "place" in which she places him, and the place she thereby generates for herself. "A loyal servant to the house, particularly pleasant to me because he was personally so clean and neat, and because I found in him a rare talent for gratitude," he is also a skilled mathematician and a whiz at chess, a game he was never taught but at which he acquired great skill by watching Finch Hatton play opponents at the farm.

> When Abdullahi had been at Ngong for a year he confided to me his passionate ambition to go to school. I felt it to be in a way legitimate, but since there was no Mohammedan school in the Highlands, I should have to send him to the Islamic school in Mombasa, and at the time I could ill afford to do so. When I told him: "I have not got the money, Abdullahi," he took in the fact resignedly, but from time to time, on an evening when Farah was not in the house, he came up to ask me: "Have you got more money now, Memsahib?"[49]

Years after leaving Africa Dinesen, at his request, had a typewriter sent to Abdullahi from Denmark. The absence of schooling for Abdullahi is portrayed in Dinesen's gossip here, however, not as a structural problem, and surely not as a consequence of specific colonial policies. It is an *individual* problem to be solved, if at all, through the ingenuity, largesse, whim, or ability of Isak Dinesen—or Lioness Blixen. The largest part of *Shadows on the Grass* constructs for her the classic identity of the pioneer going it alone, solving individual health, economic, and educational problems for the natives as if neither she nor they were playing roles specifically designed for them by those policies that were systematically and indeed purposively generating exactly those problems she was setting herself to solve. "For some of my years on the farm I had been holding the office of *fermier général* there—that is, in order to save the Government trouble I collected the taxes from my squatters locally and sent in the sum total to Nairobi," she says in *Shadows on the Grass* (p. 85), completely obscuring the fact that it was exactly those taxes she was collaborating in collecting that were impoverishing the natives she cared so much about.

Dinesen's gossip about this young African man, then, writes her self into two different but interconnected scenarios. In one she is the educated consumer revealing her discriminating good taste, who can judge among the "good" and "bad" properties—habits, looks, bearing—of the various African "tribes" she lived among. In the other she is the familiar romantic fabulist spinning a tale of noblesse oblige on the one side and fealty and gratitude on the other. In the latter role she oscillates: sometimes she is the knowledgeable colonial who can help natives negotiate their bureaucratic tangles, bemused at their ignorance or naïveté; at other times she identifies herself as one similarly victimized by and entangled in the same bureaucracy and the same policies.

If Dinesen's oscillations between identity with and alterity from East Africans were determined by which groups and which gender she was representing as well as by an oscillation between identity and alterity set in motion by what she saw as the Africans' *own* oscillation between acceptance and defiance, modesty and conceit, Olive Schreiner's positionality in South Africa was also an oscillating affair. Being English in South Africa at all was, as she pointed out, itself a form of oscillation: like being a Jew, being "either Christ or Judas." This particular oscillation generated its own form of alterity/identity. The Boers too were an either/or people like the Jews, seeing themselves as either chosen or damned. It was not until the late nineteenth century—during Schreiner's own lifetime—that Afrikaners began to regard themselves as "the chosen people." By that time "nationalist political myth makers were at work rewriting folk history to provide evidence of a deep-rooted national ethos."[50] Except for the Huguenots, Afrikaners were uneducated and had not previously seen themselves as "a people" at all. But as they became more successful commercially they found themselves in a tension of absolutes. Their success was proof that they *were* a chosen people. But wealth was associated with Baal, with corruption. There grew in them a fear of what they called *overvloed,* a term having simultaneous positive and negative connotations, meaning both overabundance and flood. The closest way to render that spirit aesthetically or visually, Sparks suggests, would be by reference to Brueghel's swarming canvases filled with celebrating peasants whose very seething, writhing joyousness strikes one as singularly discomfiting. The weird language play characteristic of Afrikaners to this day—calling apartheid "multinational democracy" for instance—is in Sparks's view not only an attempt at self-deception but an effort to ease their inner moral tensions about this oscillation between feeling themselves a chosen people (because successful) and feeling damned (because successful).[51]

At precisely the moment when this oscillation between contradictory senses of themselves would have been forming in the minds of Afrikaners, Olive Schreiner not only was living among them but was in her own formative years as well. If Dinesen's Maasai and Somali were that complex mix of projection and introjection characteristic of fetishism, Schreiner's Boers were much the same. "I learnt to love the Boer," she says. "I learnt that in the African Boer we have one of the most intellectual virile and dominant races the world has seen; a people who beneath a calm and almost stolid surface hide the intensest passions and the most indomitable resolution." Over and over the same praise recurs in her descriptions of the Boers. They have "indomitableness," an "unlimited power of self-control . . . characteristic of the average Boer man and above all the average Boer woman."[52] Those stolid, secretly passionate, long-suffering Boers were poised with Schreiner on that deictical/deixical axis: both her and not her.

Schreiner's discursive positionings can also be traced to the cultural position of the early British settlers of 1820, who in a very real sense had been tricked into coming to South Africa at all. High-mindedly they had thought their country was persuading them to come to Africa to be missionaries. But their more immediate value to England was that they would serve as a barrier, separating black from Boer.

This position would have profoundly affected how Schreiner saw herself—as a border person, as a peacemaker or conciliator, the way she constructs herself throughout *An English South-African's View of the Situation,* where she tries valiantly to interpose herself between England and the Transvaal, urging the British not to try to annex the Boer Republic (p. 74). But this self-identification as a border treader and mediator goes far back: it is the liminal position she learned early to turn into literary capital. The British had annexed the Dutch Cape Colony in 1795. By that time the Afrikaners or Trekboers had become probably at least as tribal in spirit as the native Africans they lived among. Since the Afrikaners had left Europe before the Enlightenment developments of the eighteenth century and had not maintained much contact with Europe since their arrival in Africa, they had become something of a backwater of European culture. Sparks calls them "a backward fragment of Western Civilization," missing out completely on the Age of Reason, liberalism, democracy, and the Enlightenment in general. Their isolation "froze them in time, causing their imagination to lie fallow and their intellects to become inert."[53]

Coming to South Africa somewhat later than these Trekboers, the British brought Enlightenment principles with them. They ended up dominating South Africa economically and militarily while losing out to the Afrikaners politically, a condition that continues to the present. To this day the British remain a minority, apart from but sandwiched between Boers and Africans. The civil service is dominated by Afrikaners, and white English-speaking South Africans seem to have only language in common. By contrast, the Africans and the Afrikaners share in many ways the common experiences of trekking, war, farming, and the like.

These "backward" Boers were fiercely independent, forming few institutions, behaving as rugged individualists, by and large indifferent to forming communities. They were in this sense absolutely *opposite* from the black Africans, whose ethos and philosophy was that of *ubuntu:* the word signifies the communal and is usually translated as "people are people through other people."[54]

Schreiner fiercely fought British attempts in April 1877 to annex the Transvaal, which was a Boer republic: to make, that is, the move that finally inspired the individualistic Boers to coalesce as a group. This is the moment when nationalism was born. Mining began in earnest in South Africa in 1870, and by 1886 the diamond and gold rush was on. After the British won the Boer War of 1899–1902, as part of the peace settlement they "gave" the Boers all of South Africa to rule over the blacks,[55] a move Schreiner protested as vehemently as she had protested the war. *Closer Union* had warned of the dire consequences that would follow passage of the Land Act, which prohibited further land purchases by blacks, put a stop to tenant farming and sharecropping, and eventuated in the movement of over one million black Africans into a captive labor market. Schreiner's dire predictions were all quite true.

Schreiner's psychic oscillations between identity with and alterity from Africans were also produced partly by her physical position in the South African landscape—between Boer and black African and between the different ethos the groups represented. Her desire to be a physician or a nurse, which her precarious health thwarted, for instance, was a manifestation of the *ubuntu,* communal, help one another spirit she would have absorbed from black Africans. So was her desire to help all women as a class, to serve as a kind of mediator between men and women and as an explicator of women's position and needs. Clearly she believed that, as someone closer to being a man than most women, she was best suited for such a role.

But Schreiner's desire, socially and politically, just to be *left alone* was at least as strong as her desire to help. The equal valence of those conflicting desires was a root cause of her propensity to get exasperated when she was asked to help others and didn't want to. That desire to be left alone has its roots in part in the individualistic, every man for himself spirit of the Trekboers among whom she lived. One can see that the black African spirit of *ubuntu* and the Trekboer spirit of individualism were perpetually at war in her, making her in yet one more way a nomad, at home neither in cooperation with women nor in isolation from them, neither in South Africa nor in Europe, neither among men nor among women. Positioned as they were between Europe and Africa, and psychically positioned between the single and the married life and between identifying both as males and as females, Dinesen and Schreiner came to think of themselves as in-betweens who could turn that status into something positive by becoming go-betweens, intercessors, and mediators. Dinesen was forever positioning herself in her discourses of Africa as intercessor or go-between: between the district commissioners of Kenya and the Maasai, between wounded Kikuyu and the hospitals they mistrusted, between the district commissioners and the squatters on her coffee plantation, between feuding Somali and Kikuyu.[56]

What can be recognized in all these oscillations between identification and alterity—between Africans (Somali and Maasai) as simultaneously conqueror and victim; between Africans (Afrikaners) as simultaneously chosen and damned; between, ultimately, imaginary (narcissistically represented) and symbolic (syncretically represented) Africans—is something partly explicable as a form of fetishism, which is itself a kind of oscillation, as Homi Bhabha notes: "always a 'play' or vacillation between the archaic affirmation of wholeness/similarity—in Freud's terms: 'all men have penises'; in ours: 'All men have the same skin/race/culture; and the anxiety associated with lack of difference'—again, for Freud: 'some do not have penises'; for us, 'Some *do not* have the same skin/race/culture.'" Within discourse, Bhabha sees the stereotype as "[giving] access to an 'identity' which is predicated as much on mastery and pleasure as it is on anxiety and defence, for it is a form of multiple and contradictory belief in its recognition of difference and disavowal of it. This conflict of pleasure/unpleasure, mastery/defence, knowledge/disavowal, absence/presence," has a fundamental significance for colonial discourse.[57]

The histories of Dinesen's and Schreiner's gossip of Africans and their own personal history constitute a Benjaminian one I write in and out of my own reception of those histories in the present. This history catches these two subjects in various acts of self-formation, and those acts absolutely require a particular mix of race and class, as well as sexual relations. It is a history that sees these women as neither financially nor emotionally able to control entirely their own destinies, and as displacing that identity onto native Africans, whose protectors and defenders they construct themselves to be. Ruth First and Ann Scott ask themselves, How could Olive Schreiner "'live like a man, but like a woman as well?' (The question was Schreiner's own.)." Their conclusion is that she found it impossible to do both successfully, because "her sexual identity was split, and there was no way for her as a woman to integrate the powerful, aspiring part of herself." They conclude that "in her personal relationships at least, she became a child and gave up her claims to control."[58] But behind the "child" or abject female in her personal letters was someone resourceful, competent, disdainful of humility and anyone who would demand it of her: someone masculine. Schreiner's gossip of Africans oscillates between portraits of deference and defiance because she did too. Dinesen's gossip produces Africans who oscillate between childlike stubbornness and childlike gratitude, between what she sees as self-defeating arrogance and a stoic surrender to whatever the powers that be handed them, because that was what she herself was.

I propose that Schreiner's and Dinesen's representations of Africans as identical can be seen as something more and other than purely narcissistic productions of the Lacanian or Kristevan imaginary—if specific historical and physical contexts are included in the equation—and like Robert Young in *White Mythologies* I am ambivalent about the efficacy of psychoanalytic explanations in analyses of the colonial situation. They do, however, manage to keep open the possibility of seeing what Dinesen represented as the philosophical bearing of the African peoples among whom she lived, and Schreiner as the characteristic bearing of the Boers, as philosophical stances projected onto African people. They are stances that Dinesen recognized as distinctly Kierkegaardian or Nietzschean (and therefore distinctly her own), and Schreiner as distinctly Schopenhauerian (and therefore distinctly *her* own).

In fact, everything in Dinesen's lifework is a gloss on Kierkegaard, whose writings echo her inborn love of mystification, paradox, and innuendo—her amusement at fate's perverse whimsicality. Dinesen's conviction that African and European differences produce "unity," for instance, could have come straight out of *Either/Or:* "Generally speaking, the imperfection in everything human is that its aspirations are achieved only by way of their opposites. I shall not discuss the variety of formations, which can give a psychologist plenty to do (the melancholy have the best sense of the comic, the most opulent often the best sense of the rustic, the dissolute offer the best sense of the moral)."[59] Fate's perverse humor she saw when Denys Finch Hatton found it convenient for a time to move his things to her farm. You would think she'd have been pleased. The remark his move elicits is Kierkegaardian: "When the gods want to punish you," she says, "they answer your prayers." As he put it:

> I was transported to the seventh heaven. There sat all the gods assembled. . . . What do you want, asked Mercury. "Do you want youth, or beauty, or power, or long life, or the most beautiful girl, . . . Choose but one thing." . . . For a moment I was bewildered; then I addressed the gods, saying: "My esteemed contemporaries, I choose one thing—that I may always have the laughter on my side. Not one of the gods said a word; instead, all of them began to laugh. From that I concluded that my wish was granted.[60]

Loving Socrates because the sage would not *directly* help anyone but would instead quiz people on the street on some universal truism until some contradiction or consequence confused them—this willful cultivation of paradox is a fondness Dinesen shares with modernism itself.

Dinesen's Somali and Maasai might have been produced by Nietzsche himself: they embody that ecstatic nihilism he praises at the end of *The Will to Power.* "*What is noble?*—That one constantly has to play a part. That one seeks situations in which one has constant need of poses. That one leaves happiness to the great majority. . . . That one knows how to make enemies everywhere, if the worse comes to the worst even of oneself. That one constantly contradicts the great majority not through words but through deeds."[61] "Muhammadanism makes the people who embrace it or have been brought up to it," says Dinesen, "clean and proud and gives them a kind of heroic or stoic view of life, but also . . . makes them, to us, quite intolerably doctrinaire and intolerant."[62] The Muslim Somali becomes the embodiment of Nietzsche's "nomad thought."[63]

Schreiner too saw life, and Africans, through the eyes of European philosophers. "I have been looking at that life of Schopenhauer to-day," she confesses in a letter to Havelock Ellis. "If I had ever read him, or even knew before I came to England that such a man existed, one would say I had copied whole ideas in the *African Farm* and *From Man to Man* from him."[64] Schopenhauer was convinced, in *The World as Will and Representation,* that we cannot see the world, but only what our eyes *see* and *think* of as "world." What passes for our knowledge is our recognition of the relation we—our eyes and our minds—have with objects; in other words, our knowledge is all *idea.* Common sense is a blind force, or what Schopenhauer calls, paradoxically, "will." Existence is inevitably then a continuous yearning for some undefinable relation with the real toward which we platonically stretch but recognize as unreachable.

In the *content* of Schopenhauer's philosophy Schreiner must have felt a harmonic with the material conditions of her own life: the straining toward a oneness with the "ideal man" she knew could never be: "the dream, the faith, that I should find someone just like myself [that] was with me all through my childhood," adding, "I think one would hardly believe how young it was there."[65] The Schopenhauerian straining after an ideal companion conflates two dreams into one. The dream of an ideal companion would have provided a *place* to call home: "how young it was *there,*" she says. Habitually, Schreiner became fascinated by particular men, thought them great minds, got to know them better, and revised her estimate downward. Of one she wrote to Havelock Ellis: "He is very selfish, I think. I told him so.—where is the ideal man? Just a wild dream."[66]

Schreiner borrows also Schopenhauer's notion of the function of art and the artist. If oneness and harmony with the real are perpetually thwarted dreams, the artist's work may perhaps provide a kind of temporary liberation from the suffering, the longing that the absence of that union brings. Art allows us to connect with some mysterious, intuitive vision of a meaning to life, something scientific knowledge by its very nature can never do. Her letters are riddled with Schopenhauerian references: to Edward Carpenter, "We have each to fight out our lives alone, we can never intentionally help others, the help comes by accident when it comes."[67] Doing her own self-policing—"If I can only be strong, I can . . ."—the emphasis on *will* that she would have found in Schopenhauer perfectly matches what she gained psychically from her mother.

But these Schopenhauerian, Nietzschean, and Kierkegaardian impulses need to be circulated through Africa, need to be "contaminated" one with the other, as Kwame Anthony Appiah calls it in *In My Father's House.* Constituting creative deformations of the cultural materials they inherited and amid which they lived, and a layering of African cultural materials over European, Dinesen's and Schreiner's lifeworks are every bit as radically syncretic as African art as Europeans have characterized it. But, as Valentin Mudimbe noted in private conversation, so also of course is the art of *any* culture.

The *particular* forms borrowed from African sources, and Schreiner's and Dinesen's particular versions of Afro-European or Euro-African syncretism, constitute a huge topic I hope others take up more extensively than I can here. But let me begin with the most basic. In the African colonial situation, art across Africa at least since the nineteenth century has habitually represented woman as suffering: "Man works; woman weeps." As Bogumil Jewsiewicki suggests, in Central African countries in particular, in artistic constructions of the feminine in Zaire and the Belgian Congo, for example, one sees *only* representations of woman as suffering.

"In many ways," Dinesen confesses to her mother, "my relationship with Bror was a problematic task,—one that I believed to be the most important of my life,—and that I have been quite unable to fulfill."[68] Olive Schreiner is likely to have confessed similar sentiments in one or another of her many letters, but the seriously censored persona that Cronwright-Schreiner produced in his collection of her correspondence, her urging recipients of her letters to burn them, and the absence of a full collection of her letters all make it unavailable.

Dinesen's love for Denys Finch Hatton assured her of a healthy dose of suffering. "Once God Almighty said: 'I will produce a self-working . . . machine for enduring suffering, . . . capable of the largest amount of suffering in a given space,'" Schreiner says, "and he made woman. But he wasn't satisfied that he [had] reached the highest point of perfection; so he made a man of genius. . . . [Not] satisfied yet . . . he combined the two—and made a woman of genius—and he was satisfied!"[69] "You know, darling, when I say I'm happy I don't think you understand," Schreiner writes to Havelock Ellis. "I think you think I mean something like what is ordinarily called happiness. I don't think the feeling I call 'happiness' has much likeness to that. It means *that I am for a time in a condition to master my own feelings and keep them from rending me* [her italics]."[70] Explicitly regarding feelings as something to be conquered, in *On Modern Marriage* Dinesen puts the word *feelings* in citation, apparently believing even the word needed to be walled off from the rest of her discourse. In marriage, "on principle, both spouses were probably obliged to close their eyes amiably to that aspect of their partner's nature that was ruled by the heart and what were known as 'feelings'—provided that there was no betrayal of the idea that for both of them represented what was most important and ideally elevated in their life."[71]

What seems to have been an active cultivation of a state of unrequited love on each woman's part may have had as its aim the production of themselves as some version of the African mythic figure of suffering woman. As Walter Benjamin suggests, the cultivation of the thing not fulfilled always generates a *surfeit* of something else—in this case an abundance of creative energy and an opportunity for identification with the mythic man for work, woman for suffering characteristic of some African myths and of the stolid, long-suffering Boer women Schreiner professed to admire so much.

Schreiner found her way out of her construction of woman as suffering by articulating suffering endlessly (thereby externalizing and expelling it) in letters, by enduring it after the model of the stolid Boer women among whom she lived, by intellectually transforming suffering into virtue courtesy of Schopenhauer, and by creating female characters—Lyndall and Rebekah—who embody that articulated and articulate suffering in fiction.

But Dinesen's most spectacular syncretic performance troping Western and African traditions to evoke and palliate suffering, disappointment, and desire is her story "The Diver," which will have to stand in metonymically for what must be dozens of such instances of her debt to African religion and folktales. A belief in Mami Wata is widespread throughout the African continent, constituting one of the most significant fictions in African popular art since the earliest years of the twentieth century, and in his "Mermaids, Mirrors, and Snake Charmers: Igbo Mami Wata Shrines" Henry John Drewal considers the many ways the Mami Wata is represented and worshiped across Africa. The earliest evidence of her influence exists in a 1901 photograph of a chromolith taken at Bonny in the Niger delta, a photograph subsequently copied and "distributed widely in sub-Saharan West and Central Africa where in less than eighty years it became the key image of Mami Wata." Often a collage of wig, glitter, bright paint, and mirrors in which she can enjoy her own handsome image and that the artist hopes will entice the terribly vain Mami Wata to make herself present to her devotees, she is regarded as non-African in origin, often represented with a face painted bright pink and wearing a bright yellow wig. She is, that is, often a white woman. In the paintings of her in the collection of Professor Bogumil Jewsiewicki, both those reproduced in *Africa Explores* and in the numerous paintings not yet published that make up his private research collection, her facial features frequently suggest she is ethnically Indian, as is the case in figure 9, reproduced from his collection here. But as Professor Jewsiewicki has indicated to me, this means she is still regarded as "socially white."[72] Considered a water spirit, she is characteristically shown emerging from the water combing her long, luxuriant hair as she gazes at her reflection in a mirror. Icons of wealth, earrings, golden armlets, and the like "link her with mermaid myths and imagery"[73] (see fig. 9). She carries with her connotations of foreign woman, of mermaid, and in more recent representations, of prostitute or "perverse woman" at the same time.

I believe Dinesen embraced this figure of the Mami Wata in all its multiple ambiguous references, fusing it with the mermaid of Hans Christian Andersen's "The Little Mermaid," who herself has some of those same implications of innocence, sexuality, and suf-

Figure 9. Mamba muntu, a genre painting from Lubumbashi, Zaire. Mamba muntu is the local equivalent of the Mami Wata. From the collection of Bogumil Jewsiewicki. Photograph courtesy of Bogumil Jewsiewicki.

fering all together, threw into the mix a bit of the legend of Icarus, thereby invoking her own charged personal mythology surrounding Denys Finch Hatton the flier, and produced in the process one of her most astonishingly complex and perverse tales. Because of its own fusing of Western and African images—which are in their turn fusings of the figures of angel and mermaid, air and water, sexuality and sin, suffering and joy—the story succeeds in making external, artful, and endurable exactly those qualities of "woman" that most vexed Dinesen personally and most needed to be exteriorized. Drewal suggests that in their religious practices Africans "take exotic images and ideas, interpret them according to indigenous precepts, invest them with new meanings, and then re-create and re-present them in new and dynamic ways to serve their own aesthetic, devotional, and social needs," thereby "transform[ing] external forces, using them to shape their own lives."[74] Dinesen traveled that same road in the opposite direction, taking the figure Africans transformed from Western and Indian sources and refiguring or translating it back—re-reinterpreted it if you will—to serve her own aesthetic, social, and psychic needs. Predictably, this collage evokes the mermaid not just as a sufferer or a kind of creature perpetually out of her element, but her more subversive and liberating aspects as well. These are suggested perhaps most vividly by Thackeray in *Vanity Fair:* "They look pretty enough when they sit upon a rock, twanging their harps and combing their hair, and sing, and beckon to you to come and hold the looking glass," he says, "but when they sink into their native element, depend on it those mermaids are about no good, and we had best not examine the fiendish marine mammals, travelling and feasting on their wretched pickled victims."[75]

All of which obscures the fact that "The Diver" is a great and complex story, nearly impossible even to summarize. For one thing it is one of the many Dinesen stories that structurally constitute a *mise en abyme,* whose first line announces that the story the storyteller will tell is not his own. It comes "from Mira Jama." That story is of a young student of theology, Saufe, who decides to construct wings "to lift [men] into high regions, where dwells a clear and eternal light."[76] But town officials worry about his plan. "If . . . this flying boy meets and communicates with angels, the people of Shiraz . . . will go mad with wonder and joy. And who knows what new and revolutionary things the angels may not tell him?" (p. 6). While Saufe dreams on a rooftop one evening the townsmen send one of the king's most beautiful young dancers—the "perverse woman," in other words—to convince him that she *is* an angel, inspiring him to fall in love with her.

She succeeds, and the young man and the dancer-cum-angel carry on a brief passionate affair that does just what the townspeople had hoped. It distracts him from his wing-building project long enough for them to slip into his workshop and destroy the wings. "We angels," she tells him, "do not really need wings to move between heaven and earth, but our own limbs suffice" (p. 8).

Those who remember the painful process whereby Andersen's little mermaid acquires her "limbs" will appreciate Dinesen's perverse humor at this point. Saufe discovers too late that his angel is not an angel but a dancer: or is, rather, both angel and seductress.

At this point we have all the elements of the Mami Wata but the mermaid. But Dinesen's story continues. This tale turns out to be another of Dinesen's characteristic tales within a tale. The first line of "The Diver" is "Mira Jama told this story:" (p. 3). What this beginning does, of course, is signal that it is *not* Mira Jama telling the story, but another storyteller who is recounting Mira Jama's story to us, the inner one being recounted retrospectively by the storyteller who is our narrator, who has decided to tell it "to make the world wiser." It is *our* storyteller who years later hears yet another story: the story of a diver who claims to be "the happiest man on earth." Our storyteller resolves to find this diver and learn the secret of his absolute happiness, and when he finds him, that diver tells the storyteller *his* story—the story of the young man who tried to make wings so he could reach the angels. When Mira Jama tells his tale to the diver, the diver tells the storyteller that it is *his* story he is telling: the diver *was* that young man years ago. Dinesen interjects: "It is to a poet a thing of awe to find that his story is true." The diver is happy too: he is "pleased to know that he has got into a story, for that is probably what he was made for." The diver/storyteller agrees to finish out his story/life for the storyteller, all the while insisting that that story "makes no story at all."

That "no story" related by the diver/storyteller to the initiating storyteller who heard it from the storyteller Mira Jama is a story Mira Jama heard from yet another storyteller: a tale told by the fish the diver caught in his net. And it is the fish's story to the diver/storyteller that finally explains the source of the diver's great happiness. The diver had gone deep into the sea "in search of a certain rare pearl." But what he encountered at the bottom of the sea was instead "an old cowfish." This female fish had been caught in the net of two old fishermen and had spent a whole night "in the bilgewater of their boat, listening to [their] talk" until the morning, when she "slipped through the meshes and swam away" (p. 16).

Since that time the she-fish "smiles at the other fishes' distrust of men. For really . . . if a fish knows how to behave herself, she can easily manage them. She has even come to take an interest in the nature and customs of men, and often lectures on them to an audience of fishes. She also," says the storyteller, "likes to discuss them with me."

Here, then, finally, is the Mami Wata: the female dweller in the seas who "knows men" and "can easily manage them." And fishes, as the fish/storyteller tells us, "are the happiest creatures in the universe": "We have no hands, so cannot construct anything at all, and are never tempted by vain ambition to alter anything whatever in the universe of the Lord. We sow not and toil not; therefore no estimates of ours will turn out wrong, and no expectations fail. The greatest amongst us in their spheres have reached perfect darkness" (p. 18).

Saufe, the diver, the storyteller, the boy who had sought to fly and had been seduced from his goal by an angel/seductress, gains a more genuine happiness and wisdom not from angels, but from and in the sea: with the Mami Wata, mermaid, angel, sufferer, diver, fish, savvy female who "knows men." "He who 'floats in his element,' says the fish, is happy. Without hope there are no expectations, without expectations no disappointments; without desire, no betrayal." Men, alarmed by time's passage and "unbalanced by incessant wanderings between past and future," should learn from "the inhabitants of a liquid world [who] have brought past and future together in the maxim: *après nous le déluge*." This same conflation of past, present, and future into a single moment recurs in Dinesen's story "Tempests."

Each image and source that makes up part of Dinesen's syncretic performance here comes trailing with it something of the original context in which that image or source figures. In the collapsing of past, present, and future into a perpetual present, we have something of the modernist impulse. In the collapsing of sea, sky, and land, we have some of the power Walter Benjamin talks about in the *Passagen-Werk,* where the sea is regarded as the threshold between earth and sky in his analysis of myth, Benjamin's "ladder extending downward to the interior of the earth and disappearing into the clouds," his "image for a collective experience to which the deepest shock of every individual experience, death, constitutes no impediment or barrier."[77] In the figure of the mermaid/seductress/angel there is not only the figure of the Mami Wata—woman, fish, sexuality incarnate—but an evocation of Hans Christian Andersen's mermaid who hungers after the prince, her very hungering precluding her having him and causing her intense pain and suffering. It can't have been far from Dinesen's consciousness that in invoking a mythical dancer/mermaid/angel she would be harking, especially for her Danish readers, back to Andersen's mermaid.

This is not the sanitized mermaid of the Disney film who only loses her beautiful voice. Dinesen would have known her countryman's little mermaid very well. That mermaid willingly consents to have her tongue cut out to have a shot at winning the love of the prince and agrees to drink a witch's potion so her fish's tail will turn into beautiful legs that would entice the prince to marry her. She pays a very dear price for those great legs:

> Every step she took felt, as the witch had told her it would, like treading on pointed needles and sharp knives, but she bore it gladly. . . . [The prince] and every one else marvelled at her graceful, gliding walk . . . so she danced more and more, though every time her foot touched the ground it was like treading on sharp knives. The prince said she was always to be with him and she was allowed to sleep outside his door on a velvet cushion. . . . With the prince she climbed high mountains; and though her delicate feet would bleed for all to see, she would laugh and follow him till they saw the clouds sailing beneath them like a flock of birds making their way to foreign lands.[78]

In "The Diver" Dinesen explores the costs and consequences of desire, the costs and consequences of "knowing men." In the evocation of the pain and price of desire, she evokes Andersen's mermaid and gestures toward Ibsen's "Lady of the Sea" as well. In the conflation of desire and flight she invokes Icarus and Denys Finch Hatton, fused into one. "An artist sees that which his race has never seen," Schreiner says, suggesting that artists in every age have seen wings on their gods and great spiritual beings. "It is useless for the superficial onlooker to say those wings wouldn't carry them. . . . The artist says, 'I see them.' "[79] In the collapsing of sea and sky, air and water are not only the same challenging of the terms of visuality and perspective characteristic of cubist and other avant-garde visual art of the early twentieth century, but evocations of African folktales, the stock-in-trade of which is often the inversion of up and down, sky and land. In the invocation of salvation figured in the form of the fish, we have of course not only one of the most ancient symbols of salvation, appropriated by early Christians, but an evocation of the specific form of salvation embodied in the fish/mother Mami Wata, whose devotees worship her precisely because alliance with her promises access to the gaudy power and wealth only Westerners possess. And in the perverse delight the storyteller takes in telling a story of happiness as a thing found in the end in suffering and the absence of desire, at the same time we have Kierkegaard.

This vision of a perfect contentment "in [one's] element" also erases the presence of any female *other* than the fish/mermaid/angel, neatly bypassing the highly charged relation between mother and daughter that psychoanalytic readings of Andersen's story emphasize. In discussing Andersen's story in "Race, Class, and Psychoanalysis?" for instance, Elizabeth Abel notes that "although the story focuses on the romance between the mermaid and the prince, . . . the choice of images in the story in fact highlights the relationship of the mermaid and the sea witch instead."[80] Any story in which an older woman mutilates a younger one to make her more physically desirable to the male by rendering mobility painful and speech impossible must be read in part as a story of the painful process of female psychosexual maturation and menstruation. But to turn toward Dinesen's own history rather than toward theory is to come face-to-face yet one more time with Dinesen's revenge on her mother for forcing her to sit upstairs—mute—while Georg Brandes was down in the sitting room having tea. Dinesen's mother *is* that sea witch who cut out her daughter's tongue. Dinesen's angel/fish/mermaid—and seductress—swims safely in her sea, having escaped through her own wiles both capture by men and mutilation at the mother's hand. Captured only long enough to have acquired men's wisdom by eavesdropping on them, she is in the end free, wise, and unmutilated.

"I have a real horror of being 'an object,'" Dinesen confesses to her brother. "I believe . . . I am conditioned by nature in this, but it may perhaps have been emphasized in me through having been transplanted as I was, partly because of what happened to my marriage and relationship with Bror; I have become hesitant about staking a great deal on a personal relationship."[81] Africa becomes her sea, in which she is, like the Mami Wata but unlike Andersen's mermaid, all-powerful, something Schreiner may have had in mind as well when she called the young heroine of her earliest novel Undine. Schreiner's Undine is in fact a kind of mermaid, feeling more than a bit out of her element in Europe, and also in Africa.

When God created heaven and earth, says Dinesen's fishy storyteller, "man, capable of falling, fell almost immediately. . . . But the fish did not fall, and never will fall, for how or whereto would we fall?"[82] Denys Finch Hatton died, Icarus-like, falling out of the sky. Dinesen flies too, to be sure. But she does so self-constructed as fish, mermaid, angel, seductress, and tale-teller "in her element," and as such she does not fall. Dinesen's generic Africans represent the same kind of projective dream productions constructed in "The Diver." They too have attained a perfect freedom, she thinks, because they too are "within their own element, such as we can never be, like fishes in deep water."[83]

As Schreiner grew up perched between Boer and black and trying to mediate between the two, Dinesen oscillates between African religion, tale-telling, and art and European philosophy, tale-telling, and art, producing in the process a third space and place—neither African nor European but clearly troping and amalgamating elements of both—that must have offered her at least as much delight as it offers her readers. It is a space in which she herself might reside in relative comfort precisely because it did not require that she give up either pole of any of those sets of absolute nonnegotiables—submission/defiance, desire for desire/desire for the absence of desire, desire for belonging/desire to be left alone, financial independence/financial dependency, desire to fly while escaping the dangers of plummeting—that were at the same time part of her "nature" and culturally produced. I call this a *space,* but Eve Sedgwick thinks it might best be thought of more as *place.* It is not bisexual, not gendered at all. Sedgwick sees it instead as the place of surprise at recognizing what we have found ourselves imagining and fantasizing—what Sedgwick calls that *really* perverse place.[84]

8

Conclusion: "Remembering" and the Chain of Tradition

To find the split within singularity: to live in this in-between, in the tear. . . . To one side of signification, in a region of unsigning. . . . This gap, this suspension that will not be brought to book, that is beyond the book, beyond this book marks the end of culture and the beginning of writing: art undoing culture, scattering always and again what the book, as gathering, necessarily has to gather. And it poses the question of how a book, a book seeking to exemplify its modernity, could begin to scatter itself. For isn't this what the modern writer takes on?

Michael Phillipson,
In Modernity's Wake

> Between night and light . . . memory rises up as a sign. . . . Memory remains, master, sovereign, working the material of the past, naming subjects and objects of desire. In the writing that can reflect it, it becomes a proposition of a will for truth and a history yet to come. "Not the oeuvre," . . . but a chapter of a driving, moving account, the text will, little by little, between "night" and "light," "history" and "fiction," "referent" and "reference," make the reader glimpse the narrative identity of a people in action.
>
> V. Y. Mudimbe,
> "Letters of Reference"

Mudimbe's meditations here echo Walter Benjamin's. Far from being opposites, memory and forgetting stand on the same side of a set of polarities. Remembering fights to be no more than a retrieval and replication of the same signs, structures, beliefs, constructions of self and other produced by an initial, prior forgetting of all that would complicate who we see our selves and our others to be. The opposite of both remembering and forgetting, then, is time present and immediate, dawning each day "like a clean shirt."[1] We all know this. Our first act on waking every morning is remembering to take on the familiar, stable identity by which we and others have come to know us—an act of remembering what it is I must forget in order to cling to that "I" I know myself to be.

Between the "night and day" of Mudimbe, resonating with the Nat-og-Dag of Dinesen's "Dreamers," there is that space of shuttling where glimpses of something quite different can be caught: not either the culturally produced self or the culturally produced other, but a glimpse instead of the molten self-in-production. Dinesen and Schreiner became "white" "women," I believe, only by struggling *not* to remember the opposition of woman to man, Europe to Africa, or black to white that "history" would have them not forget. Sometimes, unfortunately, they failed to forget. Sometimes, unfortunately, so have I. The temptations are great. Writing here, I've known white readers would ask: How then *did* these two European women see African men? Did they get it right? Did they at least come close? Closer than others have? I've tried to answer those questions, even though I believe the questions themselves force a forgetting of what most needs to be remembered. Most unfortunately, those questions tend to lead one to recapitulate the familiar anthropological exploration in which white folks look at Africans yet again, an enterprise that can yield nothing but replacing one production of Africans with another. The newer might be slightly better than the old, but both will still have been born of a remembering that forgets that the longing for darkness white folks attribute to Africans is their own longing *not* to be studied—not to study themselves.

Tempting as it has been for this white woman to sweep her glance past these two other white women and look at those really interesting (substitute exotic, long-suffering, mythic) others, I have tried to train my light steady on us dark folks who long for, and devise strategies for staying in, the darkness. Isak Dinesen and Olive Schreiner oscillate between absolutes: between needing men and finding them irrelevant; between loving being women and resisting it. Both found their consolation and their line of flight from the nonnegotiable contraries of their natures and psyches in the artful oscillations represented by and in modernism and in their construction and use of African and European philosophies, by oscillating between identification with and alterity from the Africans among whom they lived. Each negotiated the various absolute irreconcilables generated by their psychic natures by oscillating between and thereby parceling out their conflicting attitudes and feelings, some(times) into their fictions; some(times) into their letters or memoirs. Each tried to produce an identity by defining herself over against African men and over against women, African and European.

By now the secret's surely out: this writer is a closet oscillator. *Malgré moi* perhaps, I've written the *autoviography* my Freudian-slipping fingers alerted me to when I first began to hit the keys here. Like Dinesen and Schreiner always an absolutist, a member of at least two opposed parties and trapped by their oppositions, I pace back and forth in this prisoner's box. My conclusion, then, can't help but be an oscillating affair. On (in) one hand is the hammer, poised to nail down all these oscillations. The other hand wants to keep them all in motion and just whirr right on out of here.

The nailing down can come first. In *Building a National Literature* Peter Uwe Hohendahl questions the wisdom and explores the consequences of the way we have traditionally thought of the institution of literature. That institution has constellated itself almost exclusively around a number of assumptions that have given priority to the literary text while assuming everything else is "background material": "helpful" to literary scholars to a greater or lesser degree, but always relegated in the end to the status of "supplemental." The consequence is that we assume there is some *ontological* difference between literature and everything else that surrounds it and provides its material contexts: other kinds of writings, the various public, personal, and national histories out of which it grew and which it helped to shape, as well as the context of particular readers at its moment of reception: readers reading it not just in a different and later moment, but reading into it and out of it different concerns.

The practical consequences of this more usual way of doing criticism were what prompted me to try a different way. Under any of the various versions of the traditional paradigm I had a number of options. I could have produced a study of Dinesen's and Schreiner's literary art. But that wouldn't have got me access to anything I felt to be most vital or powerful about their lifeworks. I could have talked about their language as an instance of women's language, but to do so apart from a look at where that language came from and why it took the particular forms it did would have been to propagate the notion that woman's language is somehow genetically acquired at conception or imposed entirely from without rather than being a set of active, conscious strategies devised in response to specific material conditions. I had no interest in participating in that essentializing project. I could have detailed the socioeconomic and psychosexual impediments generating their ambivalence about being women, but by now the former are depressingly familiar, the latter predictable, and the repetition of neither particularly appealing. I could have examined what from one perspective is clearly the pathology of Dinesen's and Schreiner's survival strategies, but like all decisions to label something pathological, that one would have walled me off from my own imbrication in their issues. The strictly socioeconomic or strictly psychosexual study would also not have allowed for a more celebratory study of their successful troping, which so triumphantly transformed what may have been pathology into art and play and which was what had first drawn me to the both of them. "What function does literature have as an ideological form?" Hohendahl asks. "For Etienne Balibar and Pierre Macherey the ironing out and apparent resolution of ideological contradictions is in the foreground. Real social contradictions, which are insoluble in concrete historical situations, are thrust aside so that imaginary solutions can be found for them. The circumstances reverse the relationship between reality and literature: instead of mirroring reality, literature—as social practice—creates a fictive semblance of reality. In other words, realism and fictitiousness are concepts constituted through the praxis of literary production."[2] Hohendahl concludes by defining the institution of literature as the locus where the literary practices of authors, texts, and readers are constituted. A study of literary practices, then—which I've construed here to include the way we comb our hair and position our bodies in the landscape as well as how we write our novels—can take us far toward identifying and then tapping into the charge certain writings and writers have for us; far toward bringing those ideological contradictions into the foreground and our Western, white, and/or female selves into the light we've feared.

I admit also to being intrigued by the possibilities of looking at how both Schreiner's and Dinesen's lifeworks—taken entire and despite the great lengths I have gone to in talking about them as obsessed either with impossibly traditional roles for women, in Dinesen's instance, or with some impossibly ideal long-past prehistoric vision of the eternally suffering and enduring larger-than-life woman in Schreiner's—seem to claim the status of the avant-garde. In saying this I have in mind a definition that regards the avant-garde as characterized not so much by particular formal features as by its insistence on inhabiting a kind of counterethnographic space. The cutting edge of the modern is the avant-garde, and it becomes so by insisting that its audience confront what it cannot understand—by resisting any attempts to categorize it comfortably according to national, ethnic, class, gender, or genre categories, enacting in art exactly what these two women themselves lived.[3]

But all this is part of an admonitory, cautionary conclusion. At the other pole is the model *not* of exploration and articulation of the *langscape* constituting literary practices but the pole represented by my choice of epigraphs for this conclusion. One model for this second way of thinking is that suggested by Balkan women's singing. In earlier centuries when a young woman in the Balkans married someone from another village, women of her home village sang her on her way as she left it forever. They did not sing in chords having distinct intervals, in what we think of as harmony. Instead one stood and struck a note, then first one and then another woman would strike a different note, each in her turn finding a place where a harmonic could be set in motion so that the combination of the two notes, and then a third, would set up a vibration, ricocheting off the mountains, creating a sound far more powerful than the sum of the separate notes each woman added to the mix. That harmonic is not just heard: it is visceral as much as audible. It is felt in the gut.

The oscillations traced here have been intended to set up that kind of harmonic. As should be evident, these oscillations bear little relation to the ironic, superficial hovering over or cavalier using of older figures or images that is characteristic of the postmodern. Schreiner, Dinesen, and I are adamantly, distinctly *in* all of the figures and images, forms and figurations of "woman" we have produced.

In fact it is precisely because some of us are so profoundly *in* what we produce, and consequently because everything *matters* so much, that the formation of self, memory, and experience seems so fraught with difficulty or danger. Never a matter of simply retrieving what is "there" awaiting simple transmission to others, memory is not only an absence (caused by the forgetting that produced memory), it is at the same time what we retroactively use to fill that absence. Ideally (and I do share Dinesen's and Schreiner's dream of an ideal) memory, if it is not overwhelmed by the forgetting that produced it, can be a distillation or concentrated form of the "what really happened" that could not be fully apprehended at the time of an original experience, precisely because that experience was too hot to handle.

The work of art never just taps into experiences or invokes memories so much as it serves as midwife to the fuller experience memory has blocked. At best it also serves as host to the performance of the self that the fuller experience makes possible. Benjamin suggests that in *Matter and Memory* Henri Bergson regards memory less as the product of facts anchored in memory than as "a convergence in memory of accumulated and frequently unconscious data." More than anything else, memory is "a matter of tradition," existing "in collective existence as well as in private life": consciousness is what comes into being at the site of a memory trace. It is remembering that "creates the chain of tradition."[4] The form adopted by good storytellers like Dinesen and Schreiner, regardless of whether the stories appear in letters, memoirs, fictional narratives, or fables, involves them in what Andrew Benjamin describes as taking over, retaining, and repeating. But that repeating is never simply a repetition of the same. It is instead a perpetual representation of the narrative form, and like Dinesen's own heroine Scheherazade, prototype of the storyteller, both women tell stories to stay alive. Scheherazade is the one " 'who thinks of a fresh story . . . whenever her tale comes to a stop.' "[5]

Like the ladder that Benjamin suggests "extends downward to the interior of the earth and disappears into the clouds," the same ladder I believe is invoked by Dinesen's story "The Diver," memory is itself a ladder: "the image for a collective—and remembered—experience."[6] If Dinesen and Schreiner were producing no real Africans and no real husbands in their lifeworks, neither were they, finally, producing memoirs of their time in Africa. Nor were their letters communicating only some account of their experiences, whether those were in or out of Africa. Like all residents of the avant-garde edge of the modernist project, in collapsing a time past and a time future both were conflating retrospection and anticipation into a pregnant present moment in which they *became* themselves in the act of "remembering" and communicating a past that was a construction in and of the moment of writing. More broadly and more importantly, they were contributing rungs for the ladder we all might climb as we produce our collective history.

In 1914 Dinesen went to what Europeans of her time thought of as the past—to Africa—to construct a past for herself and to make herself a future more exciting than she found her present to be. Returning to Denmark seventeen years later, in composing a memoir of her time in Africa she created her experience of Africa retrospectively. In doing so she simultaneously brought her self into her performance of Africa and transformed her performance of Africa into her self. As Ralph Ellison says in *Shadow and Act*, "That which we do is what we are. That which we remember is, more often than not, that which we hope to be."[7]

I "remember" Isak Dinesen, Olive Schreiner, and their Africans, then, as performers of and in a future I hope to see. Since history is memory multiplied, Schreiner's and Dinesen's memoirs, letters, and fictions were inevitably memories contributing to the writing of an African "history." This must be looked at in the light so we can ensure that our memory of them and their work is constructed out of as little forgetting as possible. "Westerners, not unlike adults vis-à-vis children or psychiatrists in relation to their patients, have imposed upon non-Westerners aberrant ways of being non-Westerners," says Mudimbe.[8] But he notes too the impossibility of *erasing* those aberrant identities with which we grace one another. The project of the white Western critic cannot then be limited to attempts to erase such identities from Africans.

Even if we could do it, Mudimbe suggests, we should not. If we decline to look at those aberrant identities Europeans have produced for Africans, women for men, white women for black men, how will we know who "we" are? The project of the white Western critic also cannot be entirely made up of compensatory attempts to posit real Africans to counter earlier misconstructions. How could white folks presume, and how could we possibly succeed?

The project confronting all of us is one that is in some ways far more difficult, and one requiring in the end much more discipline. It is the rigorous analysis of ourselves: of the white folks who produce those aberrant identities. How did the distortions come to be, and what needs do they serve?

Mudimbe's more recent work suggests that African critics' project will include an effort "to consider . . . the silence of the conquered who . . . represent another silence, the massive and shameful silence of men who discover themselves incapable of explaining to their children what happened."[9] The white critic's work will be to explain to her own children the source of her incessant chatter about "Africans," about "men," on the one hand, and her own silence about herself, on the other. It will no longer be sufficient to simply name otherness and, however respectfully and benevolently, slip away home. However timorously, white critics need to begin to address head-on exactly how we have used one another in our own self-formations: whites, blacks, women, men.

This requires large quantities of self-awareness, to be sure. In one of Dinesen's favorite novels, Jens Peter Jacobsen's *Niels Lyhne,* Madame Odero, a woman of a certain age, catches herself in a moment of revelation: "It was astonishing how she came to realize that she had actually known herself very little in the past," says the narrator. "Her life had, in fact, been too eventful and exciting to give her time for exploring herself, and besides, she was only now approaching the age when women who have lived much in the world and seen much commence to recollect their memories, to look back at themselves *and assemble a past* [my italics]."[10]

Just as in the glorious little film *Cinema Paradiso* memory is produced partly as a consequence of the *blocking* of the originary experiences (by others, by circumstances, by social and psychosexual prohibitions) one is presumably trying to recall, memory is always an invocation of the incomplete. It is not a place or a time we go back to, but a *space* we clear in order to do the work that remains undone: the construction of fuller, more generous self, one built less out of forgetting and repression. The space of African *hantu* where space and time fall together. For Westerners, this is of course often the "far away" (Africa) that we have tended to think of as "long ago." [11]

It is in that space/time that Dinesen made her "home," and so did Schreiner. That home was the *tent* that is the root of *tentative,* their self-constructions emerging out of the emergencies of their existence. If Dinesen and Schreiner pitched their tents and found consolation in the oscillations offered by modernism and generated by their own psychic makeup, one of the products of those oscillations is the confounding of the two absolute contraries that form their poles: "confound[ing] fiction and reality," as Judith Thurman suggests Dinesen did, "in order to render them, for an hour, mysteriously happy." [12] I believe their carnival of different self-presentations makes Dinesen and Schreiner exceptionally successful at this. Myth, story, performance, physical self-presentation, letters, lectures, radio broadcasts, allegories—all become strategies that open up a space and a place for a self-performance in which the wall between memory and experience, self and performance drops away and presence, paradoxically, becomes momentarily possible. If the eye can oscillate rapidly enough between irrelevant men and essential men, a third space—a hospitable habitation either for no man or for everyman—might be found. Such oscillations also constitute the way out of the supreme self-consciousness blocking consciousness that is the hallmark of late nineteenth- and early twentieth-century fiction, instanced in Henry James's confession that, falling to the floor as he was having his stroke, he was thinking, "So this is it; the great thing." This is exactly the kind of self-consciousness experienced by Niels Lyhne in his most crushing moment of abandonment by his beloved, a moment when he is not *experiencing* the pain of his rejection but thinking to himself, "Exit Niels Lyhne, . . . hearing the latch of the hall-door click behind him." [13]

This book has been meant to entertain; it has made every effort to reside "between the spaces," [14] exactly like the chord produced by the Balkan women, and it has done so to keep that hall door from clicking behind us. As should be clear by now, the click to be resisted here includes that of either art history or history in general, narrowly construed. "The specific historicity of works of art . . . does not disclose itself in 'art history,' " says Benjamin, "but only in interpretation," which is the place where "interrelations of works of art among each other appear that are atemporal and yet not without historical relevance."[15] Interpretation for Benjamin is best defined as "our own rethinking of history" in what he calls an "unchaste mingling of all spheres."[16] The word *unchaste* is particularly well chosen here, since it implies both the unlicensed probings and the unlicensed—in Benjamin's model even *forced*—comminglings carried out by the interpreter who is the maker of history. Michel de Certeau sees objects and words as having "hollow places in which a past sleeps." These pasts are those "others are not allowed to read, accumulated times that can be unfolded like stories held in reserve, remaining in an enigmatic state, symbolizations encysted in the pain or pleasure of the body." The interpreter's unchaste pryings into those hidden hollows are what enable her to arrive at a place where she can say, as de Certeau suggests, " 'I feel good here.' "[17]

I can say "I feel good here" in the pasts my interpretations have opened up. But it is important that I not plant any flags in this space, thereby appropriating Dinesen's or Schreiner's words or trying to make their Africa and Africans mine. I am required to end by trying not to forget "the radical difference and otherness of the textual order (as well as that of nature)," not to forget again that in the end inevitably "recognition disappears and we are confronted with the black marks on the page, with spots of color on a surface . . . until the violence of our signifying desire makes them speak and return the stare of our glance."[18]

Having spent a couple of hundred pages "gathering" until the black marks on Dinesen's and Schreiner's pages have returned my own gaze as much as Dinesen's Africans do hers, I must end by scattering what has been gathered. In such a project Schreiner, despite herself, and Dinesen, with great abandon, would fully participate. What cannot be forgotten is that notwithstanding the jutted-jaw title it now bears, *From Man to Man* was first called

"Or Perhaps Only . . ." And Dinesen tells us that Princess Benedetta in her "Cardinal's First Tale" finds her self in music and can do so because "here, she felt, was a reasonable human language, within which things could be truthfully expressed. She was in good understanding with the cadenza, both the full or perfect cadenza and the deceptive cadenza, the *cadenza d'inganno,* of which musical dictionaries will tell you that it makes every preparation for a perfect finish and then, instead of giving the expected final accord, suddenly breaks off and sounds an unexpected, strange and alarming close. Here, quite obviously, the girl's heart told her, was the infallible rule of the irregular." [19]

A Note on Texts

Most citations are given in endnotes, and all are self-explanatory except for those to Olive Schreiner's letters. Spanning the years between 1876 and her death in 1920, these letters were first edited and published by her husband Samuel Cronwright-Schreiner in 1924. In 1988 Richard Rive published a first volume of a more accurate and expanded collection covering the years 1871 to 1899. My references are keyed to this latter edition for all letters written during that time. Unfortunately Mr. Rive was stabbed to death during a robbery attempt at his home in Cape Town in June 1989, and a second volume of this edition has not yet been published. Citations to Schreiner letters written after 1899 refer, then, to Cronwright-Schreiner's edition. In a few instances that edition includes letters written between 1871 and 1899 that are not found in Richard Rive's edition, and in such instances I cite Cronwright-Schreiner's edition. A collection of Schreiner's correspondence with Havelock Ellis, one of her major confidants, appeared in 1992, edited by Yaffa Draznin and published by Peter Lang under the title *My Other Self*. This is a rich and useful source for those striving to know Schreiner better, but not wanting to introduce a third set of references to Schreiner's letters, I have not keyed citations to this edition. Letters from Isak Dinesen are taken from the standard source, *Letters from Africa, 1914–1931,* edited by Frans Lasson and translated by Anne Born. For biographical information that negotiates the complicated psychological and geographical terrain trod by these two women I am deeply indebted to and remain impressed by the work done by Judith Thurman in her *Isak Dinesen: The Life of a Storyteller* (1982) and Ruth First and Ann Scott in their *Olive Schreiner* (1980).

Notes

Preface

1. Dinesen, *Shadows on the Grass*, p. 92.

2. See Mitchell, *Iconology*, p. 166.

3. Comaroff and Comaroff, *Of Revelation and Revolution*, pp. 186–87.

4. Mphahlele, *African Image*, p. 27.

5. Brooks, "Aesthetics and Ideology," p. 520.

Chapter 1: Disclaiming, Claim Staking, and Vacillatin' Rhythms

1. Dinesen, "The Dreamers," in *Seven Gothic Tales*, p. 271.

2. Hobman, *Olive Schreiner*, p. 42.

3. Isak Dinesen sent the manuscript of *On Modern Marriage* to her brother Thomas so he could find a publisher for it. This was not an arbitrary decision. Thomas Dinesen was a member of the World League for Sexual Reform and a participant in that organization's second world congress, held in Copenhagen in 1928. This group had been formed one year earlier and included among its honorary presidents Havelock Ellis, Olive Schreiner's closest intellectual companion and correspondent and her partner in exploring questions of sexuality and marriage. See the afterword to *On Modern Marriage*, pp. 115–16.

4. Dinesen, *Letters*, p. 376.

5. Susan Gubar's discussion of "The Blank Page" and Susan Hardy Aiken's of "The Dreamers" especially come to mind here.

6. I have in mind here the categories of Deleuze and Guattari in their *Kafka,* especially p. 22, and of Henry Louis Gates Jr. in his *Figures in Black,* p. 236. Each suggests that any minority caught in the defining categories of the majority may find a line of flight out of those categories by twisting, turning, troping, or otherwise pushing those categories to the limit to overturn, surpass, or reverse them while outwardly feigning acceptance. Gates, for instance, defines metalepsis to include not only what he refers as the "master's tropes"—metaphor, metonymy, synecdoche, and irony—but also the "slave's tropes"—hyperbole, litotes, metalepsis, aporia, chiasmus, and catechresis. With his gigantic timepiece used as a form of neckwear, for instance, rapper Flavor Flav pokes fun at the hugely expensive and consequently mostly hidden Rolex watches on some wrists, at the same time signifying prodigiously, "I've got time on my hands," "you won't give me the time of day," "it's long past time," and much else. Schreiner and Dinesen each devised an arsenal of survival strategies that can be seen as instances of these same tropes—including a kind of signifying that becomes possible as a result of recognizing the possibilities of textuality that inhere in gesture, behavior, and dress—to overturn categories of "woman" holding sway in their time and place.

7. See Thurman, *Isak Dinesen,* p. 231.

8. Dinesen, *Letters,* p. 386.

9. Baker, "African-American Studies and the Development of English."

10. Dinesen, *Out of Africa,* p. 79.

11. This is Frederic Jameson's point in his conversation with Anders Stephanson in Ross, *Universal Abandon?* p. 15.

12. Spivak, "French Feminism in an International Frame," p. 179.

13. Before the European scramble for Africa most Africans lived in small monarchic states of five to ten thousand people resembling Athenian polities, which tended to form larger clusters based on common languages or cultures. What Westerners have thought of as the partitioning of Africa across tribal territories can be seen then as in actuality "a ruthless act of political amalgamation," and tribes as a convenient invention of district commissioners and other colonial administrators. See Roland Oliver's *African Experience* and also Neal Ascherson's review of that book in *New York Review of Books.* Olive Schreiner recognized this pattern too. She saw the arrival of whites in South Africa as causing the three distinct groups of native peoples to be, as she described

it, "split up into endless tribelets" (see her *Thoughts on South Africa,* p. 106).

14. Spillers, "Mama's Baby, Papa's Maybe," p. 66.

15. Barthes, *Mythologies,* p. 123.

16. Appiah, *In My Father's House,* p. 181.

17. Kapp, *Eleanor Marx,* 2:24.

18. See Grosskurth, *Havelock Ellis,* p. 314.

19. See Jahn, *Muntu,* p. 174.

20. Thurman, *Isak Dinesen,* p. 422.

21. Schreiner, *Letters,* ed. Rive, 1:147.

22. Ibid., p. 157.

23. Ibid., p. 162.

24. Dinesen, *Shadows on the Grass,* p. 14.

25. Markham, *West with the Night,* p. 201.

26. Ibid., p. 195.

27. See Thurman, *Isak Dinesen,* p. 127n. Interestingly, whereas the more complimentary epithets Africans applied to Bror Blixen get circulated and recirculated in the writings of Europeans, only Thurman makes mention of Blixen as "the waddler."

28. Schreiner, *Letters,* ed. Rive, 1:143.

29. Schreiner, *Story of an African Farm,* p. 71.

30. Kapp, *Eleanor Marx,* 2:700.

31. Schreiner, *Letters,* ed. Rive, 1:145.

32. First and Scott, *Olive Schreiner,* p. 319. When Cronwright-Schreiner describes his marriage as "so many weary years," he may well have had in mind Christina Rossetti's "Heart's Chill Between," which had been published in the *Athenaeum* on October 21, 1848:

But it is over, it is done—
So many weary years have run
Since then, I think not how
Things might have been,—but
greet each one
With an unruffled brow.

33. First and Scott, p. 319.

34. Dinesen, *On Modern Marriage,* p. 37.

35. Martin, *Woman and Modernity,* p. 111.

36. See Gay, *Tender Passion,* pp. 83–88.

37. Schreiner, *Woman and Labour,* p. 22.

38. Benjamin, *Origin of German Tragic Drama,* p. 103.

39. Eagleton, *Ideology,* p. 91.

40. Schreiner, *Story of an African Farm,* p. 15.

41. Dinesen, *Letters,* pp. 322–23.

42. Judith Thurman is convinced Dinesen "never really overcame her loneliness. Sometimes," she says, "she could laugh at it, sometimes even welcome it. But this . . . was a question of feeling 'an excess of strength' or none at all" (p. 295).

43. See Hannah Arendt's foreword to Isak Dinesen's *Daguerreotypes,* p. viii.

44. "She approved of him, admiring his 'physical manliness, his muscular prowess,' " say Ruth First and Ann Scott in their biography. "She asked him to have himself photographed in his shirt sleeves rolled up to show his arms," p. 208. The photograph reproduced here may represent one of his many gestures of compliance with her requests.

45. Gregg, *Memories of Olive Schreiner,* p. 22.

46. Schreiner, *Story of an African Farm,* pp. 231–32.

47. Schreiner, *English South-African's View of the Situation,* p. 17.

48. If Schreiner was Ralph Iron, Karen Blixen was not only Isak Dinesen in her published writings and Tanne and Tania to her friends and family, but finally Pierre Andrezel, the name under which she published *The Angelic Avengers* during the German occupation of Denmark. Mary Poovey in *Uneven Developments,* Nancy Armstrong in *Desire and Domestic Fiction,* and Peggy Kamuf in *Signature Pieces* have each considered in detail the forms of authority or subjectivity acquired by the woman writing under a male name and the costs and payoffs of such a decision. I will not rehearse their arguments here except to point out that the fact that Schreiner and Dinesen were writing in, from, and about Africa complicates in all the ways I intend to detail here the inhabiting of the "domestic" sphere out of which they all suggest the European female was expected to write.

49. Thurman notes that Dinesen's diary "document[ed] the almost daily fluctuations of Tanne's moods," suggesting that "in the periods when she was neither working nor in love . . . [her] sense of worthlessness won out" (p. 96). All her life Dinesen was fond of dressing as Pierrot. Robert Storey suggests that the history of the Pierrot figure "is

the record of his vacillations between two . . . 'types.'" At one pole is Harlequin, "a creature of insouciance and activity . . . comic irrepressibility and unselfconscious verve." At the other pole "stands Hamlet—a figure of melancholy indolence . . . a symbol of human vulnerability and mortality, a moralist tortured by conscience—but just as curiously, an egoist who is profoundly asocial and solipsistic" (*Pierrot*, p. xiv). It would be hard to find a better description of Dinesen or Schreiner.

50. See Pakenham, *Scramble for Africa*, p. 47.

51. Schreiner, *Thoughts on South Africa*, p. 30.

52. Schreiner, *Letters*, ed. Rive, 1:53.

53. Ibid., p. 62.

54. One way to read the text of Schreiner's life is as an elaborate experiment testing whether a woman could manage to hold on to both a marriage and her freedom. This was an experiment prompted partly by her reading of Herbert Spencer's *First Principles*, a book that becomes a kind of bible for her first and largely autobiographical heroine Undine in the novel of that name.

55. See Dubow, *Racial Segregation and the Origins of Apartheid in South Africa*, p. 7.

56. Ascertaining the racial attitudes of Schreiner or anyone else during this particular period based on their racial naming is not easy, though such naming will figure in some of my analyses in chapter 7, "African Gossip and the Two-Way Street." South Africanists today tend to use the term Khoikhoi to refer to what Schreiner and other Europeans in the nineteenth century called Hottentots, San when referring to what were then called Bushmen, and Khoisan to refer to both groups. But in *Frontiers* Noël Mostert, who spent the first seventeen years of his life on the same dusty Karoo where Schreiner grew up, suggests that the term Hottentot was probably inescapable because for several centuries no other term seemed available to Europeans. He suggests as well that some words that today are thought to be better choices in fact have a different set of undesirable connotations. San, for instance, was a pejorative word used by Khoikhoi when speaking of Bushmen, so it is not necessarily any better than Bushman. Even though the latter was a name given to this group by the Dutch, who had worked hard to exterminate them, and is never used by the people themselves, it remains for Mostert "an intensely evocative word [with] . . . affectionate associations," and like a number of other African historians he continues to prefer it. See Mostert, p. 34.

57. See Mbembe, "Banality of Power and the Aesthetics of Vulgarity in the Postcolony," pp. 1–30.

58. I am hardly unaware that cross-cultural analysis of the kind I propose to embark on constitutes "one of the most charged . . . fields of scholastic inquiry in the humanities today" or that analyses of what Uzo Esonwanne refers to as " 'things' African" are inevitably "fraught with disputational dangers" ("Madness of Africa[ns]," p. 109). I have tried valiantly to heed these warnings, especially those such as E. San Juan Jr.'s particularly cogent ones in "The Cult of Ethnicity and the Fetish of Pluralism" against the dangers of blithely drifting into transhistorical or transcultural analyses. But balanced against those warnings is the urge—the *obligation,* I would even say—for white folks to identify, and then give credit to, the actual or putative borrowings of things African by particular white settlers in Africa in order to acknowledge debts that are very real, even when the Africans they borrowed and learned from were in some measure constructions of the white imagination.

59. Adorno, *Minima Moralia,* p. 154.

60. Mphahlele, *African Image,* p. 53.

61. See Hountondji, *African Philosophy.* Mudimbe's remarks were part of the commentary he offered during the Brown University Conference on African Writings, November 6, 1991.

62. Bhabha, "Remembering Fanon," p. 138.

63. Krauss, *Optical Unconscious,* pp. 13–14.

64. Krauss uses the term *deictical axis,* inspired by the linguist's vocabulary, the deictic being that which gestures or points: *this* but not *that,* as in that famous line in *Hamlet* in which Polonius points first to his head and then to his body, saying, "Take *this* from *this* if this be not so."

65. See Bryson, *Vision and Painting,* pp. 88–89.

66. Krauss, *Optical Unconscious,* p. 14.

67. Ibid.

68. Hartsock, "Rethinking Modernism," p. 19.

69. Mudimbe, "Which Idea of Africa?" pp. 91–92.

70. Brute political realities finally outran even Benjamin's prodigious capacity to imagine a safe home for himself. He took his own life, probably on September 26, 1940, after the Nazis intercepted him as he tried to cross the Pyrenees to Spain to find refuge from Vichy France, to which Spanish border guards were threatening to return him. See Smith, *On Walter Benjamin,* p. 365.

71. I take Schreiner's lifework to be a part of the modernist project despite her insistence that she didn't like modernist art and had a "pecu-

liar antipathy" to novels in general and to Virginia Woolf's in particular (see *Letters,* ed. Rive, 1:363). I find it hard to believe Schreiner would not have read *The Voyage Out,* since it was published in 1915 in Britain, at exactly the moment when Schreiner was in London meeting with British pacifists and conscientious objectors (see First and Scott, *Olive Schreiner,* p. 369). Woolf's novel is a catalog of the same questions that suffuse all of Schreiner's writings. Woolf disperses into the mouths of Terence Hewet, Evelyn Murgatroyd, and Rachel Vinrace her own youthful speculations on the nature of men and women (she was only twenty-six when the book was published), the possibility of anything like genuinely companionable relations between the two, questions about the desirability of marriage, and the conditions under which personal freedom and marriage might be combined. Woolf's Hewet wonders what would happen if he were to say to Rachel, "I worship you but I loathe marriage, I hate its smugness, its safety, its compromises and the thought of you interfering in my work, hindering me" (p. 278). "I'd keep you free. We'd be free together. We'd share everything together," he imagines saying to her (p. 279). Evelyn confides, "I've never met a man fit to compare with a woman . . . they've no dignity," he says, "no courage, they've nothing but their beastly passions and their brute strength" (p. 282). Echoing Schreiner's conclusions, he announces that "the finest men [are] like women" (p. 243). People in Schreiner's intellectual circle in London were worrying the same questions and drawing the same conclusions.

72. The spelling *Kikuyu* will be used here, since it is more familiar to Western readers. In *Facing Mt. Kenya,* however, Jomo Kenyatta suggests the spelling closest to rendering the sound would be Gikuyu or Gekuyu.

73. Dinesen, *Out of Africa,* p. 244. Some years ago a collection of Kamante Gatura's renditions of the fables Dinesen told while in Africa was published. It reproduces these tales, translated from the Swahili, in the handwriting of Kamante's sons, illustrated with dozens of Kamante's watercolors interspersed with photographs of the Karen Coffee Plantation and its African and Danish visitors and residents, most of them taken by Dinesen herself. The book is *Longing for Darkness: Kamante's Tales from out of Africa.* It provides an all too rare instance in which the voices, tales, and art of Africans and the voices and art of the Europeans who borrowed them stand in something approximating a dialogue, though that dialogue is not unproblematic, since the childlike hand in which both stories and drawings are rendered tends to perpetuate the altogether predictable misperceptions about Africans.

74. Dinesen, *Out of Africa,* p. 135.

75. Spivak, "Love Me Love My Ombre, Elle," pp. 22–24.

76. Suleri, *Rhetoric of English India,* p. 109.

77. Bermingham, *Landscape and Ideology,* pp. 174–75.

78. Dinesen, *Out of Africa,* p. 135.

79. Bentsen, *Maasai Days,* p. 276.

80. Dinesen, *Letters,* p. 170.

81. Tempels, *Bantu Philosophy;* see also Miller, *Theories of Africans,* p. 12.

82. Schreiner, *Letters,* ed. Rive, 1:363.

83. Amuka, "Oral Literature and Fiction," p. 244.

84. Johannesson, *World of Isak Dinesen,* p. 8.

85. Schreiner, *Letters,* ed. Cronwright-Schreiner, p. 50.

86. Dinesen, "The Diver," in *Anecdotes of Destiny,* p. 12.

87. Eagleton, *Ideology,* p. 333.

88. Benjamin, "Doctrine of the Similar," p. 69.

89. De Certeau, *Heterologies,* pp. 23–25.

90. Ojo-Ade, "Of Culture and Commitment, and Construction," p. 21.

Chapter 2: Alone by Design: Precarious Enclosures

1. See Crary, *Techniques of the Observer,* p. 3. "Modernity . . . coincides with the collapse of classical models of vision and their stable space of representations. Instead, observation is increasingly a question of equivalent sensations and stimuli that have no reference to a spatial location. What begins in the 1820s and 1830s is a repositioning of the observer, outside of the fixed relations of interior/exterior . . . into an undemarcated terrain on which the distinction between internal sensation and external signs is irrevocably blurred. If there is ever a 'liberation' of vision in the nineteenth century," says Crary, "this is when it first happens" (p. 24). See also Foucault, *History of Sexuality,* 2:93 and 2:5–6, in which Foucault argues that individual dispositions of the physical body reveal how individual subjects "recognize themselves as subjects of a 'sexuality,' . . . in which it is every day practices that lead individual subjects to focus their attention on themselves, to decipher, recognize and acknowledge themselves as subjects of desire, bringing into play between themselves a certain relationship that allows them to discover . . . the truth of their being."

2. See Comaroff and Comaroff, *Of Revelation and Revolution,* pp. 199–200.

3. McGregor, *The Wacousta Syndrome.*

4. Dinesen, *Out of Africa,* p. 272.

5. Ibid., p. 79.

6. Foster, " 'Primitive' Scenes," p. 81.

7. See, for instance, Swaisland, *Servants and Gentlewomen to the Golden Land.*

8. Schreiner, *Thoughts on South Africa,* p. 118.

9. Schreiner, *Letters,* ed. Rive, 1:45.

10. Jacobsen, *Niels Lyhne,* pp. 129–30.

11. Gregg, *Memories of Olive Schreiner,* p. 53.

12. Dinesen, *Out of Africa,* p. 15.

13. Ibid.

14. Schreiner, *Thoughts on South Africa,* p. 106.

15. Karl, *Modern and Modernism,* p. 16.

16. Bhabha, *Nation and Narration,* pp. 308–9.

17. Meintjes, *Olive Schreiner,* p. 98.

18. Lasson and Svendsen, *Life and Destiny of Isak Dinesen,* p. 144.

19. Thurman, *Isak Dinesen,* p. 165.

20. Brittain, *Testament of Youth,* p. 579.

21. Dinesen, "The Dreaming Child," in *Winter's Tales,* p. 163.

22. Schreiner, *Letters,* ed. Rive, 1:37–38.

23. Dinesen, *On Modern Marriage,* p. 83.

24. Krauss, *Originality of the Avant-Garde,* p. 236.

25. Ibid., p. 263.

26. Benjamin, "On Some Motifs In Baudelaire," p. 188.

27. Dinesen, *Letters,* p. 390.

28. Jameson, "Modernism and Imperialism," p. 64.

29. Krauss, *Originality of the Avant-Garde,* p. 268.

30. Said, "Yeats and Decolonization," p. 78.

31. Linker, citing Lacan, in "Representation and Sexuality," pp. 411–12.

32. Bryson, "Theory of the Image," lecture at Harvard University, March 1992.

33. Dinesen, *Out of Africa,* p. 179.

34. My quotations here are taken from the exhibition pamphlet for "Secrecy: African Art That Conceals and Reveals," Museum for African Art, February 13, 1993, through August 8, 1993. Most of these remarks are undoubtedly to be found in the book published to accompany the exhibition: *Secrecy: African Art That Conceals and Reveals,* edited by Mary H. Nooter (New York: Prestel, 1993).

35. Lasson and Svendsen, *The Life and Destiny of Isak Dinesen,* p. 153.

36. Thurman, *Isak Dinesen,* p. 88.

37. Dinesen, *Letters,* p. 381.

38. Dinesen, *Out of Africa,* p. 3.

39. Eagleton, "Nationalism," p. 37.

40. Devi, "Draupadi." The lines I cite are the final words of the story, in Spivak, *In Other Worlds,* p. 196.

41. Dinesen, in *Last Tales,* p. 133.

42. Goethe, *Elective Affinities,* p. 160.

43. Lacan, *Four Fundamental Concepts of Psycho-Analysis,* p. 101.

44. Cited in First and Scott, *Olive Schreiner,* p. 131.

45. Ibid., p. 343.

46. Schreiner's reiteration of her feelings of separateness is probably particularly strong here because in setting herself in opposition to World War I she had set herself against even Havelock Ellis. Sounding remarkably Benjaminian, she insists that "if a man and woman quarrel, or any two human beings, I cannot [but] go back to the past where *the root of the present always is*" [her italics]. Cited in *Letters,* ed. Cronwright-Schreiner, p. 353.

47. Cited in First and Scott, *Olive Schreiner,* p. 193.

48. In *Letters,* ed. Cronwright-Schreiner, p. 366.

49. Woolf, *Voyage Out,* p. 138.

50. Schreiner, *Undine,* pp. 69–70.

51. Dinesen, "Peter and Rosa," in *Winter's Tales,* p. 253.

52. Woolf, *Voyage Out,* p. 154.

53. See, for instance, Homi Bhabha in "Art and National Identity," pp. 80–83 and 141–43.

54. First and Scott, *Olive Schreiner,* pp. 126, 141, 143–44, 167.

55. In Schreiner, *Letters,* ed. Cronwright-Schreiner, pp. 194–95.

56. Comaroff and Comaroff, *Of Revelation and Revolution*, p. 107.

57. Woolf, *Voyage Out*, p. 133.

58. Schreiner, *Letters*, ed. Cronwright-Schreiner, p. 323.

59. Worringer, *Abstraction and Empathy*, pp. 15–17.

60. Ibid., p. 22.

61. Clingman, "Literature and History in South Africa," p. 112.

62. Ibid., pp. 112–13.

63. Showalter, *Literature of Their Own*, p. 204.

64. Sparks, *Mind of South Africa*, p. 122.

65. Schreiner, *Letters*, ed. Rive, 1:28.

66. Schreiner, *From Man to Man*, p. 288.

67. Schreiner's heroine's protestations that she needs a space of her own are said to have been Virginia Woolf's inspiration for the famous "room of her own." Schreiner began *From Man to Man* in 1873 in England and worked on it concurrently with *Story of an African Farm* and revisions to *Undine*. Although the latter two reached some stage of completion in her own mind, *From Man to Man* still seemed unfinished to her even at the time of her death.

68. Schreiner, *From Man to Man*, pp. 158–59.

69. Schreiner, *Letters*, ed. Cronwright-Schreiner, p. 66.

70. Dinesen, *Out of Africa*, p. 231.

71. Foucault, *History of Sexuality*, 1:93.

72. See Childers and hooks, "Conversation about Race and Class," p. 78.

73. Garbo, quoted in Gronowicz, *Garbo*, p. 10.

74. Cited in Grosskurth, *Havelock Ellis*, p. 315.

75. According to Mary Ann Caws in *The Art of Interference*, this is how the surrealists referred to their works.

76. Adorno, "Introduction to Benjamin's *Schriften*," p. 12.

Chapter 3: The Subversion of "Woman" and the Triumph of Women

1. Schreiner, *Letters*, ed. Cronwright-Schreiner, p. 39.

2. Schreiner, *Letters*, ed. Rive, 1:18–19.

3. Schreiner, *Letters*, ed. Cronwright-Schreiner, p. 157.

4. Nietzsche, *Beyond Good and Evil*, p. 82.

5. Schreiner, *Closer Union,* pp. 19–20. In a speech offered on February 14, 1994, shortly before the first open elections held in South Africa in April 1994, Breyten Breytenbach presented an argument very like the one Schreiner had offered in *Closer Union.* "Why," he asked, "is it so difficult for our supposed 'revolutionary' policy-makers to incorporate the federal option in their considerations?" Making an important distinction between "cultures" that can be blended into one country and "communities" that probably cannot (he cites the failure of the civil rights movement to achieve such a blending in the United States), he argues that "when all is said and done and despite the mutually transformative influences with the coming about of new identities, despite the change of regime . . . at sundown and for so long as the inner eye of memory can look ahead, we will still encounter the existence of discernibly separate cultural *groups* identified by languages, customs, perhaps skin color, or by their stubbornly singular hierarchy of values." See Breytenbach, "Dog's Bone," p. 3.

6. Monsman, *Olive Schreiner's Fiction,* p. 69.

7. Hobman, *Olive Schreiner,* p. 109.

8. Schreiner, *Letters,* ed. Rive, 1:68–69.

9. Schreiner bore one live child, a daughter who lived less than twenty-four hours. D. L. Hobman's biography of Schreiner says she carried this baby's coffin from one of her African homes to another all through her life, writing to her husband in 1907, for instance, that she had "just painted my baby's little inner coffin, the shell, a beautiful pure white with Aspinall's Enamel and written on it for her birthday on April 30." "It is so nice," she says, "to think it will lie close beside me in my coffin." See Hobman, p. 160. Samuel Cronwright-Schreiner followed her wishes in this matter, burying the infant beside Schreiner on the peak of Buffels Kop near the farm at Krantz Plaats where the two of them had spent the first few months of their married life.

10. Mudimbe, "Letters of Reference," p. 68.

11. Schreiner, *Woman and Labour,* p. 216.

12. Blake, "Olive Schreiner."

13. Mostert, *Frontiers,* p. 30.

14. Schreiner, *Letters,* ed. Rive, 1:218.

15. Hobman, *Olive Schreiner,* p. 17.

16. Ibid., p. 98.

17. Schreiner, *Thoughts on South Africa,* p. 27.

18. Schreiner, *Letters,* ed. Rive, 1:240.

19. Schreiner, *From Man to Man,* p. 43.

20. Quoted in Thurman, *Isak Dinesen,* p. 127.

21. Ibid., p. 268.

22. Bradbury and McFarlane, *Modernism.*

23. See Migel, *Tania,* p. 27, and Thurman, pp. 49–50.

24. Dinesen, *Letters,* p. 315.

25. Quoted in Thurman, *Isak Dinesen,* p. 14.

26. Cited in Thurman, p. 16.

27. Ibid., p. 27.

28. Ibid., p. 25.

29. See Lechte, *Julia Kristeva,* p. 160.

30. Schreiner, *Letters,* ed. Rive, 1:69, 145, 68.

31. Schreiner, *Letters,* ed. Cronwright-Schreiner, p. 365.

32. Ibid., p. 316.

33. Schreiner, "In a Far off World," in *Dreams,* p. 61.

34. Schreiner, *Letters,* ed. Rive, 1:116–17.

35. Ibid., 1:60–61.

36. Quoted in Grosskurth, *Havelock Ellis,* p. 79.

37. Ibid., p. 85.

38. See Dearborn, *Love in the Promised Land,* p. 74.

39. Cited in Vicinus, *Independent Women,* p. 187.

40. Isak Dinesen also believed financial independence was a prerequisite for any successful relationship between a particular man and a particular woman, though her reasoning was somewhat different from Schreiner's. Dinesen believed that as long as a woman's livelihood depended on staying in the good graces of the man who supported her, any relationship between the two would have to be taken too seriously by the woman. She would be unable, that is, to be spontaneous—would be unable to play. Those who were new women in the 1880s believed they had to behave seriously to be taken seriously, but in these later times, Dinesen thought, their daughters could be and needed to be "men's playmates." See *On Modern Marriage,* pp. 80–83.

41. Schreiner was far from the only person writing a "sex book" at this time, of course. The works of Freud were just beginning to appear in England in translation in 1913 and 1914. Samuel Hynes in *A War Imagined* surmises that during the Great War it was likely that only those psychologists working with soldiers returning from the front ex-

hibiting symptoms of what was then called "shell shock" were aware of Freud's works, the writings in German of a Viennese Jew being slow to make their way into great numbers of British hands. It was only after the war—between 1919 and 1925 in particular—that a flood of translations of Freud's work began to appear (see pp. 365–66). But Olive Schreiner died in 1920. Frequent references to Freud's works in Havelock Ellis's psychological studies make it clear that he was reading Freud, but I can find no references to his works in letters Ellis wrote to Schreiner, and her biographers conclude that "Olive could not have read Freud" (see First and Scott, *Olive Schreiner,* p. 294). The most popular sex book late in Schreiner's lifetime would have been Marie Stopes's *Married Love,* published in 1918, which is wonderfully satirized in E. M. Delafield's hilarious *The Way Things Are.* It is set in the 1920s, and the harried young housewife who is its heroine discovers that the young son she has sent to her room to think about his crimes has occupied his time there perusing the copy of Stopes's tome she had hidden in her underwear drawer. Stopes's sources were the works of Edward Carpenter and Havelock Ellis rather than those of Freud (see Hynes, p. 166).

42. Cited in First and Scott, *Olive Schreiner,* p. 179 n. 159. This letter does not appear in any edition of Schreiner's letters yet published.

43. Schreiner, *Letters,* ed. Cronwright-Schreiner, p. 274.

44. Schreiner, *Letters,* ed. Rive, 1:69.

45. Schreiner, *Woman and Labour,* pp. 163–64.

46. In Grosskurth, *Havelock Ellis,* p. 79.

47. Ellis, *Impressions and Comments: Second Series,* p. 44.

48. Grosskurth, pp. 81, 80.

49. Schreiner, *Letters,* ed. Rive, 1:54.

50. Grosskurth, p. 101.

51. Schreiner, *Letters,* ed. Rive, 1:68, 69.

52. Kapp, *Eleanor Marx,* 1:217.

53. Pearson, *National Life from the Standpoint of Science,* pp. 47–48.

54. In Pakenham, *Scramble for Africa,* p. 654.

55. In Grosskurth, p. 225.

56. Ellis, *Impressions and Comments: Second Series,* p. 179.

57. In Thurman, *Isak Dinesen,* p. 148, and in *Letters,* p. 51.

58. Schreiner, *Thoughts on South Africa,* p. 203.

59. Quoted in First and Scott, *Olive Schreiner,* p. 198.

60. Ibid.

61. Schreiner, *Letters,* ed. Rive, 1:39–40.

62. Schreiner, *From Man to Man,* pp. 275, 267.

63. Quoted in First and Scott, pp. 161–62.

64. Schreiner, *Letters,* ed. Rive, 1:115, 162.

65. See First and Scott, p. 171. Schreiner's regular references to her asthma attacks and various nervous conditions might be understood in the terms suggested by Tom Lutz's *American Nervousness.* Lutz sees these symptoms, which Schreiner's age called "neurasthenia," as a condition so closely related to the culture of the era in which it was "identified" that the "disease" might best be seen as a symptom of that culture itself. But I'm made uncomfortable by this, and similarly uncomfortable by feminist critics' tendency until recently to psychologize Schreiner's physical ailments too completely. This tendency may have been a product of the critics' tendency to absorb her husband's impatience with her many physical ailments. By and large the history of Schreiner criticism over the years has found feminists tending to fault Schreiner for not finishing *From Man to Man,* or for not writing faster or more than she did. Elaine Showalter in *A Literature of Their Own* adopted this perspective. Another camp has tended to valorize Schreiner's tendency toward incompletion, seeing it as a sign of woman's *jouissance.* Rachel Blau DuPlessis did this in *Writing beyond the Ending.* But neither approach gives sufficient attention to the material conditions under which Schreiner tried to write. In a bracketed note in his collection of her letters, Cronwright-Schreiner mentions that he has not reproduced letters Schreiner wrote during her time in England in 1916 and 1917. "She wrote to me to South Africa by every mail," he says, "but the vast majority of such war-time letters contained but little of general interest. Beyond personal matters between wife and husband, they dealt mainly in vague and general terms with the war and had frequent and very sad references to her ill health and apparently almost incessant sufferings, mental and physical" (p. 357). The "apparently" here I find particularly distressing, considered in the context of the one letter he does reproduce from this period. That letter details Schreiner's ills: X rays had just revealed "big holes" in her lungs from the tuberculosis she had as a child; "every organ [is] misplaced by the lifelong asthma"; she has a heart "twice the size and the point two full inches from where it ought to be"; "the blood flow[ing] back into it through . . . defective valves"; "arterial sclerosis, a floating kidney and kidney stones,

attacks of angina"; and much else she refers to relatively unmelodramatically, all considered, as "what I've suffered unbrokenly in the last twenty-five years" (p. 358).

66. In *Letters,* ed. Rive, 1:116–17.

67. Ibid., 1:35.

68. Ibid., 1:43, 55.

69. De Certeau, *Heterologies,* p. 23.

70. Schreiner, *Letters,* ed. Cronwright-Schreiner, pp. 14–15. Richard Rive cites part of this letter (p. 36), but the lines I cite here appear only in Cronwright-Schreiner's edition of the letters.

71. Schopenhauer, "On Psychology," in *Essays and Aphorisms,* p. 168.

72. Schreiner, *From Man to Man,* p. 250.

73. In Grosskurth, *Havelock Ellis,* p. 323.

74. Schreiner, *Letters,* ed. Rive, 1:42–43.

75. Cited in First and Scott, *Olive Schreiner,* p. 135.

76. Schreiner, *Letters,* ed. Rive, 1:110, 115.

77. Dinesen, *Letters,* pp. 214–15.

78. In Thurman, *Isak Dinesen,* p. 55.

79. Blixen, *En Baaltale med 14 Aars Forsinkelse,* p. 18.

80. Dinesen, *Letters,* p. 194.

81. In Maxon, "Agriculture," p. 32.

82. Penley, "Certain Refusal of Difference," pp. 387, 389.

83. Dinesen, "Copenhagen Season," in *Last Tales,* p. 249.

84. Fanon, *Black Skin, White Masks,* p. 32.

85. Taussig, *Mimesis and Alterity,* p. xiii and xvii.

86. Foucault, "Subject and Power," pp. 424, 427.

87. Richard Wright, quoted in Mphahlele, *African Image,* p. 47.

88. Dinesen, "On Orthography," in *Daguerreotypes,* p. 149.

Chapter 4: Mythic Times, Gothic Images, and the Role of the Dice

1. Benjamin, "On Some Motifs in Baudelaire," in *Illuminations,* p. 159.

2. Benjamin, "Theses on the Philosophy of History," in *Illuminations,* p. 255.

3. See Menninghaus, "Walter Benjamin's Theory of Myth," p. 296.

4. Nietzsche, *Will to Power,* pp. 545–46.

5. See Tiedemann, "Dialectics at a Standstill," p. 287.

6. Benjamin, "The Storyteller," in *Illuminations,* pp. 84–85.

7. Dinesen, "The Supper at Elsinore," in *Seven Gothic Tales,* p. 237.

8. Dinesen, "The Dreamers," in *Seven Gothic Tales,* p. 354.

9. See Benjamin, "On Some Motifs in Baudelaire," in *Illuminations,* pp. 160–65.

10. See Meintjes, *Olive Schreiner,* p. 17.

11. Schopenhauer, "On Religion," in *Essays and Aphorisms,* p. 104.

12. Monsman, *Olive Schreiner's Fiction.*

13. See, for instance, Benjamin, *Origin of German Tragic Drama,* p. 131.

14. Goethe, *Elective Affinities,* pp. 266, 217.

15. See Hannah, "In Memoriam Karen Blixen." Hannah takes his summary of Dinesen's "Sorrow Acre" from F. Ohrt's *Udvalgte Sonderrydske Folkesagn.*

16. Benjamin, "The Storyteller," in *Illuminations,* pp. 98, 182.

17. Benjamin, "On Some Motifs in Baudelaire," in *Illuminations,* p. 165.

18. Benjamin, *Passagen-Werk,* cited in Menninghaus, "Walter Benjamin's Theory of Myth," p. 297.

19. Dinesen, *Out of Africa,* p. 104.

20. Dinesen, *Shadows on the Grass,* p. 91.

21. Schreiner, *From Man to Man,* p. 155.

22. Dinesen, quoted in Thurman, *Isak Dinesen,* p. 284.

23. In Bogue, *Deleuze and Guattari,* pp. 29–30.

24. Dinesen, "The Dreamers," in *Seven Gothic Tales,* p. 271.

25. See Benjamin, "Some Motifs from Baudelaire," in *Illuminations,* and Susan Buck-Morss's discussion in *Dialectics of Seeing,* p. 193.

26. See Hamacher, "Word *Wolke,*" p. 163.

27. Buck-Morss, *Dialectics of Seeing,* p. 195.

28. Ibid., p. 188.

29. Adorno, cited in Smith, *On Walter Benjamin,* p. 12.

30. Aiken, "Writing (in) Exile," pp. 120–21.

31. Jahn, *Muntu,* p. 61.

32. Ibid., p. 106.

33. See Kvideland and Sehmsdorf, *Scandinavian Folk Belief and Legend,* esp. pp. 66–68.

34. Benjamin, *Passagen-Werk,* cited in Tiedemann, "Dialectics at a Standstill," pp. 283–84.

35. Schreiner, *Letters,* ed. Cronwright-Schreiner, p. 146.

36. Dinesen, "The Caryatids," in *Last Tales,* p. 133.

37. Langbaum, *The Gayety of Vision,* pp. 53, 285, 5.

38. See the discussion of Schreiner's strange confession to Havelock Ellis in chapter 3 above.

39. Benjamin, cited in Buck-Morss, *Dialectics of Seeing,* p. 179.

40. Buck-Morss, p. 182.

41. Benjamin, "Theses on the Philosophy of History," in *Illuminations,* p. 255.

42. See Adorno, "Introduction to Benjamin's *Schriften,*" pp. 10–11.

43. Jahn, *Muntu,* pp. xix, 160.

44. Ibid., pp. 102–3.

45. Mostert, *Frontiers,* p. 31.

46. Ibid.

Chapter 5: Sketching Landscapes, Stretching Genres

1. Suleri, *Rhetoric of English India,* p. 76.

2. Ibid., pp. 78, 94.

3. See Comaroff and Comaroff, *Of Revelation and Revolution,* p. 271.

4. See, for instance, Gordimer, "English-Language Literature and Politics in South Africa," pp. 118–19.

5. Schreiner, *Undine,* p. 244.

6. Comaroff and Comaroff, *Of Revelation and Revolution,* p. 287.

7. Mphahlele, *African Image,* p. 123.

8. Schreiner, *Undine,* pp. 36–37.

9. Cited in February, *Afrikaners of South Africa,* p. 48.

10. See Wilmsen, *Land Filled with Flies*, p. 122.

11. Schreiner, *Undine*, p. 281.

12. Schreiner, *Thoughts on South Africa*, p. 50.

13. Schreiner, *Woman and Labour*, p. 123.

14. Gaskell, *Mary Barton*, p. 254.

15. Schreiner, *Closer Union*, pp. 10–11.

16. Schreiner, *Undine*, p. 290.

17. Schreiner, *English South-African's View of the Situation*, pp. 4–5.

18. Ibid., p. 6.

19. Pratt, *Imperial Eyes*, p. 61.

20. Schreiner, *English South-African's View of the Situation*, p. 6.

21. Woolf, *Growing*, pp. 173–74.

22. Gauguin, *Intimate Journal*, p. 50.

23. Maugham, *Summing Up*, pp. 130–31.

24. Pratt, *Imperial Eyes*, p. 104.

25. Ibid.; see particularly p. 121.

26. Comaroff and Comaroff, *Of Revelation and Revolution*, p. 75.

27. Stanley, *Through South Africa*, p. xii.

28. Ibid., p. xiii.

29. Schreiner, *Closer Union*, p. 48.

30. Schreiner, *From Man to Man*, p. 88.

31. Coetzee, "Betrayed People," p. 10.

32. Mostert, *Frontiers*, pp. 158–59.

33. Gregg, *Memories of Olive Schreiner*, p. 34.

34. Cited in Meintjes, *Olive Schreiner*, p. 95.

35. Schreiner, *From Man to Man*, p. 170.

36. Quoted in Gregg, p. 25.

37. Schreiner, *Thoughts on South Africa*, p. 14.

38. Dinesen, *Shadows on the Grass*, p. 17.

39. Mostert's history in *Frontiers* is my source here.

40. Schreiner and Cronwright-Schreiner, *Political Situation*, pp. 13–14.

41. Crais, *White Supremacy and Black Resistance in Pre-industrial South Africa*, p. 65.

42. In Bonner, "Politics of Black Squatter Movements on the Rand," p. 61.

43. Schreiner and Cronwright-Schreiner, *Political Situation,* p. 20.

44. Kanogo, *Squatters and the Roots of Mau Mau,* p. 3.

45. Suleri, *Rhetoric of English India,* p. 184.

46. Dinesen, quoted in Thurman, *Isak Dinesen,* p. 274.

47. Cronwright-Schreiner, introduction to *Story of an African Farm,* p. v.

48. Schreiner, *Letters,* ed. Rive, 1:72.

49. Schreiner, *From Man to Man,* p. 81.

50. Quoted in Grosskurth, *Havelock Ellis,* p. 59.

51. Dinesen, *Out of Africa,* p. 21.

52. Dinesen, *Letters,* pp. 177–78.

53. Ibid., p. 178.

54. Ibid., p. 179.

55. Dinesen, *Out of Africa,* pp. 89–90.

56. Woolf, *Growing,* pp. 21–22.

57. Woolf, *Village in the Jungle,* p. 3.

58. Woolf, *Growing,* p. 72.

59. Dinesen, *Out of Africa,* pp. 148–50.

60. Ibid., p. 131.

61. These posters are reproduced in M. P. K. Sorrenson, *Origins of European Settlement in Kenya.* I encountered references to them in Dane Kennedy's essay "Isak Dinesen's African Recovery," p. 39.

62. Suleri, *Rhetoric of English India,* p. 82.

63. Dinesen, *Out of Africa,* pp. 131, 134.

64. Cited in First and Scott, *Olive Schreiner,* pp. 258, 260.

Chapter 6: African Landscapes, Fauve Painters

1. Bryson, *Vision and Painting,* pp. 88–89.

2. Vauxcelles's coining of the term appeared in a special supplement to *Gil Blas* on October 17, 1905. A shortlist of the painters he had in mind at that time would include Kees van Dongen, Othon Friesz, Maurice de Vlaminck, André Derain, Raoul Dufy, Charles Camoin, Albert Marquet, Henri Manguin, Auguste Chabaud, Franz Nolken, Oskar Moll, Louis Valtat, Maurice Denis, and Georges Braque. Included

also were a group of Scandinavian painters, some trained by Matisse himself during his own fauve phase at the Académie Julian. In his review of the exhibition catalog printed to accompany the 1990 and 1991 exhibitions of the fauve landscape painters' works at the Los Angeles County Museum of Art, the Metropolitan Museum in New York, and the Royal Academy of Arts in London, Jack Flam notes that Vauxcelles in fact used the term *fauve* in two ways. In his review of "Le Salon d'Automne" in this issue of *Gil Blas,* he used it first to refer to the reaction he anticipated from the shocked academics, who would "pounce" on Matisse's paintings like wild beasts. In his review of "Le Salon des Indépendants" in *Gil Blas* in 1907, he used the word to refer to the visual effects of these wild and wildly colorful paintings. See Flam, "Taming the Beasts," pp. 40–42.

3. First and Scott, *Olive Schreiner,* p. 250.

4. See Serge Fauchereau's essay "Scandinavian Art Seen from Afar" for a listing and discussion of Scandinavian modernist representers of the fauve impulse—Karl Isakson and Jens Adolf Jerichau in Denmark, Hilding Linnqvist and Sigrid Hjerten in Sweden.

5. See Barr, *Matisse,* p. 82.

6. Dijkstra, *Idols of Perversity,* p. 281.

7. Fanon, *Wretched of the Earth,* p. 57.

8. Dinesen, *Out of Africa,* pp. 354–55.

9. This is entirely explicable, since Matisse had advised Derain to go see the Turners in 1905 and 1906 when he was in London, having been so much affected by them during his own visit in 1898. See Giry, *Fauvism,* p. 155.

10. Gregg, *Memories of Olive Schreiner,* p. 34.

11. Mostert, *Frontiers,* p. 167, xxii, 158.

12. See Schreiner, *Thoughts on South Africa,* particularly pp. 38–39.

13. Quoted in Freeman, *Fauve Landscape,* p. 92.

14. Derain in a letter to Vlaminck, cited by Freeman, p. 29.

15. Schreiner, *From Man to Man,* pp. 360–61.

16. Dinesen, *Shadows on the Grass,* pp. 109–10.

17. Schreiner, *Story of an African Farm,* p. 73.

18. Matisse, cited in Giry, *Fauvism,* p. 198.

19. Stewart, *On Longing,* p. 54.

20. With the appearance of Errol Trzebinski's *Lives of Beryl Mark-*

ham in 1993, an old debate has resurfaced: Did Markham really write her memoirs and her African stories at all, was most or all of the writing attributed to her ghostwritten by her third husband Raoul Schumacher, or was theirs a collaborative effort she published under her own name? But the precise authorship of "Brothers Are the Same" need not figure in a consideration either of how the story functions or of the kind of "African scene" it produces.

21. Trzebinski, *Lives of Beryl Markham,* p. 221.

22. Lovell, Introduction to Markham, *Splendid Outcast,* p. 51.

23. Markham, "Brothers Are the Same," in *Splendid Outcast,* pp. 56–61.

24. Clark, *Painting of Modern Life,* p. 14.

25. Cited in Freeman, *Fauve Landscape,* p. 134.

26. Ibid., pp. 24, 239, 237.

27. Said, "Yeats and Decolonization," pp. 77–78.

28. In Freeman, *Fauve Landscape,* p. 22.

29. Clark, *Painting of Modern Life,* pp. 202, 204.

30. Ibid., p. 184.

31. Bongie, *Exotic Memories,* p. 5.

32. Dinesen, *Out of Africa,* p. 322.

Chapter 7: African Gossip and the Two-Way Street

1. In Luhan, *Lorenzo in Taos,* pp. 18–19.

2. Quoted in the Black Audio/Film Collective's "Expeditions: On Race and Nation," p. 81.

3. This experience of feeling real only insofar as one sees oneself reflected in the eyes of another I have argued elsewhere is one by-product of nineteenth-century explorations into the physiology of the eye and the working of vision, and of the mechanical means for replicating the image and tricking the eye that became possible as a consequence. See Horton, "Were They Having Fun Yet?" This is a topic that deserves much more extensive treatment than I can give it here. A few years ago I became friends with a young woman who makes her living as a bondage and discipline prostitute in Manhattan, serving clients who are largely successful businessmen in the city. When she comes to stay with me while her bruises heal, she frequently talks about the extent to which the "dominants" who are her clients need her far more than she needs them. They, she insists, need her display of attention and submissiveness to confirm the "power" that forms a place in their identity so central they

are willing to pay handsomely for the display. She, on the other hand, insists her own identity requires nothing from them but their cash.

4. Carlyle, *Sartor Resartus,* p. 126.

5. Dinesen, *Out of Africa,* p. 137.

6. Ronell, "Street Talk," p. 129.

7. Said, "Orientalism Reconsidered," p. 214.

8. Ronell, "Street Talk," p. 121.

9. Ellis, *Man and Woman,* p. 3.

10. Schreiner, *Woman and Labour,* pp. 261–62.

11. "When the settler seeks to describe the native fully in exact terms, he constantly refers to the bestiary." Fanon, *Wretched of the Earth,* p. 42.

12. Schreiner, *Woman and Labour,* pp. 259–60, 330–31.

13. Ibid., pp. 294, 386.

14. Ellis, *Psychology of Sex,* 1:182.

15. Ibid., 1:206–7.

16. Ellis, *My Life,* p. 183.

17. In Grosskurth, *Havelock Ellis,* p. 76.

18. Ellis, *Psychology of Sex,* 1:15–16.

19. Comaroff and Comaroff, *On Revelation and Revolution,* p. 171.

20. Ibid., p. 189.

21. This kind of apparent denigration occurs especially frequently in *Undine.* But Mostert notes that Hottentots or Khoikhoi did smear animal fat on their bodies and used entrails as necklaces. Both obviously would tend to get rancid. In *The Afrikaners of South Africa* Vernon February relates that writers of seventeenth-century travel narratives regularly described "Bushmen" as having "dried garbage around their necks," as being "dirty to excess [and] seeming to take pleasure in making themselves hideous" (see pp. 20–21). As it happens, the animal fat was an extremely efficient way of keeping their bodies free of the insects that plagued everyone else. They also believed fat was a sign of luck: rich men tended to be fat; thus fat itself came to be a kind of talisman and promise of riches.

22. Dinesen, "On Mottoes of My Life," in *Daguerreotypes,* pp. 7–8.

23. Fanon, *Black Skin, White Masks,* p. 63.

24. In Mostert, *Frontiers,* pp. 358–59.

25. Ibid.

26. JanMohamed, "Economy of the Manichean Allegory," pp. 66–67.

27. Lacan, "On the Possible Treatment of Psychosis," p. 194.

28. The strongest current advocate for such a project may be Mudimbe, in his "Letters of Reference," pp. 67, 66. See also many of the essays in the collection titled *History from South Africa,* ed. Brown et al.

29. The schema being constructed here borrows from Rosalind Krauss's "No More Play," in *The Originality of the Avant-Garde and Other Modernist Myths,* and from Hal Foster's recent "Primitive Scenes," pp. 69–102. Foster identifies Westerners' traumatic encounter with the machine and the traumatic encounter with the primitive as constituting the two original "scenes" of modernism. These twin traumas are often conflated in modern art in the form of the machinic black body—explaining the popularity of Josephine Baker in Paris, for instance, and the appeal of paintings such as Fernand Léger's *Création du monde.* One might assume that the rap and hip-hop of young African Americans and the break dancing of a few years ago are forms of the same metaleptic commentary addressed to these same twin terrors still alive and well in the hearts of white America.

30. JanMohamed, *Manichean Aesthetics,* p. 83.

31. Kanogo, *Squatters and the Roots of Mau Mau,* pp. 46–47.

32. Ibid., p. 83.

33. Fanon, *Wretched of the Earth,* p. 51.

34. See Hynes, *War Imagined.*

35. Schreiner, *Thoughts on South Africa,* pp. 374–75.

36. Fanon, *Wretched of the Earth,* p. 51.

37. Dinesen, *Shadows on the Grass,* p. 12.

38. Ibid., pp. 12–13.

39. Suleri, *Rhetoric of English India,* pp. 77, 96.

40. Dinesen, *Letters,* p. 334.

41. Ibid., p. 379.

42. Dinesen, *Shadows on the Grass,* p. 13.

43. Dinesen, *Out of Africa,* p. 159.

44. In Njoku, *World of the African Woman,* p. 87.

45. Dinesen, *Shadows on the Grass,* pp. 9–10.

46. Cited in Mudimbe, "Letters of Reference," pp. 67–68.

47. Dinesen, *Shadows on the Grass,* p. 12.

48. Kanogo, *Squatters and the Roots of Mau Mau,* p. 83.

49. Dinesen, *Shadows on the Grass,* pp. 123, 124.

50. Sparks, quoting André DuToit, in *Mind of South Africa,* pp. 28–29.

51. Sparks, pp. 33–34, 36.

52. Schreiner, "Boer Race," in Krige, p. 115.

53. Sparks, *Mind of South Africa,* p. 42.

54. Ibid.

55. Ibid., p. 125.

56. Dinesen, *Out of Africa,* pp. 161, 158, 149ff.

57. Bhabha, "Other Question," pp. 161–62.

58. First and Scott, *Olive Schreiner,* p. 335.

59. Kierkegaard, *Either/Or,* p. 20.

60. Ibid., p. 43.

61. Nietzsche, *Will to Power,* pp. 544, 498.

62. Dinesen, *Letters,* p. 381.

63. See Rice, " 'Nomad Thought,' " p. 156, and Deleuze, "Nomad Thought."

64. Schreiner, *Letters,* ed. Rive, 1:61.

65. Ibid., 1:17.

66. Schreiner, *Letters,* ed. Cronwright-Schreiner, p. 75.

67. Schreiner, *Letters,* ed. Rive, 1:125.

68. Dinesen, cited in introduction to *On Modern Marriage,* p. 9.

69. Schreiner, *Letters,* ed. Cronwright-Schreiner, p. 146.

70. Ibid., p. 65.

71. Dinesen, *On Modern Marriage,* p. 68.

72. Bogumil Jewsiewicki, private correspondence, May 30, 1994.

73. Drewal, "Mermaids, Mirrors, and Snake Charmers," p. 38.

74. Ibid.

75. Thackeray, *Vanity Fair,* pp. 696–97.

76. Dinesen, "The Diver," in *Anecdotes of Destiny,* p. 4.

77. Benjamin, *Art, Mimesis, and the Avant-Garde,* pp. 159–60.

78. Andersen, "The Little Mermaid," in *Fairy Tales and Stories,* pp. 92–93.

79. Schreiner, *From Man to Man,* p. 451.

80. Abel, "Race, Class, and Psychoanalysis?" p. 196.

81. Dinesen, *Letters,* p. 390.

82. Dinesen, "The Diver," p. 18.

83. Ibid., p. 21.

84. Sedgwick, "Socratic Raptures, Socratic Ruptures."

Chapter 8: Conclusion: "Remembering" and the Chain of Tradition

1. Benjamin, cited in Bahti, "Theories of Knowledge," p. 72.

2. Hohendahl, *Building a National Literature,* p. 23.

3. Claiming Dinesen's and Schreiner's works as a part of the avant-garde requires a view of the avant-garde that comes closest to Barbara Kirshenblatt-Gimblett's definition in the issue of *Art in America* on art and national identity that considers the ways African art itself might be seen as avant-garde so as to push its viewers to challenge their own comfortable categories of what that art is and does. Kirshenblatt-Gimblett follows Frederick Karl and others who see the avant-garde as the cutting edge of modernism that is "always contingent, in danger, endangering itself" (p. 13).

4. Benjamin, "On Some Motifs in Baudelaire," in *Illuminations,* p. 157.

5. Benjamin, *Art, Mimesis and the Avant-Garde,* pp. 157–58.

6. Ibid.

7. Ellison, *Shadow and Act,* p. 199.

8. Mudimbe, *L'odeur du père,* p. 174.

9. Mudimbe, "Letters of Reference," p. 64.

10. Jacobsen, *Niels Lyhne,* p. 222.

11. See Susan Hiller, introduction to *Myth of Primitivism,* p. 11.

12. Thurman, *Isak Dinesen,* p. 285.

13. Jacobsen, *Niels Lyhne,* p. 131.

14. Phillipson, *In Modernity's Wake,* p. 102.

15. Benjamin, cited in Nägele, *Benjamin's Ground,* p. 15.

16. Ibid., pp. 11–12.

17. de Certeau, *Practice of Everyday Life,* p. 108.

18. Benjamin, cited in Nägele, *Benjamin's Ground,* p. 18.

19. Dinesen, "The Cardinal's First Tale," in *Last Tales,* p. 7.

Works Cited

Abel, Elizabeth. "Race, Class and Psychoanalysis? Opening Questions." In Hirsch and Keller, *Conflicts in Feminism,* pp. 184–204.

Abildgaard, Hanne. "The Modernist Movement in Denmark." In *Scandinavian Modernism,* pp. 23–32.

Abrahams, Roger D. *African Folktales: Traditional Stories of the Black World.* New York: Pantheon, 1983.

Adams, Parveen, and Elizabeth Cowie, eds. *The Woman in Question.* Cambridge: MIT Press, October Books, 1990.

Adorno, Theodor, "Introduction to Benjamin's *Schriften.*" 1955. In Smith, *On Walter Benjamin,* pp. 2–17.

———. *Kierkegaard: Construction of the Aesthetic.* Translated, edited, and with a foreword by Robert Hullot-Kentor. Minneapolis: University of Minnesota Press, 1989.

———. *Minima Moralia.* Translated by E. F. N. Jephcott. London: Verso, 1974.

Adorno, Theodor, and Max Horkheimer. *Dialectic of Enlightenment.* Translated by John Cumming. New York: Continuum, 1972.

Agawu, Kofi. "Representing African Music." *Critical Inquiry* 18 (winter 1992): 245–66.

Aiken, Susan Hardy. "Dinesen's 'Sorrow-Acre': Tracing the Woman's Line." *Contemporary Literature* 25 (summer 1984): 156–86.

———. *Isak Dinesen and the Engendering of Narrative.* Chicago: University of Chicago Press, 1990.

———. "Writing (in) Exile: Isak Dinesen and the Poetics of Displacement." In Broe and Ingram, *Women's Writing in Exile,* pp. 113–31.

Amuka, P. S. O. "Oral Literature and Fiction." In Ochieng', *Themes in Kenyan History,* pp. 242–51.

Andersen, Hans Christian. *Fairy Tales and Stories.* Translated by Reginald Spink. New York: E. P. Dutton, 1960.

Anthony, David. "South African People's History." In Brown et al., *History from South Africa,* pp. 277–86.

Appiah, Kwame Anthony. *In My Father's House: Africa in the Philosophy of Culture.* New York: Oxford University Press, 1992.

———. "Out of Africa: Topologies of Nativism." *Yale Journal of Criticism* 2 (fall 1988): 153–78.

———. "The Uncompleted Argument: DuBois and the Illusion of Race." *Critical Inquiry* 12 (autumn 1985): 21–37.

Arendt, Hannah. "Isak Dinesen: 1885–1962." *New Yorker* 44 (November 9, 1968): 223–36.

Armstrong, Nancy. *Desire and Domestic Fiction: A Political History of the Novel.* New York: Oxford University Press, 1991.

Aschan, Ulf. *The Man Whom Women Loved: The Life of Bror Blixen.* New York: St. Martin's, 1987.

Ascherson, Neal. "Africa's Lost History." *New York Review of Books* 39 (June 11, 1992): 26–29.

Ashcroft, Bill, Gareth Griffiths, and Helen Tiffin, eds. *The Empire Writes Back: Theory and Practice in Post-colonial Literatures.* New York: Routledge, 1989.

Bahti, Timothy. "Theories of Knowledge: Fate and Forgetting in the Early Works of Walter Benjamin." In Nägele, *Benjamin's Ground,* pp. 61–82.

Baker, Houston A., Jr. "African-American Studies and the Development of English." English Institute Lecture, Harvard University, August 1991.

———. *Blues, Ideology, and Afro-American Literature.* Chicago: University of Chicago Press, 1984.

Balibar, Renée. "National Language, Education, Literature." In Barker et al., *Literature, Politics, and Theory,* pp. 126–47.

Barker, Francis, Peter Hulme, Margaret Iversen, and Diane Loxley, eds. *Literature, Politics, and Theory*. New Accent Series. New York: Methuen, 1986.

Barr, Albert H., Jr. *Matisse: His Art and His Public*. New York: Museum of Modern Art, 1951.

Barthes, Roland. *Mythologies*. Selected and translated by Annette Lavers. New York: Hill and Wang, 1972.

Beer, Gillian. "The Death of the Sun: Victorian Solar Physics and Solar Myth." In Bullen, *The Sun Is God*, pp. 159–80.

Benjamin, Andrew. *Art, Mimesis and the Avant-Garde: Aspects of a Philosophy of Difference*. New York: Routledge, 1991.

Benjamin, Jessica. "A Desire of One's Own: Psychoanalytic Feminism and Intersubjective Space." In De Lauretis, *Feminist Studies, Critical Studies*, pp. 78–101.

Benjamin, Walter. "Central Park." Translated by Lloyd Spencer. *New German Critique* 34 (winter 1985): 32–58.

———. "Doctrine of the Similar." Translated by Knut Tarnowski. *New German Critique* 17 (spring 1979): 65–69.

———. *Illuminations*. Translated by Harry Zohn and edited by Hannah Arendt. New York: Schocken Books, 1969.

———. "On Some Motifs in Baudelaire." In Benjamin, *Illuminations*, pp. 155–200.

———. *The Origin of German Tragic Drama*. Translated by John Osborne, with an introduction by George Steiner. New York: Verso, 1977.

———. *Reflections*. Translated by Edmund Jephcott and edited by Peter Demetz. New York: Schocken Books, 1978.

———. "The Storyteller." In Benjamin, *Illuminations*, pp. 83–109.

———. "Theses on the Philosophy of History." In Benjamin, *Illuminations*, pp. 253–64.

Bentsen, Cheryl. *Maasai Days*. New York: Anchor/Doubleday, 1989.

Bergson, Henri. *Matter and Memory*. Translated by N. M. Paul and W. S. Palmer. New York: Zone Books, 1991.

Berkman, Joyce Avrech. *The Healing Imagination of Olive Schreiner: Beyond South African Colonialism*. Amherst: University of Massachusetts Press, 1989.

———. *Olive Schreiner: Feminism on the Frontier*. St. Albans, Vt.: Eden Press, 1979.

Bermingham, Ann. *Landscape and Ideology: The English Rustic Tradition, 1740–1860.* Berkeley and Los Angeles: University of California Press, 1986.

Bhabha, Homi K. "Art and National Identity: A Critics' Symposium." *Art in America* 79 (September 1991): 80–83, 140–43.

———, ed. *Nation and Narration.* New York: Routledge, 1990.

———. "The Other Question: Difference, Discrimination and the Discourse of Colonialism." In Barker et al., *Literature, Politics, and Theory,* pp. 148–72.

———. "Remembering Fanon: Self, Psyche, and the Colonial Condition." In Barbara Kruger and Phil Mariani, *Remaking History,* pp. 131–48.

———. "Signs Taken for Wonders: Questions of Ambivalence and Authority under a Tree outside Delhi, May 1817." *Critical Inquiry* 12 (autumn 1985): 144–65.

Bjørnvig, Thorkild. *The Pact: My Friendship with Isak Dinesen.* Translated by Ingvar Schousboe and William Jay Smith, with an introduction by William Jay Smith. Baton Rouge: Louisiana State University Press, 1983.

Black Audio/Film Collective. "Expeditions: On Race and Nation." In Hiller, *The Myth of Primitivism,* pp. 72–83.

Blake, Kathleen. "Olive Schreiner—a Note on Sexist Language and the Feminist Writer." In *Women and Literature,* vol. 1, *Gender and Literary Voice,* edited by Janet Todd, pp. 81–86. New York: Holmes and Meier, 1980.

Blixen, Karen. *En Baaltale med 14 Aars Forsinkelse.* Copenhagen: Berlingske, 1954.

Blixen-Finecke, Bror von. *The African Hunter.* New York: Alfred Knopf, 1938.

Bogue, Ronald. *Deleuze and Guattari.* Critics of the Twentieth Century Series. New York: Routledge, 1989.

Bongie, Chris. *Exotic Memories: Literature, Colonialism, and the Fin de Siècle.* Stanford: Stanford University Press, 1991.

Bonner, Philip. "The Politics of Black Squatter Movements on the Rand." In Brown et al., *History from South Africa,* pp. 59–81.

Bozzoli, Belinda, and Peter Delius. "Radical History and South African History." In Brown et al., *History from South Africa,* pp. 5–25.

Bradbury, Malcolm, and James McFarlane, eds. *Modernism: a Guide to European Literature, 1890–1930.* London: Penguin, 1976.

Bradford, Helen. "Highways, Byways, and Culs-de-Sac: The Transition to Agrarian Capitalism in Revisionist South African History." In Brown et al., *History from South Africa*, pp. 39–58.

Brantlinger, Patrick. *Rule of Darkness: British Literature and Imperialism, 1830–1914*. Ithaca, N.Y.: Cornell University Press, 1988.

———. "Victorians and Africans: The Genealogy of the Myth of the Dark Continent." *Critical Inquiry* 12 (autumn 1985): 166–203.

Breytenbach, Breyten. "Dog's Bone." *New York Review of Books* 41 (May 26, 1994): 3–6.

Brittain, Vera. *Testament of Youth*. London: Virago, 1978.

Broe, Mary Lynn, and Angela Ingram, eds. *Women's Writing in Exile*. Chapel Hill: University of North Carolina Press, 1991.

Brooks, Peter. "Aesthetics and Ideology: What Happened to Poetics?" *Critical Inquiry* 20 (spring 1994): 509–23.

Brown, Joshua, Patrick Manning, Karin Shapiro, John Wiener, Belinda Bozzoli, and Peter Delius, eds. *History from South Africa: Alternative Visions and Practices*. Philadelphia: Temple University Press, 1991.

Bryson, Norman. *Vision and Painting: The Logic of the Gaze*. New Haven: Yale University Press, 1983.

Buchanan-Gould, Vera. *Not without Honor: The Life and Writings of Olive Schreiner*. London: Hutchinson, 1949.

Buck-Morss, Susan. *The Dialectics of Seeing: Walter Benjamin and the Arcades Project*. Cambridge: MIT Press, 1989.

Bullen, J. B., ed. *The Sun Is God: Painting, Literature, and Mythology in the Nineteenth Century*. New York: Oxford University Press, 1989.

Bürger, Peter. *Theory of the Avant-Garde*. Translated by Michael Shaw with a foreword by Jochen Schulte-Sasse. Theory and History of Literature 4. Minneapolis: University of Minnesota Press, 1984.

Burstein, Janet Handler. "Two Locked Caskets: Selfhood and Otherness in the Work of Isak Dinesen." *Texas Studies in Literature and Language* 20 (winter 1978): 615–32.

Burton, Sir Richard F. *Personal Narrative of a Pilgrimage to Al-Madinah and Meccah*. Edited by Isabel Burton. 2 vols. 1893. Reprint, New York: Dover Publications, 1964.

Busia, Abena P. A. "Silencing Sycorax: On African Colonial Discourse and the Unvoiced Female." *Cultural Critique* 14 (winter 1989–90): 81–104.

Butler, Christopher. *After the Wake: An Essay on the Contemporary Avant Garde*. Oxford: Clarendon Press, 1980.

Butler, Judith. *Bodies That Matter: On the Discursive Limits of "Sex."* New York: Routledge, 1993.

———. "Disorderly Woman." *Transition* 53 (1991): 86–95.

———. *Gender Trouble: Feminism and the Subversion of Identity*. New York: Routledge, Chapman and Hall, 1990.

Callinicos, Luli. "Popular History in the Eighties." In Brown et al., *History from South Africa*, pp. 258–67.

Carlyle, Thomas. *Sartor Resartus*. 1833–34. Edited with an introduction and notes by Kerry McSweeney and Peter Sabor. New York: Oxford University Press, 1987.

Carpenter, Edward. *Intermediate Types among Primitive Folk: A Study in Social Evolution*. 1911. Reprint, London: G. Allen, 1914.

———. *Love's Coming of Age*. Manchester: Labour Press, 1896.

———. *My Days and Dreams*. London: Allen and Unwin, 1916.

———. *Towards Democracy*. New York: Boni, 1935.

Carter, Paul. *The Road to Botany Bay: An Exploration of Landscape and History*. Chicago: University of Chicago Press, 1987.

Caws, Mary Ann. *The Art of Interference: Stressed Readings in Verbal and Visual Texts*. Princeton: Princeton University Press, 1989.

Chambers, Ross. *Room for Maneuver: Reading (the) Oppositional (in) Narrative*. Chicago: University of Chicago Press, 1991.

Childers, Mary, and bell hooks. "A Conversation about Race and Class." In Hirsch and Keller, *Conflicts in Feminism*, pp. 60–81.

Churchill, Winston S. *The Boer War: London to Ladysmith via Pretoria: Ian Hamilton's March*. London: Longmans, Green, 1900. Reprint, New York: Octopus, 1989.

Clark, T. J. *The Painting of Modern Life: Paris in the Art of Manet and His Followers*. Princeton: Princeton University Press, 1984.

Clingman, Stephen. "Literature and History in South Africa." In Brown et al., *History from South Africa*, pp. 105–18.

Coetzee, J. M. "A Betrayed People." Review of Noël Mostert, *Frontiers: The Epic of South Africa's Creation and the Tragedy of the Xhosa People*. *New York Review of Books*, January 14, 1993, 8–10.

———. *White Writing: On the Culture of Letters of South Africa.* New Haven: Yale University Press, 1990.

Colby, Vineta. *The Singular Anomaly.* New York: New York University Press, 1970.

Comaroff, Jean, and John Comaroff. *Of Revelation and Revolution: Christianity, Colonialism, and Consciousness in South Africa.* Vol. 1. Chicago: University of Chicago Press, 1991.

Crais, Clifton C. *White Supremacy and Black Resistance in Pre-industrial South Africa: The Making of the Colonial Order in the Eastern Cape, 1770–1865.* New York: Cambridge University Press, 1992.

Crary, Jonathan. *Techniques of the Observer: On Vision and Modernity in the Nineteenth Century.* Cambridge: MIT Press, 1990.

Cronwright-Schreiner, S. C. *The Life of Olive Schreiner.* London: Allen and Unwin, 1924.

Deane, Seamus. "Introduction." In Eagleton et al., *Nationalism, Colonialism, and Literature,* pp. 3–19.

Dearborn, Mary V. *Love in the Promised Land: The Story of Anzia Yezierska and John Dewey.* New York: Free Press, 1988.

de Certeau, Michel. *Heterologies: Discourse on the Other.* Translated by Brian Massumi, with a foreword by Wlad Godzich. Minneapolis: University of Minnesota Press, 1986.

———. *The Practice of Everyday Life.* Translated by Steven Rendall. Berkeley and Los Angeles: University of California Press, 1984.

De Duve, Thierry. *Pictorial Nominalism: On Marcel Duchamp's Passage from Painting to the Readymade.* Translated by Dana Polan, with a foreword by John Rajchman. Minneapolis: University of Minnesota Press, 1991.

Delafield, E. M. [psued. of Edmée E. M. de la Pasture]. *The Way Things Are.* 1927. Reprint, London: Penguin Books, Virago Press, 1988.

De Lauretis, Teresa, ed. *Feminist Studies: Critical Studies.* Bloomington: Indiana University Press, 1986.

———. *Technologies of Gender.* Bloomington: Indiana University Press, 1987.

Deleuze, Gilles. "Nomad Thought." In *The New Nietzsche: Contemporary Styles of Interpretation,* edited with an introduction by David B. Allison, pp. 142–49. New York: Delta, 1977.

Deleuze, Gilles, and Felix Guattari. *Anti-Oedipus: Capitalism and Schizophrenia.* Translated by Robert Hurley, Mark Seem, and

Helen R. Lane, with a preface by Michel Foucault. Minneapolis: University of Minnesota Press, 1983.

———. *Kafka: Toward a Minority Literature*. Translated by Dana Polan with a foreword by Reda Bensmaia. Minneapolis: University of Minnesota Press, 1986.

———. *A Thousand Plateaus: Capitalism and Schizophrenia*. Translated by Brian Massumi. Minneapolis: University of Minnesota Press, 1987.

Devi, Mahasweta. "Draupadi." Translated by Gayatri Chakravorty Spivak. In Spivak, *In Other Worlds*, pp. 179–96.

Diawara, Manthia. "Reading Africa through Foucault: V. Y. Mudimbe's Reaffirmation of the Subject." *October* 55 (winter 1990): 79–82.

Diehl, Gaston. *The Fauves: The Movement, the Masters, the Precursors and Their Followers*. New York: Harry N. Abrams, 1975.

Dijkstra, Bram. *Idols of Perversity: Fantasies of Feminine Evil in Fin-de-Siècle Culture*. New York: Oxford University Press, 1986.

Dinesen, Isak. *Anecdotes of Destiny*. New York: Random House, 1958.

———. *The Angelic Avengers*. New York: Random House, 1946. Reprint, Chicago: University of Chicago Press, 1982.

———. *Carnival: Entertainments and Posthumous Tales*. Chicago: University of Chicago Press, 1977.

———. *Daguerreotypes and Other Essays*. Translated by P. M. Mitchell and W. D. Paden, with a foreword by Hannah Arendt. Chicago: University of Chicago Press, 1979.

———. *Last Tales*. 1957. New York: Vintage, 1975.

———. *Letters from Africa, 1914–1931*. Translated by Anne Born and edited by Frans Lasson. Chicago: University of Chicago Press, 1981.

———. *On Modern Marriage and Other Observations*. 1977. Translated by Anne Born with an introduction by Else Cederborg and afterword by Frank Egholm Anderson. New York: St. Martin's Press, 1977. Reissued, Rungstedlund Foundation, 1986.

———. *Out of Africa*. 1937. New York: Vintage, 1965.

———. *Seven Gothic Tales*. 1934. New York: Vintage, 1961.

———. *Shadows on the Grass*. New York: Vintage, 1960.

———. *Winter's Tales*. 1942. New York: Vintage, 1961.

Dinesen, Thomas. *My Sister, Isak Dinesen*. Translated by Joan Tate. London: Michael Joseph, 1975.

Draznin, Yaffa, ed. *My Other Self: Letters of Olive Schreiner and Havelock Ellis*. London: Peter Lang, 1992.

Drewel, Henry John. "Editor's Comment, Object and Intellect: Interpretation of Meaning in African Art." *Art Journal* 47 (summer 1988): 70–74.

———. "Interpretation and Re-presentation in the Worship of Mami Wata." *Journal of Folklore Research* 25 (January 1, 1988): 101.

———. "Mermaids, Mirrors, and Snake Charmers: Igbo Mami-Wata Shrines." *African Arts* 21 (fall 1988): 38–45.

———. "Performing the Other: Mami Wata Worship in Africa." *Drama Review* 32 (summer 1988): 160–85.

Dubow, Saul. *Racial Segregation and the Origins of Apartheid in South Africa 1919–36*. Oxford: Macmillan, 1989.

DuPlessis, Rachel Blau. *Writing beyond the Ending: Narrative Strategies of Twentieth-Century Women Writers*. Bloomington: Indiana University Press, 1985.

Eagleton, Terry. *Ideology*. New York: Verso, 1991.

———. "Nationalism: Irony and Commitment." In Eagleton et al., *Nationalism, Colonialism, and Literature,* pp. 23–39.

———. *Walter Benjamin, or Towards a Revolutionary Criticism*. New York: Verso, 1981.

Eagleton, Terry, et al., *Nationalism, Colonialism, and Literature*. Minneapolis: University of Minnesota Press, 1990.

Eliot, George. *Middlemarch*. Afterword by Frank Kermode. New York: New American Library, 1964.

Ellis, Havelock. *Impressions and Comments: Second Series (1914–1920)*. Boston: Houghton Mifflin, 1921.

———. *Impressions and Comments: Third Series (1920–1923)*. London: Constable, 1924.

———. *Man and Woman: A Study of Secondary and Tertiary Sexual Characters*. Boston: Houghton Mifflin, 1929.

———. *My Confessional: Questions of Our Day*. Boston: Houghton Mifflin, 1934.

———. *My Life: Autobiography of Havelock Ellis*. Boston: Houghton Mifflin, 1939.

———. *Sex and Marriage: Eros in Contemporary Life*. Edited by John Gawsworth. New York: Random House, 1952.

———. *Studies in the Psychology of Sex*. 2 vols. New York: Random House, 1901.

———. *A Study of British Genius*. Boston: Riverside Press, 1926.

Ellison, Ralph. *Shadow and Act*. 1953. Reprint, New York: Vintage Books, 1972.

Esonwanne, Uzo. "The Madness of Africa(ns), or Anthropology's Reason." *Cultural Critique* 17 (winter 1990–91): 107–26.

Fabian, Johannes. *Language and Colonial Power: The Appropriation of Swahili in the Former Belgian Congo, 1880–1938*. Cambridge: Cambridge University Press, 1986.

Fanon, Frantz. *Black Skin, White Masks*. Translated by Charles Lam Markmann. New York: Grove/Weidenfeld, 1967.

———. *The Wretched of the Earth*. Translated by Constance Farrington. New York: Grove Press, 1963.

Fauchereau, Serge. "Scandinavian Art Seen from Afar." In *Scandinavian Modernism*, pp. 13–22.

Faulkner, Peter, ed. *The English Modernist Reader, 1910–1930*. Iowa City: Iowa University Press, 1986.

February, Vernon. *The Afrikaners of South Africa*. New York: Kegan Paul International, 1991.

First, Ruth, and Ann Scott. *Olive Schreiner*. London: Andre Deutsch, 1980.

Flam, Jack. "Taming the Beasts." *New York Review of Books* 38 (April 25, 1991): 40–42. (Review of *The Fauve Landscape: Matisse, Derain, Braque and Their Circle, 1904–1908*, exhibition catalog, Los Angeles County Museum of Art, October 4–December 3, 1990; the Metropolitan Museum of Art, New York, February 19–May 5, 1991; the Royal Academy of Arts, London, June 10–September 1, 1991; and of *The Fauve Landscape*, exhibition catalog by Judi Freeman [New York: Los Angeles County Museum of Art and Abbeville Press, 1991].)

Forster, E. M. *Aspects of the Novel*. 1927. New York, Harcourt Brace, 1954.

———. *The Hill of Devi*. New York and London: Harcourt Brace Jovanovich, 1953.

Foster, Hal, ed. *The Anti-aesthetic: Essays on Postmodern Culture*. Port Townsend, Wash.: Bay Press, 1983.

———. "Primitive Scenes." *Critical Inquiry* 20 (autumn 1993): 69–102.

———, *Vision and Visuality*. Seattle: Bay Press, 1989.

Foucault, Michel. *The History of Sexuality*. Vol. 1. *An Introduction*. Translated by Robert Hurley. New York: Random House, 1990.

———. *The History of Sexuality*. Vol. 2. *The Use of Pleasure*. Translated by Robert Hurley. New York: Random House, 1985.

———. "The Subject and Power." In *Michael Foucault: Beyond Structuralism and Hermeneutics*, 2d ed., by Hubert L. Dreyfus and Paul Rabinow, with Afterword by and interview with Michel Foucault, pp. 208–26. Chicago: University of Chicago Press, 1983.

Fox-Genovese, Elizabeth. *Feminism without Illusions: A Critique of Individualism*. Chapel Hill: University of North Carolina Press, 1991.

Fradkin, B. M. "Havelock Ellis and Olive Schreiner's Gregory Rose." *Texas Quarterly* 21 (autumn 1978): 145–53.

Frankenberg, Ruth. *White Women, Race Matters: The Social Construction of Whiteness*. Minneapolis: University of Minnesota Press, 1993.

Fraser, Nancy. *Unruly Practices: Power, Discourse and Gender in Contemporary Social Theory*. Minneapolis: University of Minnesota Press, 1989.

Freeman, Judi. *The Fauve Landscape*. Exhibition catalog. New York: Los Angeles Museum of Art and Abbeville Press, 1991.

Freud, Sigmund. "Fetishism." In *Collected Papers*, vol. 5, edited by James Strachey. New York: Basic Books, 1959.

———. *Totem and Taboo*. Edited by A. A. Brill. New York: Modern Library, 1938.

Friedman, Susan Stanford. *Penelope's Web: Gender, Modernity, and H.D.* Cambridge: Cambridge University Press, 1990.

Friedmann, Marion V. *Olive Schreiner: A Study in Latent Meanings*. Johannesburg: Witwatersrand University Press, 1955.

Frow, John. *Marxism and Literary History*. Cambridge: Harvard University Press, 1986.

Furedi, Frank. *The Mau Mau War in Perspective*. London: James Currey, 1989.

Gallagher, Catherine, and Thomas Laqueur, eds. *The Making of the Modern Body*. Berkeley and Los Angeles: University of California Press, 1987.

Gaskell, Elizabeth. *Mary Barton*. 1848. Edited by Stephen Gill. New York: Penguin, 1985.

Gates, Henry Louis, Jr. *Figures in Black: Words, Signs, and the Racial Self*. New York: Oxford University Press, 1989.

———. *The Signifying Monkey: A Theory of Afro-American Literary Criticism*. New York: Oxford University Press, 1988.

Gatura, Kamante. *Longing for Darkness: Kamante's Tales from out of Africa*. Collected by Peter Beard. New York: Chronicle Books, 1990.

Gauguin, Paul. *Paul Gauguin's Intimate Journals*. 1921. Translated by Van Wyck Brooks. Preface by Emil Gauguin. New York: Boni and Liveright, 1949.

Gay, Peter. *The Tender Passion*. Vol. 2 of *The Bourgeois Experience: Victoria to Freud*. New York: Oxford University Press, 1986.

Giry, Marcel. *Fauvism: Origins and Development*. Translated by Helga Harrison. New York: Alpine Fine Arts Collection, 1982.

Goethe, Johann Wolfgang von. *Elective Affinities*. 1809. Translated by R. J. Hollingdale. New York: Penguin, 1971.

Gordimer, Nadine. "English-Language Literature and Politics in South Africa." In *Aspects of South African Literature*, edited by Christopher Heywood, pp. 99–120. London: Heinemann, 1976.

———. *Selected Stories*. New York: Penguin, 1978. Originally published as *No Place Like: Selected Stories*. Johannesburg: Jonathan Cape, 1975.

Gregg, Lyndall [Dot Schreiner]. *Memories of Olive Schreiner*. London: W. and R. Chambers, 1957.

Grohmann, Will. *Wassily Kandinsky*. Cologne: Du Mont Schauberg, 1961.

Gronowicz, Antoni. *Garbo*. Afterword by Richard Schickel. New York: Simon and Schuster, 1990.

Grosskurth, Phyllis. *Havelock Ellis: A Biography*. New York: Alfred A. Knopf, 1980.

Gubar, Susan. "The Blank Page and the Issues of Female Creativity." In *The New Feminist Criticism: Essays on Women, Literature and Theory*, edited by Elaine Showalter, pp. 292–313. New York: Pantheon, 1985.

———. "Blessings in Disguise: Cross-Dressing as Re-dressing for Female Modernists." *Massachusetts Review* 22 (autumn 1981): 477–508.

Habermas, Jürgen. *The Philosophical Discourse of Modernity: Twelve*

Lectures. Translated by Frederick G. Lawrence. Cambridge: MIT Press, 1987.

Hamacher, Werner. "The Word *Wolke*—If It Is One." In Nägele, *Benjamin's Ground,* pp. 147–76.

Hannah, Donald. "In Memoriam Karen Blixen: Some Aspects of Her Attitude to Life." *Sewanee Review* 71 (autumn 1963): 585–604.

———. *Isak Dinesen and Karen Blixen: The Mask and the Reality.* New York: Random House, 1972.

Hartsock, Nancy. "Rethinking Modernism: Minority vs. Minority Theories." In JanMohamed and Lloyd, *The Nature and Context of Minority Discourse,* pp. 17–36.

Hayes, R. D. "Elements of Romanticism in *The Story of an African Farm.*" *English Literature in Transition* 24, 2 (1981): 59–79.

Hecht, David. "Mermaids and Other Things in Africa." *Arts Magazine* 5 (November 1990): 80–6.

Hiller, Susan, ed. and comp. *The Myth of Primitivism: Perspectives on Art.* New York: Routledge, 1991.

Hirsch, Marianne, and Evelyn Fox Keller, eds. *Conflicts in Feminism.* New York: Routledge, Chapman and Hall, 1990.

Hobman, Daisy Lucie. *Olive Schreiner: Her Friends and Times.* London: Watts, 1955.

Hohendahl, Peter Uwe. *Building a National Literature: The Case of Germany, 1830–1870.* Translated by Renate Baron Franciscono. Ithaca, N.Y.: Cornell University Press, 1989.

Horton, Susan R. "Were They Having Fun Yet? Victorian Visuality, Modernist Selves." In *Victorian Literature and the Visual Imagination,* edited by Carol Christ and John O. Jordan. Berkeley and Los Angeles: University of California Press. Forthcoming.

Hountondji, Paulin J. *African Philosophy: Myth and Reality.* Translated by Henri Evans with the collaboration of Jonathan Ree; introduction by Abiola Irele. Bloomington: Indiana University Press, 1976.

Hulme, T. E. "Modern Art and Its Philosophy." 1914. In *Speculations: Essays on Humanism and the Philosophy of Art,* edited by Herbert Read, pp. 73–110. London: K. Paul, Trench, Trubner, 1924.

Huyssen, Andreas. *After the Great Divide: Modernism, Mass Culture, Postmodernism.* Bloomington: Indiana University Press, 1986.

Hynes, Samuel. *A War Imagined: The First World War and English Culture.* New York: Atheneum, 1991.

Isaak, Jo Anna. *The Ruin of Representation in Modernist Art and Texts.* Studies in the Fine Arts, Art Theory 13. Ann Arbor: UMI Research Press, 1986.

Jacobsen, Jens Peter. *Niels Lyhne.* Translated by Hanna Astrup Larsen, with an introduction by Borge Gedso Madsen. Library of Scandinavian Literature Series, vol. 2. Boston: G. K. Hall, 1980.

Jahn, Janheinz. *Muntu: African Culture and the Western World.* 1961. Translated by Marjorie Grene, with an introduction by Calvin C. Hernton. Reprint, New York: Grove/Weidenfeld, 1990.

Jameson, Fredric. "Modernism and Imperialism." In Eagleton et al., *Nationalism, Colonialism, and Literature,* pp. 43–66.

———. "Regarding Postmodernism—a Conversation with Fredric Jameson." In *Universal Abandon? The Politics of Postmodernism,* edited by Andrew Ross, pp. 3–30. Minneapolis: University of Minnesota Press, 1988.

JanMohamed, Abdul R. "The Economy of the Manichean Allegory: The Function of Racial Difference in Colonialist Literature." *Critical Inquiry* 12 (autumn 1985): 59–87.

———. *Manichean Aesthetics: The Politics of Literature in Colonial Africa.* Amherst: University of Massachusetts Press, 1983.

JanMohamed, Abdul R., and David Lloyd, eds. *The Nature and Context of Minority Discourse.* New York: Oxford University Press, 1990.

Jewsiewicki, Bogumil, and D. Newbury, eds. *African Historiographies.* Beverly Hills, Calif.: Sage, 1985.

———. "Painting in Zaire: From the Invention of the West to the Representation of Social Self." In Vogel, *Africa Explores,* pp. 130–75.

Johannesson, Eric O. *The World of Isak Dinesen.* Seattle: University of Washington Press, 1961.

Johnston, Sir Harry H. *A History of the Colonization of Africa by Alien Races.* New York: Cooper Square, 1966.

Kamuf, Peggy. *Signature Pieces: On the Institution of Authorship.* Ithaca, N.Y.: Cornell University Press, 1988.

Kanogo, Tabitha. *Squatters and the Roots of Mau Mau, 1905–1963.* Eastern African Studies Series. Nairobi: Heinemann Kenya, 1987.

Kapp, Yvonne. *Eleanor Marx.* 2 vols. New York: Pantheon Books, 1972.

Karl, Frederick R. *Modern and Modernism: The Sovereignty of the Artist, 1885–1925*. New York: Atheneum, 1985.

Kasfir, Sidney L. "Taste and Distaste: The Canon of New African Art." *Transition* 57 (1992): 52–70.

Kelder, Diane. "Fauvism: An Orgy of Pure Colors." In *The Great Book of Post-impressionism,* pp. 219–59. New York: Abbeville Press, 1986.

Kellner, Douglas. *Critical Theory, Marxism and Modernity.* Baltimore: Johns Hopkins University Press, 1989.

Kennedy, Dane. "Isak Dinesen's African Recovery of a European Past." *CLIO* 17 (1987): 37–50.

———. *Islands of White: Settler Society and Culture in Kenya and Southern Rhodesia, 1890–1939*. Durham, N.C.: Duke University Press, 1987.

Kenyatta, Jomo. *Facing Mt. Kenya*. Foreword by Bernard Malinowski. New York: Vintage, 1965.

Kierkegaard, Søren. *Either/Or.* 1843. Translated and edited by Howard V. Hong and Edna H. Hong. Princeton: Princeton University Press, 1987.

———. *Selections from the Writings of Kierkegaard.* Translated by Lee M. Hollander. Garden City, N.Y.: Doubleday Anchor, 1960.

Killam, G. D., ed. *The Writing of East and Central Africa*. London: Heinemann, 1984.

Kirshenblatt-Gimbel, Barbara. "Art and National Identity: A Critics' Symposium." *Art in America* 79 (September 1991): 80–83, 142–43.

Knapp, James F. *Literary Modernism and the Transformation of Work*. Evanston, Ill.: Northwestern University Press, 1988.

Kolb, David. *The Critique of Pure Modernity: Hegel, Heidegger and After.* Chicago: University of Chicago Press, 1986.

Krauss, Rosalind. *The Optical Unconscious*. Cambridge: MIT Press, 1993.

———. *The Originality of the Avant-Garde and Other Modernist Myths*. Cambridge: MIT Press, 1985.

———. "Photography in the Service of Surrealism" and "Corpus Delecti." In *L'Amour Fou: Photography and Surrealism,* ed. Rosalind Krauss, Jane Livingston, and Dawn Ades, pp. 15–54. Washington, D.C.: Corcoran Gallery of Art and Abbeville Press, 1985.

Krige, Uys, ed. *Olive Schreiner: A Selection.* New York: Oxford University Press, 1968.

Kristeva, Julia. "Oscillation between Power and Denial." In *New French Feminisms: An Anthology,* translated by Marilyn A. August and edited by Elaine Marks and Isabelle de Courtivron, pp. 165–67. New York: Schocken Books, 1981.

———. *Powers of Horror: An Essay on Abjection.* Translated by Leon Roudiez. New York: Columbia University Press, 1982.

———. *Strangers to Ourselves.* Translated by Leon Roudiez. New York: Columbia University Press, 1990.

Kruger, Barbara and Phil Mariani, eds. *Remaking History.* Dia Art Foundation Discussions in Contemporary Culture, no. 4. Seattle: Bay Press, 1989.

Kvideland, Reimund, and Henning K. Sehmsdorf, eds. *Scandinavian Folk Belief and Legend.* Minneapolis: University of Minnesota Press, 1988.

Lacan, Jacques. *The Four Fundamental Concepts of Psycho-Analysis.* Translated by Alan Sheridan. New York: W. W. Norton, 1981.

———. "On the Possible Treatment of Psychosis." In *Ecrits: A Selection,* pp. 179–225.

———. "Subversion of the Subject and the Dialectic of Desire in the Freudian Unconscious." In *Ecrits: A Selection,* translated by Alan Sheridan, pp. 292–325. New York: W. W. Norton, 1977.

LaCapra, Dominick, ed. *The Bounds of Race: Perspectives on Hegemony and Resistance.* Ithaca, N.Y.: Cornell University Press, 1991.

Lahr, John. Review of *Garbo,* by Antoni Gronowicz. *New York Times Book Review,* June 24, 1990, p. 10.

Landy, Marcia. "Anecdote as Destiny: Isak Dinesen and the Storyteller." In *Massachusetts Review* 19 (summer 1978): 389–406.

Langbaum, Robert. *The Gayety of Vision: A Study of Isak Dinesen's Art.* New York: Random House, 1965.

Larsen, Neil. *Modernism and Hegemony: A Materialist Critique of Aesthetic Agencies.* Minneapolis: University of Minnesota Press, 1990.

Lasson, Frans, and Clara Svendsen, eds. *The Life and Destiny of Isak Dinesen.* Chicago: University of Chicago Press, 1970.

Lawrence, T. E. [pseud. of T. E. Shaw]. *The Odyssey.* 1935. Translated by T. E. Shaw. Reprint, New York: Oxford University Press, 1956.

Lechte, John. *Julia Kristeva*. London: Routledge, 1990.

Lee, Judith. "The Mask of Form in *Out of Africa*." *Prose Studies* 8 (September 1985): 45–59.

Levenson, Michael H. *A Genealogy of Modernism: A Study of English Literary Discourse*. Cambridge: Cambridge University Press, 1984.

Levy, Anita. *Other Women: The Writing of Class, Race, and Gender, 1832–1898*. Princeton: Princeton University Press, 1991.

Lewis, Florence C. "Isak Dinesen and Feminist Criticism." *North American Review* 264 (spring 1979): 62–72.

Linker, Kate. "Representation and Sexuality." In Wallis, *Art after Modernism*, pp. 391–415.

Lippard, Lucy. *Mixed Blessings*. New York: Pantheon, 1990.

Loevgren, Sven. *The Genesis of Modernism*. Bloomington: Indiana University Press, 1971.

Logenbach, James. *Modernist Poetics of History: Pound, Eliot, and the Sense of the Past*. Princeton: Princeton University Press, 1987.

Lubiano, Wahneema. "Shuckin' off the African-American Native Other: What's 'Po-Mo' Got to Do with It?" *Cultural Critique* 18 (spring 1991): 149–86.

Luhan, Mabel Dodge. *Lorenzo in Taos*. New York: Alfred A. Knopf, 1932.

Lunn, Eugene. *Marxism and Modernism: An Historical study of Lukacs, Brecht, Benjamin, and Adorno*. Berkeley and Los Angeles: University of California Press, 1982.

Lutz, Tom. *American Nervousness, 1903: An Anecdotal History*. Ithaca, N.Y.: Cornell University Press, 1991.

Lydenberg, Robin. "Against the Law of Gravity: Female Adolescence in Isak Dinesen's *Seven Gothic Tales*." *Modern Fiction Studies* 24 (winter 1978–79): 521–32.

Lytton, Constance. *Prisons and Prisoners: Some Personal Experiences*. London: Heineman, 1914.

Markham, Beryl. *The Splendid Outcast*. African stories compiled and introduced by Mary S. Lovell. New York: Dell, 1987.

———. *West with the Night*. 1942. Reprint, San Francisco: North Point Press, 1983.

Marks, Elaine, and Isabelle de Courtivron, eds. *New French Feminisms*. New York: Schocken Books, 1981.

Martin, Biddy. *Woman and Modernity: The (Life)styles of Lou Andreas-Salomé.* Ithaca, N.Y.: Cornell University Press, 1990.

Matthiessen, Peter. *The Tree Where Man Was Born.* London: William Collins, 1972.

Maugham, W. Somerset. *The Summing Up.* 1938. New York: Doubleday, Doran, 1939.

Maxon, R. M. "Agriculture." In Ochieng', *Themes in Kenyan History,* pp. 29–35.

Mbembe, Achille. "The Banality of Power and the Aesthetics of Vulgarity in the Postcolony." *Public Culture* 4 (spring 1992): 1–30.

Mbiti, John. *African Religions and Philosophy.* New York: Anchor, 1970.

McCole, John. *Walter Benjamin and the Antinomies of Tradition.* Ithaca, N.Y.: Cornell University Press, 1993.

McEvilley, Thomas. "The Selfhood of the Other: Reflections of a Westerner on the Occasion of an Exhibition of Contemporary Art from Africa." In Vogel, *Africa Explores,* pp. 266–75.

McGregor, Gaile. *The Wacousta Syndrome: Explorations in the Canadian Landscape.* Toronto: University of Toronto Press, 1985.

Meintjes, Johannes. *Olive Schreiner: Portrait of a South African Woman.* Johannesburg: Hugh Keartland, 1965.

Menninghaus, Winfried. "Walter Benjamin's Theory of Myth." In Smith, *On Walter Benjamin,* pp. 299–325.

Michis, Elsie. *Outside the Pale: Cultural Exclusion, Gender Difference, and the Victorian Woman Writer.* Ithaca, N.Y.: Cornell University Press, 1993.

Migel, Parmenia. *Tania: A Biography and Memoir of Isak Dinesen.* New York: McGraw-Hill, 1967.

Miller, Christopher L. *Theories of Africans: Francophone Literature and Anthropology in Africa.* Chicago: University of Chicago Press, 1990.

Mirza, Sarah, and Margaret Strobel, eds. and trans. *Three Swahili Women: Life Histories from Mombasa, Kenya.* Bloomington: Indiana University Press, 1989.

Mitchell, W. J. T. *Iconology: Image, Text, Ideology.* Chicago: University of Chicago Press, 1986.

Mohanty, S. P. "Us and Them: On the Philosophical Bases of Political Criticism." *Yale Journal of Criticism* 2 (spring 1989): 5–13.

Monsman, Gerald. *Olive Schreiner's Fiction: Landscape and Power.* New Brunswick, N.J.: Rutgers University Press, 1991.

Mostert, Noël. *Frontiers: The Epic of South Africa's Creation and the Tragedy of the Xhosa People.* New York: Alfred A. Knopf, 1992.

Mphahlele, Ezekiel. *The African Image.* London: Faber and Faber, 1962.

Mudimbe, V. Y. "African Philosophy as an Ideological Practice: The Case of French-Speaking Africa." *African Studies Review* 26 (September–December 1983): 139–54.

———. *The Invention of Africa: Gnosis, Philosophy, and the Order of Knowledge.* Bloomington: Indiana University Press, 1988.

———. "Letters of Reference." *Transition* 53 (1991): 62–78.

———. *L'odeur du père.* Paris: Présence Africaine, 1982.

———. " 'Reprendre': Enunciations and Strategies in Contemporary African Arts." In Vogel, *Africa Explores,* pp. 276–87.

———. "Which Idea of Africa? Herskovits's Cultural Relativism." *October* 55 (winter 1990): 93–104.

Mulvey, Laura. "Visual Pleasure and Narrative Cinema." In Wallis, *Art after Modernism,* pp. 361–73.

Nägele, Rainer, ed. *Benjamin's Ground: New Readings of Walter Benjamin.* Detroit: Wayne State University Press, 1988.

Neret, Gilles. *The Arts of the Twenties.* Translated by Thomas Higgins. New York: Rizzoli, 1986.

Nietzsche, Friedrich. *Beyond Good and Evil.* Translated by Walter Kaufmann. New York: Vintage, 1966.

———. *Thus Spake Zarathustra.* Translated by R. J. Hollingdale. New York: Penguin, 1961.

———. *The Will to Power.* Translated and edited by Walter Kaufmann and R. J. Hollingdale. New York: Vintage, 1968.

Njoku, John E. Eberegbulam. *The World of the African Woman.* Metuchen, N.J.: Scarecrow Press, 1980.

Nochlin, Linda. *Women, Art, and Power and Other Essays.* New York: Harper and Row, 1988.

Nooter, Mary H. *Secrecy: African Art That Conceals and Reveals.* New York: Prestel, 1993.

Ochieng', William R., ed. *Themes in Kenyan History.* Athens: Ohio University Press, 1990.

Odhiambo, Atieno. "Kenyatta and Mau Mau." *Transition* 53 (1991): 147–52.

Ogutu, M. A. "Pastoralism." In Ochieng', *Themes in Kenyan History,* pp. 36–43.

Ohrt, F. *Udvalgte Sonderrydske Folkesagn* (Selected folktales from South Jutland). Copenhagen: Munksgaard, 1936.

Ojo-Ade, Femi. "Of Culture and Commitment, and Construction: Reflections on African Literature." *Transition* 53 (1991): 4–24.

Olaniyan, Tejumola. "Narrativizing Postcoloniality: Responsibilities." *Public Culture* 5 (fall 1992): 47–55.

Oliver, Roland. *The African Experience: Major Themes in African History from Earliest Times to the Present.* New York: HarperCollins, 1992.

Owens, Craig. "The Discourse of Others: Postmodernism and Feminism." In Foster, *Anti-aesthetic,* pp. 57–82.

Pakenham, Thomas. *The Scramble for Africa: White Man's Conquest of the Dark Continent from 1876 to 1912.* New York: Avon Books, 1991.

Parker, Kenneth, ed. *The South African Novel in English: Essays in Criticism and Society.* New York: Africana, 1978.

Pearson, Karl. *The Chances of Death and Other Studies of Evolution.* London: Edward Arnold, 1897.

———. *The Ethic of Freethought.* 1888. Reprint, London: Adam and Charles Black, 1901.

———. *National Life from the Standpoint of Science.* London: Adam and Charles Black, 1901.

Penley, Constance. "A Certain Refusal of Difference: Feminism and Film Theory." In Wallis, *Art after Modernism,* pp. 375–89.

Phillipson, Michael. *In Modernity's Wake: The Ameurunculus Letters.* New York: Routledge, 1989.

Platt, D. C. M. *The Decline and Recovery in British Overseas Trade, 1873–1914.* London: Macmillan, 1993.

Poggioli, Renato. *The Theory of the Avant-Garde.* Translated by Gerald Fitzgerald. Cambridge: Harvard University Press, 1968.

Polenska, Olga Anastasia. *Isak Dinesen: The Life and Imagination of a Seducer.* Athens: Ohio University Press, 1991.

Poovey, Mary. *Uneven Developments: The Ideological Work of Gender in Mid-Victorian England*. Chicago: University of Chicago Press, 1988.

Poster, Mark. *Critical Theory and Poststructuralism: In Search of a Context*. Ithaca, N.Y.: Cornell University Press, 1989.

Prager, Emily. "Mermaids in Fact and Fiction." *Sunday New York Times* 143 (July 17, 1994), Styles section, pp. 31, 33.

Pratt, Mary Louise. *Imperial Eyes: Travel Writing and Transculturation*. New York: Routledge, 1992.

———. "Scratches on the Face of the Country, or What Mr. Barrow Saw in the Land of the Bushmen." *Critical Inquiry* 12 (autumn 1985): 119–43.

Quinones, Ricardo J. *Mapping Literary Modernism: Time and Development*. Princeton: Princeton University Press, 1985.

Rabinbach, Anson. *The Human Motor: Energy, Fatigue and the Origins of Modernity*. New York: Basic Books, 1990.

Rice, Laura. " 'Nomad Thought': Isabelle Eberhardt and the Colonial Project." *Cultural Critique* 17 (winter 1990–91): 151–76.

Riley, Denise. *"Am I That Name?" Feminism and the Category of "Women" in History*. Minneapolis: University of Minnesota Press, 1989.

Rive, Richard M. "Olive Schreiner: A Critical Study and a Checklist." *Studies in the Novel* 4 (summer 1972): 231–51.

———, ed. *Olive Schreiner Letters: 1871–1899*. Vol. 1. New York: Oxford University Press, 1988.

Robertson, Claire, and Iris Berger, eds. *Women and Class in Africa*. New York: Africana, 1986.

Roediger, David R. *The Wages of Whiteness: Race and the Making of the American Working Class*. London: Routledge Chapman and Hall, 1991.

Ronell, Avital. "Street Talk." In Nägele, *Benjamin's Ground*, pp. 119–45.

Rose, Jacqueline. *Sexuality in the Field of Vision*. London: Verso, 1988.

Said, Edward. *Orientalism*. New York: Vintage, 1979.

———. "Orientalism Reconsidered." In Barker et al., *Literature, Politics, and Theory*, pp. 210–29.

———. "Yeats and Decolonization." In Eagleton et al., *Nationalism, Colonialism, and Literature*. pp. 69–95.

Saitoti, Tepilit Ole. *The Worlds of a Maasai Warrior: An Autobiography.* Introduced by John Galaty. Berkeley and Los Angeles: University of California Press, 1986.

San Juan, E., Jr. "The Cult of Ethnicity and the Fetish of Pluralism: A Counterhegemonic Critique." *Cultural Critique* 18 (spring 1991): 215–29.

Scandinavian Modernism: Painting in Denmark, Finland, Iceland, Norway, and Sweden, 1910–1920. Preface by Knut Berg. New York: Rizzoli, 1989.

Schleifer, Ronald. *Rhetoric and Death: The Language of Modernity and Postmodern Discourse Theory.* Urbana: University of Illinois Pres, 1990.

Schopenhauer, Arthur. *Essays and Aphorisms.* Translated by R. J. Hollingdale. New York: Penguin, 1970.

———. *The World as Will and Representation.* 2 vols. Translated by E. F. J. Payne. New York: Dover, 1966.

Schreiner, Olive. *Closer Union: A Letter on the South African Union and the Principles of Government.* London: A. C. Fifield, 1909.

———. *Dream Life and Real Life: A Little African Story.* 1891. Chicago: Academy Press, 1977.

———. *Dreams.* London: T. Fisher Unwin, 1891.

———. *An English South-African's View of the Situation: Words in Season.* London: Hodder and Stoughton, 1899. Also published as *The South African Question.* Chicago: Charles H. Sergel, 1899.

———. *From Man to Man.* 1926. Chicago: Academy Press, 1977.

———. *A Letter on the Jew.* Cape Town: Liberman, 1906.

———. *Letters.* Vol. 1. *1871–99.* Edited by Richard M. Rive. Oxford: Clarendon Press, 1988.

———. *The Letters of Olive Schreiner: 1876–1920,* Edited by S. C. Cronwright-Schreiner. London: T. Fisher Unwin, 1924.

———. *A Selection.* Edited by Uys Krige. New York: Oxford University Press, 1968.

———. Stories, Dreams and Allegories. London: T. Fisher Unwin, 1923.

———. *The Story of an African Farm.* 1883. Chicago: Academy Press, 1977.

———. *Thoughts on South Africa.* New York: Frederick A. Stokes, 1923.

———. *Trooper Peter Halklet of Mashonaland.* Introduction by Marion Friedmann. London: T. Fisher Unwin, 1897. Reprint, Johannesburg: Ad. Donker, 1974.

———. *Undine.* 1928. Introduction by Martin Tucker. New York: Johnson Reprint, 1972.

———. *Woman and Labour.* New York: Frederick A. Stokes, 1911.

Schreiner, Olive, and Samuel Cronwright-Schreiner. *The Political Situation.* London: T. Fisher Unwin, 1896.

Schwartz, Sanford. *The Matrix of Modernism: Pound, Eliot, and Early Twentieth Century Thought.* Princeton: Princeton University Press, 1985.

Sedgwick, Eve Kosofsky. *Epistemology of the Closet.* Berkeley and Los Angeles: University of California Press, 1990.

———. "Socratic Raptures, Socratic Ruptures." English Institute Lecture, Harvard University, August 25, 1991.

Seregueberhan, Tsenay, ed. *African Philosophy: The Essential Readings.* New York: Paragon House, 1991.

Shattuck, Roger. *The Banquet Years: The Arts in France, 1895–1918.* London: Faber and Faber, 1959.

Showalter, Elaine. *A Literature of Their Own: British Woman Novelists from Brontë to Lessing.* Princeton: Princeton University Press, 1977.

Smith, Angela. *East African Writing in English.* New York: Macmillan, 1989.

Smith, Gary, ed. *On Walter Benjamin: Critical Essays and Recollections.* Cambridge: MIT Press, 1988.

Snead, James. "European Pedigrees/African Contagions: Nationality, Narrative, and Communality in Tutuola, Achebe, and Reed." In Bhabha, *Nation and Narration,* pp. 231–49.

Sorrenson, M. P. K. *Origins of European Settlement in Kenya.* Nairobi: Oxford University Press, 1968.

Spacks, Patricia Meyer. *The Female Imagination.* New York: Alfred A. Knopf, 1972.

Sparks, Allister. *The Mind of South Africa.* New York: Alfred A. Knopf, 1990.

Spillers, Hortense J. "Mama's Baby, Papa's Maybe." *Diacritics* 17 (summer 1987): 65–81.

Spivak, Gayatri Chakravorty. "Can the Subaltern Speak?" In *Marxism and the Interpretation of Culture,* edited by Cary Nelson and Lawrence Grossberg, pp. 271–313. Urbana: University of Illinois Press, 1988.

———. "French Feminism in an International Frame." *Yale French Studies* 62 (1981): 154–84.

———. *In Other Worlds: Essays in Cultural Politics.* New York: Methuen, 1987.

———. "Love Me Love My Ombre, Elle." *Diacritics* 14 (winter 1984): 19–36.

———. "Woman in Difference: Mahasweta Devi's 'Douloti the Bountiful.'" *Cultural Critique* 14 (winter 1989–90): 105–28.

Stanley, Henry. *Through South Africa.* New York: Charles Scribner and Sons, 1898.

Stephenson, Anders. "Regarding Postmodernism—a Conversation with Fredric Jameson," In *Universal Abandon? The Politics of Postmodernism,* edited by Andrew Ross, pp. 3–30. Minneapolis: University of Minnesota Press, 1988.

Stewart, Susan. *On Longing: Narratives of the Miniature, the Gigantic, the Souvenir, the Collection.* Baltimore: Johns Hopkins University Press, 1984.

Storey, Robert F. *Pierrot: A Critical History of a Mask.* Princeton: Princeton University Press, 1978.

Strobel, Margaret. *European Women and the Second British Empire.* Bloomington: Indiana University Press, 1991.

Suleiman, Susan Rubin. *Subversive Intent: Gender, Politics and the Avant-Garde.* Cambridge: Harvard University Press, 1990.

Suleri, Sara. *The Rhetoric of English India.* Chicago: University of Chicago Press, 1992.

Swaisland, Cecillie. *Servants and Gentlewomen to the Golden Land: The Emigration of Single Women from Britain to South Africa, 1820–1939.* South Africa: University of Natal Press, 1993.

Taussig, Michael. *Mimesis and Alterity: A Particular History of the Senses.* New York: Routledge, 1993.

Tempels, Placide. *Bantu Philosophy.* Translated by Colin King. Paris: Présence Africaine, 1959.

Thackeray, William Makepeace. *Vanity Fair.* 1847–48. Reprint, New York: Quality Paperback Club. 1991.

Thiong'o, Ngugi wa. *Decolonising the Mind: The Politics of Language in African Literature.* Nairobi: Heinemann, 1981.

Thompson, Dorothy. *Outsiders, Class, Gender and Nation*. London: Verso, 1993.

Thompson, Leonard. *A History of South Africa*. New Haven: Yale University Press, 1990.

Thurman, Judith. *Isak Dinesen: The Life of a Storyteller*. New York: St. Martin's Press, 1982.

Tiedemann, Rolf. "Dialectics at a Standstill: Approaches to the *Passagen-Werk*." In Smith, *On Walter Benjamin*, pp. 260–91.

Tignor, Robert L. *The Colonial Transformation of Kenya: The Kamba, Kikuyu, and Maasai from 1900 to 1939*. Princeton: Princeton University Press, 1976.

Torgovnick, Marianna. *Gone Primitive: Savage Intellects, Modern Lives*. Chicago: University of Chicago Press, 1990.

Trzebinski, Errol. *The Lives of Beryl Markham*. New York: Norton, 1993.

———. *Silence Will Speak: A Study of the Life of Denys Finch Hatton and His Relationship with Karen Blixen*. Chicago: University of Chicago Press, 1977.

Vicinus, Martha. *Independent Women: Work and Community for Single Women, 1850–1920*. Chicago: University of Chicago Press, 1985.

Vogel, Susan, ed. *Africa Explores: Twentieth Century African Art*. New York: Center for African Art/Prestel, 1991.

Wallis, Brian, ed. *Art after Modernism: Rethinking Representation*. New York: New Museum of Contemporary Art and David R. Godine, 1984.

Weightman, John. *The Concept of the Avant-Garde: Explorations in Modernism*. LaSalle, Ill.: Library Press, 1973.

Westenholz, Anders. *The Power of Aries: Myth and Reality in Karen Blixen's Life*. Translated by Lise Kure-Jensen. Baton Rouge: Louisiana State University Press, 1982.

Whissen, Thomas R. "Bow of the Land: Isak Dinesen's Portrait of the Artist." *Scandinavian Studies* 46 (winter 1974): 47–58.

———. *Isak Dinesen's Aesthetics*. Port Washington, N.Y.: Kennikat Press, 1973.

Willan, Brian. *Sol Plaatje: South African Nationalist, 1876–1932*. Berkeley and Los Angeles: University of California Press, 1984.

Wilmsen, Edwin N. *Land Filled with Flies: A Political Economy of the Kalahari*. Chicago: University of Chicago Press, 1989.

Wiredu, Kwasi. *Philosophy and African Culture.* London: Cambridge University Press, 1980.

Wohlfarth, Irving. "Walter Benjamin's Image of Interpretation." *New German Critique* 17 (spring 1979): 70–98.

Wolff, Janet. *Feminine Sentences: Essays on Women and Culture.* Berkeley and Los Angeles: University of California Press, 1991.

Wolin, Richard. *Walter Benjamin: An Aesthetic of Redemption.* New York: Columbia University Press, 1982.

Woolf, Leonard. *Growing: An Autobiography of the Years 1904 to 1911.* New York: Harcourt Brace, 1961.

———. *The Village in the Jungle.* London: M. T. Parsons, 1913. Reprint, New York: Oxford University Press, 1981.

Woolf, Virginia. *The Voyage Out.* London: George Duckworth, 1915. Reprint, New York: Bantam, 1991.

Worringer, Wilhelm. *Abstraction and Empathy: A Contribution to the Psychology of Style.* 1908. Translated by Michael Bullock. New York: International Universities Press, 1967.

Young, Robert. *White Mythologies: Writing History and the West.* New York: Routledge, 1990.

Index

Abel, Elizabeth, 234
abstraction, 65–66, 180
Adorno, Theodor, 25, 73; on Benjamin, 125–26, 135
"African" landscapes, constructed by Dinesen, 25, 131–32, 140–42, 165–67, 188–91; as backdrop to her drama, 164, 131–32, 182–85; as cubist painting, 182–83; as "empty," 188–91; as Europe's "future," 112; as fauvist, 170–92; as large as she is small, 44, 164–66, 181–82, 186–87; as psychic reflections of her, 43–46, 59, 156–57, 188, 205; as psychically compensatory, 22, 170–72, 174–79; as reflecting effects of colonialism, 157–59, 162, 191–92; as release from claustrophobia, 47; as sexualized, 44; as still life, 170–76; as tableau, 181–85, 187; as in transformation, 47–48, 162–63; as woman, 44–45
"African" landscapes, constructed by Schreiner, 25, 47–48, 188–91; as backdrop to her drama, 131–32; as changeable, 156–57; as containing all history, 116–17; as "empty," 112, 154–55, 181, 188–89, 200; as Europe's "future," 112; as fauvist, 170–92; as psychic reflections of her, 44–46, 68–70, 105, 146–47, 156–57, 176–79, 189; as reflecting consequences of colonialism, 139–40, 143–49, 157–60; as release from claustrophobia, 47; as representing "mastery," 22, 28, 70, 82, 146–47; as still life, 170–76; as woman, 44, 151;
"Africans," constructed by Dinesen, 100, 206–13, 222; as actors, 32, 118; as ambitious farmers, 209–12; as aristocratic, proud, 32–33, 224; as attitudinizers, 213; as audience to her becoming, 7, 43–44, 72, 195; as children, 72, 82, 163–

"Africans" (*continued*) 64, 167, 208, 210, 216–18; as dreamers, 235; as echoes of her, 6, 25, 43–44, 47, 59, 205; as embodying ecstatic nihilism, 224–25; as embodying paradox, 32; as exhibiting "perfect freedom," 235; as fellow exiles, 159; as fellow workers, 25, 72, 209–12; as instance of fetishism, 219, 222–23; as longing for darkness, xi, 25, 34, 116, 215; as "mass," 168; as mastered, 206; as mythic creatures, 138; as objects of connoisseurship, 32, 213–16, 218; as objects for contemplation, 34; as oscillating between defiance and deference, 55, 213–15, 223; as reflectors, 104, 195, 205; as secretive, 105–6; as self-ironizing, 32–34, 55, 57–59, 166–67, 212–13, 205; as shadows, 157; as stoic accepters of fate, 32, 93–94, 118, 206, 213–16, 224–25, 227; as victims of colonial policies, 210; as victims of tragic fate, 166–67
"Africans," constructed by Schreiner, 7, 24–25, 198, 204–8, 212–13, 222–23; as children, 72; as cunning, 80, 137–38, 203–4, 273n. 21; as determined workers, 94, 110; as distant abstractions, 212; as emotional, 205; as evolving, 47–48; as fellow exiles/squatters, 159, 208; as instance of fetishism, 206–7, 222–23; as "mass," 168; as mastered, 22, 25, 206; as means to solidify relation with European eugenicists, 198–99; as mythic creatures, 138; as objects of noblesse oblige, 207–8; as pacific, "sheep-souled," 15, 31, 91; as "raw material," 155; as reflectors of her nature, 33, 44–45, 47, 95, 101, 220–23; as reserved, 205; as sexually repellant, 198–200; as stoic sufferers, 88, 227
Aiken, Susan Hardy, 127, 252n. 5
Andersen, Hans Christian, 10, 32, 111, 125, 228–34
Appiah, Kwame Anthony, 3, 11, 226
Armstrong, Nancy, 254n. 48
Ascherson, Neal, 252n. 13

Baker, Houston, Jr., 7
Barthes, Roland, 10–11, 70
Baudelaire, Charles, 121, 133–34
Beer, Gillian, 148
Benjamin, Walter: Adorno on, 125–26; on allegory, 134; on Baudelaire, 53; on binaries, 10; on consciousness and/or collective experience, 112–13, 115, 227, 232–33, 246; on desire, 233; on "the destructive character," 196–99; Eagleton on, 38–39; on eternal recurrence, 109–10, 115; on the flaneur, 30–31; on *German Tragic Drama,* 18; on gossip, 195–96, 202–3; on "history," 39, 108–9, 115, 121–29, 222–23, 246–47; on interpretation, 125, 247; on memory, 109, 238–39, 243–44, 246; on modernity, 134; on mythic image, 10, 30–31, 53, 123–26, 131, 134–36; on storyteller, xiv, 14, 108–34, 216; on suffering, 227
Bentsen, Cheryl, 34
Bergson, Henri, 243
Berkman, Joyce, 90
Bermingham, Ann, 33

Bhabha, Homi, 26–28, 48, 222
Blake, Kathleen, 80
Boer War, 4, 23, 89, 158, 170
Bongie, Chris, 191
Born, Anne, 250
Bradbury, Malcolm, 83
Brandes, Georg, 12, 83, 103, 234
Breytenbach, Breyten, 262n. 5
Brittain, Vera, 51–52
Brooks, Peter, xii
Bryson, Norman, 27, 54
Buck-Morss, Susan, 121, 134
bugingo, 127–28
Burton, Sir Richard, 153
Butler, Judith, 29
buzima, 127–28

Carlyle, Thomas, 195
Carter, Paul, 187
Clark, T. J., 187–91
Clingman, Stephen, 67–68
Coetzee, J. M., 156
Comaroff, Jean and John, xi, 42, 64, 142–44, 154, 202–3
Crary, Jonathan, 41–42, 258n. 1

de Certeau, Michel, 39, 97–98, 247
Deleuze, Gilles, 252n. 6
Derain, Andrè, 170–71, 175–76, 270–71n. 2
Derrida, Jacques, 33, 134
desire: Benjamin on, 233; Dinesen on, 6, 18–22, 84, 122–25, 228, 232–33; Mudimbe on 238; Schreiner on, 16, 18, 22, 81, 92, 101–2, 160–62, 254n. 44
Devi, Mahasweta, 59
dialectical image: Dinesen's use of, 134; "woman" as, 134–35. *See also* Benjamin, Walter
Dickens, Charles, 163
Dijkstra, Bram, 172–73
Dinesen, Isak: on art, 8, 36–37, 58, 70–71; on desire and the erotic, 18–22, 84, 123–24, 232–33; on "Fate," 114, 118, 224–25; on "feeling," 52, 227, 235; on male-female relations, 22, 111–12, 206; on marriage, 17, 52, 210–12, 226–27, 263n. 40; on the maternal, 82–83; on the "nature" of "man," 16–17; on play, 52, 84; on "woman," 28–31, 46, 78, 83–84, 100–105, 130, 133–34, 242; on will and the ideal, 12, 15, 17–18
—*works: Angelic Avengers,* 114, 254n. 48; "Babette's Feast," 19; "Barua a Soldani," 14; "The Cardinal's First Tale," 117, 248; "The Caryatids," 59, 119, 129–30; "Copenhagen Season," 102–3; "The Deluge at Norderney," 14; "The Diver," 10, 114, 228–34; "The Dreamers," 4, 108, 112, 119–27; "The Dreaming Child," 52; *On Modern Marriage,* 15, 36, 52, 210–12, 227, 251; "On Mottoes of My Life," 205; *Out of Africa,* 7, 32, 34, 43–44, 47, 55, 59, 70, 82, 111, 116, 131, 159, 162–63, 166–67, 174–76, 181–92, 195, 209; "Peter and Rosa," 63; "The Ring," 134; *Shadows on the Grass,* xi, 15, 116, 178–79, 193–95, 209, 213, 217, 218; "Sorrow-acre," 115; "The Supper at Elsinore," 111; "The Wine of the Tetrarch," 14
Dinesen, Isak, family of: Bror Blixen (husband), 6, 15–16, 19, 51–52, 58, 100, 203, 210, 226, 235; Ingeborg Westenholz Dinesen (mother), 83–85, 100, 103, 234; Thomas Dinesen (brother), 18, 100, 215, 235,

Dinesen, Isak (*continued*)
251n. 3; Wilhelm Dinesen (father), 83–84, 171; Mary Bess Westenholz (aunt), 100
Dinesen, Isak, friends and associates of: Abdullahi, 217–18; Farah Aden, 6, 15, 94, 209–10, 215, 217; Berkeley Cole, 157; Lord Delamere, 93–94; Kabero, 167; Kamante Gatura, 6, 32, 210, 257n. 73; Ingrid Lindstrom, 131. *See also* Finch Hatton, Denys
Drabble, Margaret, 123
Draznin, Yaffa, 249
Drewal, John Henry, 228–30
DuPlessis, Rachel Blau, 265–66n. 65

Eagleton, Terry, 18, 38–39
Elective Affinities. *See* Goethe
Eliot, George: *Daniel Deronda,* 22, 35, 161; *Middlemarch,* 169
Ellis, Havelock: on "Africans," 197; as companion to Schreiner, 202; as president of World League for Sexual Reform, 251n. 3; as recipient of Schreiner's letters, 23–24, 45, 48, 52, 64, 68, 70–78, 86, 88, 91–99, 105, 129, 160, 225, 227; on sexuality, 201–2; on *Undine,* 162
Ellison, Ralph, 244
Emerson, Ralph Waldo, 22–23, 81, 83
Esonwanne, Uzo, 256n. 58
eternal recurrence: 115, 119, 138; in Nietzsche, 115, 135. *See also* Benjamin, Walter
eugenics, 24, 45, 47, 93, 197

Fanon, Frantz, 26, 103, 163; on the *ngoma,* 173; on tropes of the colonial, 210, 212; on wishing to be "white," 205
Fauves, the: Dinesen's debt to, 120; history of, 170, 188–89
February, Vernon, 273n. 21
Finch Hatton, Denys, 6, 15–16, 36, 51, 100, 185, 217, 226–27, 233; and flying, 229, 233; gravesite of, 174–76; as prompter of tale-telling, 196, 213; as unreliable partner, 210
First, Ruth, 17, 223, 250
Flam, Jack, 270–71n. 2
Forster, E. M., 50
Foster, Hal, 44, 208
Foucault, Michel, 30, 70–71, 104, 258n. 1
Frankenberg, Ruth, 8
Freeman, Judi, 188–89
Freud, Sigmund, 43, 85, 97, 113, 197, 208; fetishism in, 222; reception of works in England, 263–64n. 41

Gaskell, Elizabeth, 147–48
Gates, Henry Louis, Jr., 43, 252n. 6
Gauguin, Paul, 44, 152–53, 180
Gay, Peter, 86
Gèricault, Jean Louis, 54
Giacometti, Alberto, 53, 58
Giry, Marcel, 180
Glen Grey Act, 158
Goethe, Wolfgang von, 59, 112–15
Gordimer, Nadine, 143
Gregg, Lyndall [Dot Schreiner], 41, 47, 156, 177
Grosskurth, Phyllis, 88, 92, 99
Guattari, Félix, 252n. 6
Gubar, Susan, 252n. 5

Haarhoff's Curfew Bill, 158–59
Habermas, Jürgen, 30

Hannah, Donald, 115
Hantu, 135–37, 246
Hartsock, Nancy, 29
Heine, Heinrich, 95
History, 26, 207–8, 222, 244; Benjamin and, 39, 108–9, 121–26, 134–35; Dinesen and, 162, 166–67, 189–92, 208–10, 214–18, 244; Langbaum and, 130–31; modernism and, 14–15, 26–27, 222; Mudimbe on, 79, 238–39, 244–45, 274n. 28; Schreiner on, 107
Hohendahl, Peter Uwe, 240–41
hooks, bell, 71
Hountondji, Paulin, 26, 35; on meaning of African art, 136
Hulme, T. E., 65
Huxley, Aldous, 152, 166
Hynes, Samuel, 211, 263–64n. 41

Jacobsen, Jens Peter, 34, 46, 245
Jahn, Janheinz, 13, 127–28, 135–37
James, Henry, xiii, 86, 246
Jameson, Fredric, 53, 252n. 11
JanMohamed, Abdul, 15, 131, 206–8
Jewsiewicki, Bogumil, xiii, 226

Kamuf, Peggy, 254n. 48
Kapp, Yvonne, 12, 16, 99, 202, 206
Karen Coffee, 44
Karl, Frederick, 47–48, 276n. 3
Kehlet, Reimert, 34, 48–49, 54, 58, 105
Kenyatta, Jomo, 257n. 72
Kierkegaard, Søren, Dinesen's debt to, 17, 32, 38, 79, 87, 104–5, 119, 134, 161, 223–24, 234
Kifagio, 159, 209–10
Kintu, 135–37
Kipanda, 167
Kirshenblatt-Gimbel, Barbara, 276n. 3
Konogo, Tabitha, 216–17
Krauss, Rosalind, 26–28, 50, 53, 166–68, 256n. 64, 274n. 29
Kristeva, Julia, 85, 223
Kuntu, 135–37

Lacan, Jacques, 54, 59, 85, 223
Langbaum, Robert, 15, 130–31, 208–9
Lasson, Frans, 250
Lawrence, D. H.: on "dark people," 194–95; on infection, 211
Lawrence, T. E., 154
Lechte, John, 85
Lee, Judith, 162–63
Linker, Kate, 54
Luhan, Mabel Dodge, 194
Lytton, Lady Constance, 88–89

Majara, 128
Mallarmé, Stéphane, 48
Mami Wata, xiv, 9–10, 228–35
Markham, Beryl: *Splendid Outcasts,* 185–87, 271–72n. 20; *West with the Night,* 15–16
Marquet, Albert, 175–76
Marx, Karl, 12
Matisse, Henri, 54, 170–73, 180, 190
Maugham, Somerset, 152–53, 166
Mbembe, Achille, 25
McFarlane, James, 83
McGregor, Gaile, 42
Meintjes, Johannes, 48
Memory: "African" on, 245–46; Benjamin on, 238–39; Bergson on, 243; Mudimbe on, 238–39, 244–45; relation be-

Memory (*continued*)
tween memory and experience, 243–46
Millais, John Everett, 55
Mitchell, J. W. T., xi, 195
Modernism: as aesthetic erasure of history, 187–90; as collapsing of time, space, and perspective, 50, 136–37, 232–34, 244; as contingency and becoming, 47–48; as denial of "nature," 13–15; entry into Scandinavia of, 83; and fascination with the "primitive," 180, 208; as grid, 26–28; and the ideal, 13; and the impersonal, 13–15, 37, 180–81, 211; and love, 17; as oscillation, 24, 87, 191, 246; as space-clearing and/or counter-ethnographic gesture, 42–43, 46–48, 53–54, 60–61, 142, 182–83, 242–44; and visuality, 60; and "will," 24
Modernist: Dinesen as, 13–24, 34, 45–46, 181; Schreiner as, 13–15, 24, 45–46, 181
Mohanty, S. P., 193
Monsman, Gerald, 77, 113–14, 146
Mostert, Noël: on "Bushmen," 138, 204, 255n. 56; on Karoo, 156, 176–77; on Natives Land Act, 158–59
Mphahlele, Ezekiel, xii, 25–26, 28; on Schreiner, 144
Mudimbe, Valentin, xiv, 26, 29, 35, 79; on African art and sycretism, 136, 226; on writing of "history," 238–39, 244–45, 274n. 28
Muntu, 135–37

Nägele, Rainer, 196
Natives Land Act, 158–59, 221
Ngoma, 6–7, 173–74
Niels Lyhne. *See* Jacobsen, Jens Peter
Nietzsche, Friedrich, 12, 76, 109–10; and anti-rationalism, 171–72; Dinesen's debt to, 17, 32–33, 83, 94, 103; and ecstatic nihilism, 224–25; and eternal recurrence, 115, 135; and fate, 118; and the turn to "style," 187–88
Nommo, 135–37
Ntu, 135–37

Ojo-Ade, Femi, 39
Oliver, Roland, 252n. 13
Oscillations, formal: in Dinesen, 10–11, 28, 30, 33–34, 50, 55, 191, 209, 235–36, 242–43, 246; in Schreiner, 10–11, 28, 30, 33–34, 191, 235–36, 242–43, 246
Oscillations, psychic: in Dinesen, xiii, 22, 24–26, 29, 36, 46, 48, 65, 87, 137, 140–42, 177–78, 218, 222–23, 239–40; in Schreiner, xiii, 16–17, 22–26, 29, 36, 46, 48, 52, 65, 87, 137, 140, 142, 177–78, 218–23, 239–40

Parke, T. H., 197
Penley, Constance, 102
Phillipson, Michael, 237
Plaatje, Sol, 67–68
Poovey, Mary, 254n. 48
Pratt, Mary Louise, 150–55

Rabinbach, Anson, 148
Resident Native Labor Ordinance, 159–60, 209
Retief, Piet, 144–45
Rive, Richard, 95, 249
Roediger, David, 8

Ronell, Avital, 196

Salomé, Lou-Andreas, 17
Samba, Cheri, 10
San Juan, E., Jr., 256n. 58
Schopenhauer, Arthur: Eagleton on, 18; on function of art, 225–26; on hope, 98; on the ideal, 37; as misogynyst, 86, 88; on observation, 42; Schreiner's debts to, 12, 17–18, 78, 83, 172, 223; on self-reliance and will, 18, 31, 81, 113, 225
Schreiner, Olive: on art, 18, 36, 64–65, 132–33, 225–26, 233–34; on Boer War, 23, 143, 149–50, 211, 220–21; on British presence in South Africa, 150–51, 219–21; on desire and the erotic, 18, 22, 81, 92, 160–62, 254n. 44; on federation in South Africa, 77, 148; on financial independence for women, 90, 147–49; on free love, 45–46, 52; on ideal man, 225; on male-female relations, 16, 22, 36, 96–98, 160, 206, 211; on marriage, 16–20, 37, 50–51, 211, 257n. 71; on maternity and motherhood, 78–82, 262n. 9; on Natives Land Act, 158–59, 221; on the "nature" of "man," 16–17, 45, 60–62; on psychic isolation 60–65, 68, 94–95; on "race," 24–25, 198–200, 204–5; on Schopenhauerean will and the ideal, 12, 18, 20–21, 42, 225–26; on suffering and/or self-wounding, 86–88, 160–62, 227; on "tribes," 149–50; 255n. 56; on "woman," 5–6, 24, 28–35, 76, 78, 85–91, 95–99, 103–5, 110, 128–30, 133, 225–27, 242; on woman's movement, 61–62, 148; on woman's suffrage, 23, 89; on World War I, 23, 60–61, 86–87, 260n. 46
—*works:* "The Boer Race," 219; *Closer Union,* 72, 77, 126, 155–56, 221; *Dream Life and Real Life,* 90, 128; "Dreams," 87, 89, 151; *An English South African's View of the Situation,* 22, 89, 143–44, 150, 220; *From Man to Man,* 4, 36, 62, 69–70, 79, 82, 95, 98–99, 110, 117, 119, 132–33, 157, 161, 178–79, 199–200, 203–4, 211, 247; *The Political Situation,* 151, 158–59; *Stories, Dreams, and Allegories,* 90; *Story of an African Farm,* 4, 16, 18, 22–23, 62, 77, 79, 84, 89, 144, 159, 170, 179–81; *Thoughts on South Africa,* 23, 44, 47, 82, 86, 88, 91, 94, 138, 151, 157, 177, 211, 252–53n. 13; *Thoughts about Women,* 90; *Undine,* 4, 10, 21–22, 36, 61–62, 79, 80, 143–49, 154–62, 203–4; "The Woman's Rose," 128–29; *Women and Labour,* 17–18, 37, 61, 78–79, 88, 90–91, 147–48, 198–200
Schreiner, Olive, family of: Cronwright-Schreiner, Samuel (husband), 20, 51, 64, 77, 81–82, 84, 226;—as editor of Schreiner letters, 95, 226, 249–50;—as interpreter of Schreiner marriage, 253n. 32; Gottlob Schreiner (father), 16, 81, 84–85; Rebecca Lyndall Schreiner (mother), 80–82
Schreiner, Olive, friends and associates of: Edward Aveling, 16, 45, 202; John Brown, 82; Mary Brown, 89, 156; Edward

Schreiner, Olive (*continued*) Carpenter, 14, 16, 45, 71, 96, 99–100, 227; Erilda Cawood, 89; Nikolai F. Danielson, 92; Brian Donkin, 92, 99, 160; Havelock Ellis (*See* Ellis, Havelock); Louise Ellis, 99; Alice Greene, 90; James Hinton, 45, 52, 91–92, 100; Aletta Jacobs, 89; Amy Levy, 14; Eleanor Marx, 12, 16, 92, 99, 202; Betty Molteno, 90; Karl Pearson, 24, 71, 78, 86, 87, 90, 93–96, 99–100; Mary Roberts, 86; Frances Smith, 61, 90
Scott, Ann, 17, 223, 250
Sedgwick, Eve Kosofsky, 28, 236
Showalter, Elaine, 68, 265n. 65
Spacks, Patricia Meyer, 78, 130
Sparks, Allister, 219–21
Spencer, Herbert, 81, 88
Spillers, Hortense, 10
Spivak, Gayatri Chakravorty, 8
Stanley, Henry, 153–55
Stewart, Susan, 184–85
Storey, Robert, 254–55n. 49
Suleri, Sara, 33, 141, 152, 155, 159–60, 162–64, 214

Taussig, Michael, 104
Tempels, Placide, 35
Tennyson, Alfred Lord, 54–55
Thackeray, William M., 230
Thurman, Judith, 52, 58, 82, 246, 250, 254n. 42
Thygesen, Rudolph, 54

Van Gogh, Vincent, 47
Visuality, 41–43, 57, 60
Voyage Out. See Woolf, Virginia

Westenholz, Anders, 130
Wilmsen, Edwin, 145
Wiredu, Kwasi, 136
"woman": as confined/confining, 81–84, 91; as confounder of ontological categories, 4, 6, 105–6, 230, 247–48; as eternal sufferer, 88–89, 226–27; as inferior to man, 86; as isolate, 19, 22–23, 70–71, 92, 97; as miming woman, 34, 103–4; as mythic image, 14, 29, 125–35; as other, 5–6, 75–76, 90–96, 100–104; as self-abnegating, 88, 161–62
Woolf, Leonard, 152–53, 164–65, 210
Woolf, Virginia 31, 61–64, 169, 211, 257n. 71
Worringer, Wilhelm, 65–67
Wright, Richard, 105

Yezierska, Anzia, 89
Young, Robert, 223

Library of Congress Cataloging-in-Publication Data

Horton, Susan R.
Difficult women, artful lives : Olive Schreiner and Isak Dinesen, in and out of Africa / Susan R. Horton.
p. cm. — (Parallax)
Includes bibliographical references and index.
ISBN 0-8018-5037-1 (hc : alk. paper). — ISBN 0-8018-5038-X (pbk : alk. paper))
1. Schreiner, Olive, 1885–1920—Homes and haunts—South Africa. 2. Women authors, South African—20th century—Biography. 3. Dinesen, Isak, 1885–1962—Homes and haunts—Kenya. 4. Women authors, Danish—20th century—Biography. 5. Africa—Intellectual life—20th century. 6. White women—Africa—Biography. 7. Africa—In literature. I. Title. II. Series: Parallax (Baltimore, Md.)
PR9369.2.S37Z67 1995
823—dc20
[B] 94-39707